THE 20O0 CENSUS

CENSUS
Interim
Assessment

Panel to Review the 2000 Census

Constance F. Citro, Daniel L. Cork, and Janet L. Norwood, *Editors*

Committee on National Statistics

Division of Behavioral and Social Sciences and Education

National Research Council

NATIONAL ACADEMY PRESS
Washington, DC

NATIONAL ACADEMY PRESS

The project that is the subject of this report was supported by contract no. 50-YABC-8-66010 between the National Academy of Sciences and the U.S. Census Bureau. Any opinions, findings, conclusions, or recommendations expressed in this publication are those of the author(s) and do not necessarily reflect the views of the organizations or agencies that provided support for the project.

International Standard Book Number 0-309-07649-8
Library of Congress Control Number 2001097857

Additional copies of this report are available from National Academy Press, 2101 Constitution Avenue, NW, Lockbox 285, Washington, D.C. 20055; (800) 624-6242 or (202) 334-3313 (in the Washington metropolitan area); Internet, http://www.nap.edu

Suggested Citation: National Research Council (2001). *The 2000 Census: Interim Assessment*. Panel to Review the 2000 Census, Constance F. Citro, Daniel L. Cork, and Janet L. Norwood, editors. Committee on National Statistics. Washington, DC: National Academy Press.

The **National Academy of Sciences** is a private, nonprofit, self-perpetuating society of distinguished scholars engaged in scientific and engineering research, dedicated to the furtherance of science and technology and to their use for the general welfare. Upon the authority of the charter granted to it by the Congress in 1863, the Academy has a mandate that requires it to advise the federal government on scientific and technical matters. Dr. Bruce M. Alberts is president of the National Academy of Sciences.

The **National Academy of Engineering** was established in 1964, under the charter of the National Academy of Sciences, as a parallel organization of outstanding engineers. It is autonomous in its administration and in the selection of its members, sharing with the National Academy of Sciences the responsibility for advising the federal government. The National Academy of Engineering also sponsors engineering programs aimed at meeting national needs, encourages education and research, and recognizes the superior achievements of engineers. Dr. William A. Wulf is president of the National Academy of Engineering.

The **Institute of Medicine** was established in 1970 by the National Academy of Sciences to secure the services of eminent members of appropriate professions in the examination of policy matters pertaining to the health of the public. The Institute acts under the responsibility given to the National Academy of Sciences by its congressional charter to be an adviser to the federal government and, upon its own initiative, to identify issues of medical care, research, and education. Dr. Kenneth I. Shine is president of the Institute of Medicine.

The **National Research Council** was organized by the National Academy of Sciences in 1916 to associate the broad community of science and technology with the Academy's purposes of furthering knowledge and advising the federal government. Functioning in accordance with general policies determined by the Academy, the Council has become the principal operating agency of both the National Academy of Sciences and the National Academy of Engineering in providing services to the government, the public, and the scientific and engineering communities. The Council is administered jointly by both Academies and the Institute of Medicine. Dr. Bruce M. Alberts and Dr. William A. Wulf are chairman and vice chairman, respectively, of the National Research Council.

v

Preface

This volume contains the full text of two reports of the Panel to Review the 2000 Census. On October 9, 2001, the panel released its interim report in pre-publication format. Titled *The 2000 Census: Interim Assessment*, the interim report reviewed major census operations. It also assessed the U.S. Census Bureau's recommendation in March 2001 regarding statistical adjustment of census data for redistricting. By design, the interim report did not address the Census Bureau's decision on adjustment for non-redistricting purposes, which was anticipated to occur on or about October 15 (the decision was actually announced on October 17).

Subsequently, on November 26, the panel sent a letter report to William Barron, Acting Director of the Census Bureau. In the letter report, the panel reviewed the new set of evaluations prepared by the Census Bureau in support of its October decision.

These two reports—the letter report and the interim report—are packaged together in this single volume to provide a unified discussion of statistical adjustment and other aspects of the 2000 census that the panel has considered to date. The letter report is Part I of the volume; the interim report is Part II. We have retained the title *The 2000 Census: Interim Assessment* to differentiate this volume from the panel's forthcoming final report. Both reports have been edited slightly for continuity as a single volume; in particular, the references from both individual reports are combined into a single list, and the acknowledgments section has been revised to properly credit the reviewers of both reports.

Janet L. Norwood, *Chair*
Panel to Review the 2000 Census

Acknowledgments

The Panel to Review the 2000 Census wishes to thank the many people who have contributed to the panel's work and helped make possible the preparation of this interim report.

We thank, first, staff of the U.S. Census Bureau who prepared a large number of evaluation reports about the census, the Accuracy and Coverage Evaluation (A.C.E.) Program, and demographic analysis, made informative presentations at panel meetings and workshops, and answered many specific questions about census procedures and evaluations. We thank particularly William Barron, Cynthia Clark, Robert Fay, Howard Hogan, Ruth Ann Killion, Joseph Knott, Donna Kostanich, John Long, J. Gregory Robinson, John Thompson, and Preston J. Waite. Former director Kenneth Prewitt also made valuable contributions to the panel's meetings and workshops. Rajendra Singh has been very helpful as the Census Bureau's project officer throughout the study.

We further thank the Census Bureau for arranging for panel members and staff to have access to key data files for analysis, beginning in February 2001. Such access was provided not only to the panel, but also to congressional oversight groups, under procedures to safeguard confidentiality. The ability to analyze key data sets provided knowledge of census and A.C.E. procedures and evaluations that would not otherwise have been possible for the panel to obtain.

We thank others in the professional community who participated in panel workshops: Barbara Bailar, National Opinion Research Center (retired); Stephen Fienberg, Carnegie Mellon University; David Freedman, University of California, Berkeley; Charles Jones, U.S. Census Monitoring Board, Congressional Members; Graham Kalton, Westat; Mary Mulry, Abt Associates; Jeffrey Passel, Urban Institute; Allen Schirm, Mathematica Policy Research, Inc.; Joseph Sedransk, Case Western Reserve University; Bruce Spencer, Northwestern University; Philip Stark, University of California, Berkeley; Michael Stoto, George Washington University; Joseph Waksberg, Westat; Martin Wells, Cornell University; Kirk Wolter, National Opinion Research Center; Donald Ylvisaker, University of California, Los Angeles; and Alan Zaslavsky, Harvard Medical School.

We also thank Joseph Salvo, New York City Department of City Planning, who ably chaired a working group on the Local Update of Census Addresses (LUCA) Program commissioned by the panel to evaluate LUCA from the local government perspective.

The panel is especially indebted to Constance Citro who, as senior study director, organized the work of the panel and guided its evaluation of the 2000 census. Her wide experience in census issues, her competence in statistical methods, and the clarity of her reasoning have been critical to the successful completion of this interim report. We have benefited enormously from her talent and knowledge and feel extremely fortunate to have her working with us.

The panel was assisted by a very able staff. Daniel Cork played a major role for the panel in conducting analyses of data files from the A.C.E., analyzing 1990 and 2000 census data on mail return rates, drafting the chapters on evaluation issues and mail response, developing informative graphs of key results, and preparing the report for release. His hard work and contributions, achieved under tight time pressures, were extraordinary. Andrew White, director of the Committee on National Statistics, served as study director for the panel from November 1998 through March 2000. He was assisted by Michael Cohen, who organized three panel workshops and contributed to the panel's work throughout, particularly to the chapter on issues of census evaluation. Meyer Zitter contributed to the panel's assessments of demographic analysis and the procedures for developing the Master Address File. Michele Ver Ploeg and Marisa Gerstein assisted in data analysis, as did Zhanyun Zhao, University of Pennsylvania. Heather Koball, now with the Urban Institute, prepared background material for the panel on race and ethnicity and organized and assessed trips for the panel and staff to observe census and A.C.E. operations in January-June 2000. Carrie Muntean, now with the U.S. Foreign Service, prepared background material for the panel on the development of the 1990 and 2000 census address lists and provided invaluable support to the panel's commissioned working group on the LUCA Program. Joshua Dick, Jamie Casey, and Agnes Gaskin provided valuable project assistance to the panel, particularly in making arrangements for the panel's workshops. Eugenia Grohman, associate director for reports of the Division of Behavioral and Social Sciences and Education, made important contributions to the report through her fine technical editing and eye for effective organization and presentation of technical material. To all we are grateful.

The reports in this volume have been reviewed in draft form by individuals chosen for their diverse perspectives and technical expertise, in accordance with procedures approved by the Report Review Committee of the National Research Council (NRC). The purpose of this independent review is to provide candid and critical comments that will assist the institution in making the published reports as sound as possible and to ensure that the reports meet institutional standards for objectivity, evidence, and responsiveness to the study charge. The review comments and draft manuscript remain confidential to protect the integrity of the deliberative process.

We thank the following individuals for their participation in the review of one or both of the reports in this volume: Alfred Blumstein, H. John Heinz III School of Public Policy and Management, Carnegie Mellon University; Barbara Bryant, University of Michigan Business School; Brad Efron, Department of Statistics, Stanford University; Stephen Fienberg, Department of Statistics, Carnegie Mellon University; Eugene Hammel, Department of Demography, University of California, Berkeley; William D. Kalsbeek, Department of Biostatistics, University of North Carolina; Jeffrey Passel, Urban Institute, Washington, D.C.; Stephen Stigler, Department of Statistics, University of Chicago; and Martin T. Wells, Department of Social Statistics, Cornell University.

Although the reviewers listed above provided many constructive comments and suggestions, they were not asked to endorse the conclusions or recommendations, nor did they see the final drafts of the reports before their release. The review of the panel's interim report was overseen by Samuel Preston, School of Arts and Sciences, University of Pennsylvania, and the review of the letter report was overseen by John T. Bailar, University of Chicago (emeritus). Appointed by the National Research Council, they were responsible for making certain that an independent examination of these reports was carried out in accordance with institutional procedures and that all review comments were carefully considered. Responsibility for the final content of this report rests entirely with the authoring panel and the institution.

Janet L. Norwood, *Chair*
Panel to Review the 2000 Census

Contents

List of Tables

List of Figures

List of Boxes

Part I

Letter Report

Panel to Review the 2000 Census
Committee on National Statistics
Division of Behavioral and Social Sciences and Education

November 26, 2001

Mr. William Barron
Acting Director
U.S. Census Bureau
Washington, D.C. 20233

Dear Mr. Barron:

This letter from the Panel to Review the 2000 Census comments on the Census Bureau's October 17, 2001, decision that unadjusted data from the 2000 census enumeration process should be used for the allocation of federal funds and other purposes. This decision follows an earlier decision by the Bureau on March 1, 2001, that unadjusted census counts should be used for redrawing congressional district boundaries. The Bureau released extensive evaluation materials to accompany both decisions.[1]

In our interim report (see Part II), we concluded that the 2000 census was well executed in many respects although—like every census—there were some problems. The latest set of Census Bureau evaluations make it clear that there were considerably more errors of overcounting in the census than were originally estimated by the Accuracy and Coverage Evaluation (A.C.E.) Program.[2] These evaluations—while not yet complete—suggest that because the A.C.E. did not identify a substantial number of these overcounting errors (mostly duplicates), the use of the original A.C.E. data to adjust the census could lead to overstating the population. Accordingly, the panel concludes that the Census Bureau's decision not to adjust the census at this time is justifiable. However, the panel urges the Bureau to complete the research necessary to develop reliable revised estimates of the net coverage errors in the census, particularly for population groups, in order to determine whether their use would improve the Bureau's population estimates that are regularly produced during the postcensal period.

---

[1]The Bureau's evaluations are available at http://www.census.gov.

[2]The A.C.E. was designed to provide the basis for an adjustment of the census for net population undercount through dual-systems estimation. Our panel is charged to review the statistical methods of the 2000 census, particularly the use of the A.C.E. and dual-systems estimation, and other census procedures that may affect the completeness and quality of the data.

BUREAU DECISIONS

The Census Bureau decided in March not to use the results of the A.C.E. to adjust the census redistricting data, citing two principal reasons (Executive Steering Committee for A.C.E. Policy, 2001a).[3] First, the Bureau identified discrepancies between the population estimates from the census, the A.C.E., and demographic analysis that it could not reconcile by the time (April 1) when redistricting data were required by law to be provided to all the states. Second, the Bureau identified possible problems in the A.C.E. The panel concluded in its interim report that the Bureau's decision was justifiable (see Part II).

Following its March decision, the Census Bureau accelerated some previously planned longer term analyses and conducted additional evaluations of the census, the A.C.E., and demographic analysis. From these evaluations, the Bureau estimated that the A.C.E. had failed to identify as many as 3-4 million erroneous enumerations in the census (in addition to the 12.5 million that A.C.E. did identify), mostly duplicates. Consequently, the Bureau concluded that the dual-systems estimate of the population was too high and an adjustment using the A.C.E. results as originally calculated would have overstated the population (Executive Steering Committee for A.C.E. Policy, 2001c).[4]

The Census Bureau's evaluations of the A.C.E. covered many other kinds of error, such as errors in conducting the targeted extended search, in identifying matched and nonmatched cases in the independent P-sample, in classifying movers in the P-sample, and in imputing for missing items (see, e.g., Adams and Liu, 2001; Bean, 2001; Keathley, Kearney, and Bell, 2001; Raglin and Krejsa, 2001). In general, the Bureau found that these kinds of errors were either not large or not consequential for the dual-systems estimates, although the treatment of missing data was found to increase the uncertainty of the original A.C.E. estimates.

PANEL ASSESSMENT OF THE OCTOBER DECISION

The panel reviewed the evaluation studies that were released by the Census Bureau to accompany the October 17 decision, including two papers that were made available on October 26 (Fay, 2001; Thompson, Waite, and Fay, 2001). The panel staff met with Census Bureau staff to ask clarifying questions about the key analyses of unmeasured erroneous census enumerations.

---

[3]The Executive Steering Committee for A.C.E. Policy (ESCAP) is comprised of senior Census Bureau staff.

[4]See the panel's interim report (Part II, in this volume) for explanations of the A.C.E., its two components (the independent P-sample and the E-sample of census enumerations in the A.C.E. sample block clusters), dual-systems estimation, demographic analysis, and other census and coverage evaluation features.

The panel concludes that the Census Bureau's decision that the census data from the enumeration process should be used for nonredistricting purposes, such as fund allocation, was reasonable. It seems apparent that there are sufficient errors in the A.C.E., primarily due to unmeasured erroneous census enumerations, so that the original A.C.E. results could not reliably be used for census adjustment.

It would be desirable for the Bureau to revise the dual-systems estimates for the total population and individual post-strata as quickly as possible to determine if use of the revised estimates would improve the census counts that form the basis of regularly updated postcensal estimates of the population.[5] To date, the Bureau's estimates of erroneous census enumerations not measured in the A.C.E and the effects on the estimated net undercount are based only on preliminary analyses of small subsets of the A.C.E. data. The panel understands that considerably more research will be needed to produce reliable revised estimates from the A.C.E. and, hence, that such estimates cannot be generated immediately; nonetheless, this research should be carried out as quickly as possible.

ERRONEOUS ENUMERATIONS

The Bureau has developed rough preliminary estimates of the effects of taking account of the additional erroneous census enumerations not measured in the A.C.E. on the dual-systems estimate for the total population and three major groups. These estimates show a reduction in the estimated net undercount of the total population in 2000 from 1.18 percent (March estimate) to 0.06 percent (October estimate) and a narrowing of the differences in net undercount rates for blacks and Hispanics compared with all others; see Table L-1, which also provides undercount estimates from the 1990 Post-Enumeration Survey.

The unmeasured erroneous census enumerations identified in the Bureau's A.C.E. evaluations imply a larger number of gross errors in the census than originally estimated. In fact, it appears that the number of duplicates and other erroneous census enumerations in 2000 may have been as high as (or possibly higher than) the number estimated in 1990 from the Post-Enumeration Survey (see Part II:Table 7-10).

Focusing on the net underestimation in the A.C.E. of erroneous census enumerations (mostly duplicates), we ask: How well are they estimated and how accurate are the preliminary estimates the Census Bureau provided of

---

[5]The A.C.E. post-strata comprise 416 population groups (reduced in estimation from 448 originally defined groups) for which separate dual-systems estimates were derived. Post-strata were defined by using age, sex, race/ethnicity, and housing tenure categories and, for some groups, mail return rates, geographic region, and size of metropolitan area and type of enumeration area (see Part II:Table 6-2).

TABLE L-1 Alternative Estimates of Percentage Net Undercount of the Population in the Census from the 2000 Accuracy and Coverage Evaluation (A.C.E.) and the 1990 Post-Enumeration Survey (PES)

	2000 Estimates		
Category	A.C.E. (March 2001)[a]	Revised Early Approximation (October 2001)[b]	1990 PES Estimate[c]
Total Population	1.18	0.06	1.61
Black, non-Hispanic	2.17	0.78	4.57
Hispanic	2.85	1.25	4.99
All Other	0.73	−0.28	0.68

NOTES: Net undercount rates are calculated as the estimate—from the A.C.E. or PES—minus the census count divided by the estimate. The census count of the population in 2000 was 281.4 million; the census count in 1990 was 248.7 million. Minus sign (−) indicates a net overcount of the population

[a] Data from Thompson, Waite, and Fay (2001:Table 1, col.1). Includes household population. Race/ethnicity defined according to the domain specifications for the A.C.E. (see Part II:Table 6-2).

[b] Data from Thompson, Waite, and Fay (2001:Table 1, col.3). Takes the A.C.E. estimates of percentage net undercount and subtracts adjustments estimated by Fay (2001:Table 9) for additional unmeasured erroneous enumerations, including an assumption that computer matching was 75.7 percent efficient in identifying duplicates. See also note a for A.C.E.

[c] Data from Hogan (2001a:Table 2b). Includes household and noninstitutional group quarters population. Race/ethnicity definitions are not strictly comparable with 2000; "all other" is white and some other race, not-Hispanic.

their effects in reducing the differential net undercount? How did the A.C.E. miss these errors in the census? Why did they occur in the census in the first place?

Measurement of Erroneous Enumerations

Two principal evaluations of the E-sample identified problems with the classification of erroneous census enumerations in the A.C.E.—the Evaluation Follow-Up Study (EFU) and the Person Duplication Studies.[6]

- The EFU revisited a subsample of the E-sample housing units in one-fifth of the A.C.E. block clusters using a more detailed interview. It identified instances in which the A.C.E. failed to find out that a household member should have been enumerated elsewhere in the census and, hence, that the E-sample person should have been identified as

---

[6]The Person Duplication Studies could be conducted because the optical character recognition technology used by the Bureau for the first time in 2000 to process the questionnaires made it feasible to put names on the computerized census data records.

erroneous instead of correct. The EFU also found errors in the other direction, that is, instances in which the A.C.E. identified an erroneous census enumeration when the enumeration was correct. On balance, the EFU estimated that the A.C.E. failed to measure 1.9 million erroneous census enumerations (Krejsa and Raglin, 2001). The EFU could not resolve the status of an estimated 4.6 million census enumerations—an unresolved rate of 1.7 percent (lower than the 2.6 percent unresolved enumeration status in the original A.C.E.). The EFU estimates are subject to uncertainty from sampling error; they are also subject to error due to the time lag between Census Day (April 1, 2000) and the EFU interview (January-February 2001).

Because the EFU estimate of 1.9 million (net) unmeasured erroneous census enumerations in the A.C.E. seemed high, a subset of the EFU sample (about 17,500 cases) was reanalyzed by Census Bureau staff with extensive experience in matching. The result of this work was an estimate that, on balance, the A.C.E. had failed to measure about 1.5 million erroneous census enumerations. However, the reanalysis could not resolve the enumeration status of an estimated 15 million cases (5.8%, unweighted sample size of about 1,000; see Adams and Krejsa, 2001).

- In one analysis from the Person Duplication Studies, the E-sample cases were matched by name and date of birth to all nonimputed census cases nationwide. Members of E-sample households believed to contain a duplicated enumeration were further processed, resulting in an estimate of 2.7 million E-sample enumerations that duplicated another census household or group quarters enumeration outside the A.C.E. search area (Mule, 2001).

    Analysis of these duplicated E-sample cases indicated that the A.C.E. may have failed to identify about 2.1 million of these census duplicates as erroneous (Feldpausch, 2001, as reanalyzed in Fay, 2001). Such cases included college students who were counted both at their college dormitory and at their parents' household; prisoners who were counted both at prison and at their family's residence; children in joint custody who were counted in the homes of both parents; and people with more than one house, such as those who live part of the year in the South or West and the rest of the year in the North or Midwest.

A subsequent study linked the duplicates identified in the Person Duplication Studies to the erroneous enumerations found in the EFU reanalysis subset of 17,500 persons with the goal of eliminating overlap (Fay, 2001). This linkage, which attempted to take account of the conflicting and unresolved cases in the EFU reanalysis, estimated that the A.C.E. failed to identify a total of 2.6 million erroneous census enumerations. (Separate estimates were developed for blacks, Hispanics, and all others, and for age/sex groups.) Because the Person Duplication Studies involved computer matching only (and not clerical matching, due to time constraints), an allowance was added for duplicates not detected by the computer matching. The result was an estimate of 2.9 million erroneous census enumerations that were not measured in the A.C.E. for the population as a whole.

The studies of duplications and other erroneous census enumerations not measured in the A.C.E. are not conclusive regarding the extent of errors in either the census or the A.C.E. Collectively, however, they raise sufficient questions to support the Bureau's conclusion that an adjustment of the census data using the original A.C.E. results should not be carried out at this time.

Estimated Effects of Unmeasured Erroneous Enumerations on Net Undercount

The results of the analyses by Fay (2001) were used by Thompson, Waite, and Fay (2001) to construct the revised preliminary estimates of the 2000 net undercount shown in Table L-1 above (second column, October estimate). Unlike the original A.C.E., the revised figures were not built up from estimates for individual post-strata, but were constructed crudely for the total population and three race/ethnicity groups. The calculations were based on an assumption that the factor for duplicates not detected by the computer matching applied equally to all race/ethnicity groups. They were based on other simplifying assumptions as well, such as that P-sample errors would not likely affect the dual-systems estimate.

Thompson, Waite, and Fay (2001:1) termed the revised estimates an "early approximation" of the likely effects on the estimated net undercount that might result from a corrected A.C.E. Certainly, these estimates should only be considered illustrative and not in any way definitive. Considerable work will be required to refine the estimates, particularly for population groups.

Reasons for Duplications

Research is needed to understand why so many duplications occurred in the 2000 census. One possibility is that a growing number of people with multiple residences—such as college students, children in joint custody, and others—do not fit well the concept of "usual residence" because they are considered residents at more than one location. To investigate this possibility, testing could be carried out on alternative designs for the census questionnaire. Perhaps it would be helpful to add a place on the questionnaire for households to indicate second (or additional) residences, which could permit cross-checking other residences for potential duplication. Instructions for enumerating children in joint custody could also be tested.

Research is also needed on why the A.C.E. did not estimate the full number of duplicates and other erroneous enumerations in 2000.[7] It may be that adding more probes for other residences to the A.C.E. questionnaire that is used to follow-up nonmatched E-sample cases would be helpful. There is also a need to examine the P-sample questionnaire because many of the erroneous enumerations identified in the Evaluation Follow-Up Study were cases that matched between the independent P-sample and the E-sample of census enumerations. These matches mean that the P-sample must have included cases (e.g., college students counted at home) who should have been deleted from the P-sample because their usual residence was somewhere else (see Adams and Krejsa, 2001). The EFU questionnaire itself included more detailed probes, but it could be too burdensome to use on a production basis. Also, it did not pick up as many duplicate enumerations as the Person Duplication Studies, which matched the E-sample to the census nationwide.

Because the addition of more questions or instructions to the census and A.C.E. questionnaires could discourage response, investigation of other ways to identify duplicates should be considered. One option to explore is the feasibility of using computer matching techniques for households at likely risk of duplication as a means to reduce the number of duplicate enumerations in future censuses.

It is also important to examine further the quality of the Master Address File (MAF). A special unduplication operation in summer 2000 to identify duplicate MAF addresses and associated household members resulted in 6 million person records identified initially as possible duplicates, of which 3.6 million were dropped from the census and 2.4 million were reinstated after further analysis. If this operation had not been carried out, the census would have included still more duplicates. We concluded in our interim report (see Part II:Ch.8) that the exclusion of the reinstated person records from the A.C.E. would not likely bias the dual-systems estimate of the population; this conclusion was confirmed by the Bureau in its recent evaluation studies (Raglin, 2001). However, the Person Duplication Studies found that there were errors in the special unduplication operation in both directions: that is, some census records that were dropped were not duplicates, while some records that were reinstated should have been dropped (Mule, 2001). Further analysis is needed of the complete universe of reinstated and dropped records, including their distribution across geographic areas, in order to better understand the MAF and ways to improve it for the future.

---

[7]As noted above, the 1990 Post-Enumeration Survey estimated a higher percentage of duplications and other kinds of erroneous enumerations than did the original A.C.E. Whether the level was even higher in 1990 (or earlier censuses) cannot be established because there was no way to match the E-sample to the entire census.

IMPUTATIONS

In our interim report (see Part II:Ch.8), we identified the relatively large number of census records for which all of the characteristics of the person had to be imputed as a major reason for the smaller differences in 2000 in estimated net undercount rates between historically less-well-counted and better-counted groups than in 1990. There were three times as many such whole person imputations in 2000 (5.8 million) as in 1990 (1.9 million), and we found that they occurred disproportionately among minorities, renters, and children compared with whites and other races, owners, and adults. The imputations were carried out by using information from other census records in the immediate neighborhood. Often, imputations were performed for people in households that supplied the characteristics of some but not all of their members or for households that were known to have a specific number of occupants. However, some imputations were carried out when there was no information on household size or even whether the structure was a housing unit.

Whole person imputations cannot be included in the A.C.E. matching, but they are included in the census count that is subtracted from the dual-systems estimate to calculate net undercount. Without imputations, one would have calculated an overall net undercount rate of more than 3 percent from the A.C.E.—higher than in 1990 (see Part II:Table 8-1). Adding imputations (also reinstated people) to the census count resulted in an estimated net undercount rate of 1.18 percent—less than in 1990—and reduced the differences in estimated net undercount rates for historically less-well-counted groups in comparison with better-counted groups (see Table L-1 above: A.C.E. March estimate, PES estimate). Hence, imputations are crucial to understanding the patterns of undercount in the 2000 census.

The Census Bureau should conduct a detailed analysis of census imputations, including their distribution across geographic areas. A limited analysis in the most recent set of Bureau evaluations concluded that imputations did not affect the undercount for minorities (Wetrogan and Cresce, 2001). This study compared the race and ethnicity composition of imputed persons and data-defined persons, but it did not look at the proportions of population groups that were imputed, which is the relevant analysis for the effects on net undercount rates. If it has not already done so, the Census Bureau should study imputations for other groups as well, such as owners and renters, and make the results publicly available.

The Bureau investigated reasons for different types of whole person imputations, such as the larger number of children imputed in households with other members reported (Nash, 2001). As we surmised, most such cases occurred for mail returns from households with more members than there was space on the questionnaire and for which the coverage edit and telephone follow-up was not successful. However, more analysis is needed, particularly of the 1.2 million imputations that were performed on the basis of knowing very little about the housing unit.

DEMOGRAPHIC ANALYSIS

In both the March and October decisions, the Census Bureau stressed the role of demographic analysis in evaluating the accuracy of the 2000 census and the A.C.E. Demographic analysis is used to construct an estimate of the population under age 65 by taking the demographic analysis estimate for the previous census, adding reported births, subtracting reported deaths, and adding estimates for net legal and illegal immigration. Medicare records with an adjustment for underregistration are used for the population aged 65 and older.

Demographic analysis techniques are important for developing postcensal population estimates, and they can certainly help diagnose possible problems in the census and the A.C.E. (e.g., by comparing sex ratios by age and race). However, as we concluded in our interim report (see Part II:Ch.5), there are sufficient uncertainties in the estimates of net immigration (particularly the illegal component), compounded by the difficulties of classifying people by race, so that demographic analysis estimates cannot serve as a standard for evaluation of the census or the A.C.E.

The Bureau's revised demographic analysis puts the estimated net undercount at 0.12 percent of the population; see Table L-2, October estimate. This estimate incorporates additional information for estimating net immigration (particularly illegal immigration) from the census itself (the long-form sample) and the Census 2000 Supplementary Survey. It also reflects new assumptions about the extent of undercount of legal immigrants and the completeness of birth registration.

We commend the Bureau for its work to examine each component of demographic analysis. However, its revised estimates of the immigration component are not independent of the census, and the estimates for births and immigration incorporate assumptions that are based primarily on expert judgment. Such judgments may be reasonable, but they retain sufficient uncertainty so that it is not appropriate to conclude that the revised demographic estimates are more accurate than the census. As we urged in our interim report (see Part II:Ch.5), the Census Bureau should increase its resources for demographic analysis, particularly for methods for improving estimates of net immigration. It should also devote resources to estimating the uncertainty in the demographic estimates.

FURTHER ANALYSIS OF THE A.C.E. AND THE CENSUS

We urge the Census Bureau to continue its evaluations of the A.C.E. and, particularly, to refine its estimates of the likely differential undercount for population groups. Differences in net undercount rates among groups are of more

TABLE L-2 Alternative Estimates of Percentage Net Undercount of the Population from Demographic Analysis, 2000 and 1990 Censuses

Category	2000 Estimates			1990 Estimates[a]	
	Base[b,c] (Jan. 2001)	Alternate[b,d] (Mar. 2001)	Revised[b,e] (Oct. 2001)	Base (1991)	Revised (Oct. 2001)
Total Population	−0.65	0.32	0.12	1.85	1.65
Black	2.80	3.51	2.78	5.68	5.52
All Other	−1.19	−0.17	−0.29	1.29	1.08

NOTES: Net undercount rates are calculated as the estimate from demographic analysis minus the census count divided by the estimate. The census count of the population in 2000 was 281.4 million; the census count in 1990 was 248.7 million. Minus sign (−) indicates a net overcount of the population

[a] Data from Robinson (2001b:Table 2). Includes household and group quarters population. Base is the estimate developed following the 1990 census; "revised" is the October 2001 estimate, with revisions to such components as births.

[b] Data from Robinson (2001a:Table 6; 2001b:Table 2). Includes household and group quarters population. The estimates by race are an average of estimates calculated using two different tabulations of the census (see National Research Council, 2001:Ch.5). "All other" includes Hispanics not classified as black.

[c] "Base" is the original January 2001 estimate, including an allowance for 6 million illegal immigrants—3.3 million from the 1990 demographic analysis estimate and a net increase of 2.7 million over the decade, extrapolated from estimates that mainly reflect changes between 1992 and 1996.

[d] "Alternate" is the March 2001 estimate, including an allowance for 8.7 million illegal immigrants. This estimate was developed as an illustrative alternative to the base estimate when it became apparent that the latter likely underestimated illegal immigration. The alternate estimate reflects an assumed doubling of the net increase in illegal immigrants in the 1990s—from 2.7 million to 5.4 million.

[e] "Revised" is the October 2001 estimate, which revises several components, including births and legal and illegal immigration.

concern than the overall undercount for many uses of census data, and such differences are likely present in the census even if the net undercount rate for the total population is close to zero.[8]

This work may involve respecifying the post-strata for which separate dual-systems estimates are prepared, as well as refining the estimates of various kinds of errors in the A.C.E. and their effects on the variability of the estimates. We recognize that such work cannot be completed quickly; however, it is important to pursue given the critical role of the census for the development of postcensal estimates that are used for such purposes as fund allocation and reweighting of the nation's major household surveys.

---

[8]In this regard, the Census Bureau concluded in October that "the net undercount remains disproportionately distributed among renter and minority populations" and that it is "reasonable to expect that research and analysis may lead to revised A.C.E. estimates that can be used to improve future post-censal estimates" (Executive Steering Committee on A.C.E. Policy, 2001c:i,v).

It is also important to continue investigation of the reasons for errors in the census. In particular, it is important to learn as much as possible about census operations that may have contributed to duplicate enumerations and imputations in order to identify useful modifications to census procedures for 2010.

Finally, we stress that there will always be a need to evaluate the adequacy of population coverage in the census and to have a basis for census adjustment if needed. For this reason, it is essential to continue research on ways to improve the A.C.E., as well as the census.

In all of these analyses, the Census Bureau can benefit from the contributions and insights of independent researchers. The panel urges the Bureau to make available as much A.C.E. and census data as possible to the scientific research community for evaluation purposes. The Bureau should develop publicly available analysis files (consistent with protecting confidentiality) of coverage-related information (e.g., imputations, reinstated people, match rates) for post-strata and geographic areas. It should also find ways to provide access to A.C.E. microdata for researchers. While the likely errors in the A.C.E. preclude the use of the data for adjustment purposes at this time, there is much value in the data for research.

FUTURE WORK OF THE PANEL

In its work to prepare a final report, the panel plans to address the quality of the important socioeconomic information collected in the census long form and to review the detailed information obtained on race and ethnicity. The panel will also review further Census Bureau evaluations of population coverage in the 2000 census and consider methods for improving coverage evaluation for future censuses.

SUMMARY

The panel concludes that the Census Bureau's two decisions (March and October) not to adjust the 2000 census counts for coverage errors are justifiable because of the evidence of errors in the A.C.E. that could lead to overstating the population.

The panel concludes that the Bureau's estimates of the effects of the unmeasured erroneous census enumerations on net undercount rates for population groups are far from definitive. These estimates are based on small samples and incorporate a number of simplifying assumptions. The Bureau should conduct further research on the unmeasured duplicate and other erroneous census enumerations and attempt to develop revised estimates of net undercount for the population and for major population groups. The Bureau should also conduct further research on the causes, quality, and effects of the larger number of census imputations and on demographic analysis components, particularly immigration.

The panel commends the Bureau for the extensive evaluations that it has conducted of the census and the A.C.E. to date. These evaluations underscore the critical importance for the census of having a coverage measurement program, such as the A.C.E., with a large independent survey that can provide detailed information on coverage errors for population groups and geographic areas.

Sincerely yours,

Janet L. Norwood, *Chair*
Panel to Review the 2000 Census

Part II

Interim Report

Executive Summary

The 2000 decennial census provides data for many important purposes. Population counts and other census data are used to reapportion the U.S. House of Representatives; draw new boundaries for legislative districts; allocate billions of dollars in federal and state funds; support public and private sector planning, decision making, and research; undergird estimates from other government statistical programs; and serve as a valuable reference for the media and the general public. Census information is the product of a massive, complex, and costly set of operations.

Such an effort deserves a thorough assessment to understand how and why procedures worked and to understand the quality and limitations of the data for their intended uses. Accordingly, at the request of the U.S. Census Bureau, the Committee on National Statistics established the Panel to Review the 2000 Census to provide an independent review of statistical methods and other procedures in the census that may affect the completeness and quality of the data.

The 2000 census process included an Accuracy and Coverage Evaluation (A.C.E.) Program, in which the results of an independent sample survey of household residents were matched to census enumerations in a sample of small areas nationwide. The A.C.E. provides a basis for judging the net undercount in the census enumeration, as well as for statistical adjustment of census counts to reflect net undercount using the method of dual-systems estimation. In March 2001, the Census Bureau concluded that it could not resolve uncertainties in the census, the A.C.E. results, and separate population estimates from demographic analysis by a legally mandated deadline of April 1, 2001. Therefore, the Bureau recommended that census counts for congressional redistricting should not be statistically adjusted; this recommendation was subsequently approved by the U.S. Department of Commerce. In mid-October 2001, the Census Bureau is expected to decide whether to recommend that statistical adjustment be used on census data for allocation of state and federal funds and other purposes.

SCOPE OF REPORT

This interim report assesses the operations of the census and the A.C.E. on the basis of information available to the panel from the Census Bureau as of August 2001. The Bureau is expected to release the results of additional evaluations to accompany its second decision in mid-October, and it has planned a longer range evaluation program as well. We commend the Census Bureau for its openness in providing documentation and evaluation data, as they are completed, to our panel and other advisory and oversight groups.

The panel has considered statistical data on census operations, the A.C.E. Program, imputation for missing information on census questionnaires, late additions to the census counts, mail return rates, and demographic analysis. The information on these topics does not support definitive assessments, particularly of which census operations and design features had the greatest effects on the completeness and quality of the census information. We offer this report to provide preliminary assessments and suggestions for next steps.

This interim report makes no judgment on the appropriateness of adjusting or not adjusting the census for net population undercount. The panel in its November 2000 letter report concluded that the Census Bureau's plans for evaluations that could be completed within the time available appeared to be sufficient for making a reasonably confident decision about adjustment in March 2001. However, the panel noted that whether the evaluations would permit such a decision would not become clear until the results were known. The evaluations were carried out as planned, and the Bureau determined that the results were inconclusive about important aspects of the A.C.E. and insufficient to resolve differences among the census estimate, A.C.E., and demographic analysis. The panel concludes that the Census Bureau followed its specified process and, thus, that its recommendation to release the counts from the census enumeration for redistricting was justifiable.

CENSUS AND A.C.E. OPERATIONS

We conclude that the 2000 census was well executed in many respects, particularly given the difficulties of last-minute changes in the overall design and other problems encountered prior to 2000. Ample funding enabled the Bureau staff to carry out the census on schedule.

Innovations

We examined six major innovations in the census, four of which appeared to be successful: (1) contracting for data operations and using improved technology for capturing the data on the questionnaires; (2) use of a redesigned questionnaire and mailing strategy to encourage response; (3) paid advertising and expanded outreach; and (4) aggressive recruitment of enumerators for follow-up of nonresponding households. The effectiveness of a fifth innovation—greater reliance on computers for data editing and imputation for inconsistent and missing responses—cannot be determined until information is available with which to evaluate the effects on data quality.

The sixth innovation was to develop the Master Address File (MAF)—a listing of all potential residences in the country—from new and multiple sources, including the U.S. Postal Service's Delivery Sequence File and interaction with local and tribal governments. Although the concept behind this MAF-building process made sense, there were problems in execution that may have increased duplicate and other erroneous enumerations. An ad hoc operation had to be mounted in summer 2000 to reduce duplication in the census from the MAF. Further evaluation is required to assess the success of that operation and the quality of the overall MAF.

Mail Response Rates

The mail response rate in the 2000 census—the percentage of all addresses from which a census questionnaire was received—held steady at the 1990 level. This was an important achievement in light of the decline in the response rate over several past censuses and given the expense and time required to visit addresses lacking a completed questionnaire. The mail return rate, a more refined indicator that focuses on occupied households by excluding vacant and nonresidential addresses, was very close to the 1990 rate. There was a marked decline in the return rate for recipients of the long-form questionnaire, which could have adverse affects on the quality of the long-form data. Mail return patterns were similar between 1990 and 2000: most areas that were hard to count and had low mail return rates in 1990 had low mail return rates in 2000.

A.C.E.

The A.C.E. is, like the census itself, a set of complex procedures and operations. The panel finds that the A.C.E. was well planned and documented and that it seems generally to have been well executed. However, until the Census Bureau completes additional studies of error in the A.C.E., the panel cannot offer a definitive assessment of it.

POPULATION COVERAGE

The net undercount of the population, as measured by the A.C.E., declined from about 4 million people (1.6 percent of the population) in 1990 to about 3.3 million people (1.2 percent of the population) in 2000. Moreover, net undercount rates were considerably reduced for such historically less-well-counted groups as children, minorities, and people who rent their homes. The level of gross errors—both omissions and erroneous enumerations—may also have been somewhat reduced.

Scattered evidence points to significant problems that may have occurred in enumerating people residing in group quarters, such as dormitories and nursing homes (about 3% of the population). The treatment of group quarters residents may also have been a problem in the A.C.E.

Apart from the question about group quarters residents, the reductions in the overall net undercount and in the differential undercount are puzzling because estimates of key components of the dual-systems estimation formula are similar between the 1990 Post-Enumeration Survey and the 2000 A.C.E. In investigating this puzzle, the panel focused on two groups of people whose census records were not included in the A.C.E. process: people who required imputation to complete their census records and people reinstated in the census too late for A.C.E. processing.

People Requiring Imputation

The panel found a large part of the explanation for the reduction in net undercount in the group of people who had insufficient information (concerning name and other characteristics) to carry out the individual matching required in the core of the A.C.E. process. Their census records were completed by computerized imputation routines that used information from the household or a neighboring household. The 2000 census included about three times as many people requiring imputation (5.8 million) as did the 1990 census (1.9 million). This much larger number contributed to reducing the net undercount when the dual-systems estimate from the A.C.E. was compared with the census count. Moreover, the people requiring imputation in 2000 were disproportionately found among minorities, renters, and children, thus accounting in large part for the reduction in differential net undercount for these groups relative to non-Hispanic whites, owners, and older people.

Of the 5.8 million people who required imputation for some or all of their characteristics, a large number—2.3 million—were imputed in situations when the household size and characteristics of other members were known. Another large group—also about 2.3 million—were imputed into households believed to be occupied for which household size, but not other information, was available. In these cases, the imputation used information for a similar size household in the immediate neighborhood. In terms of assessing the quality of the census, a much more problematic group—amounting to 1.2 million people in 2000—are those who were imputed into the census when there was no information about the size of the household or, in some instances, whether the address was occupied. Factors contributing to this type of imputation, which could have been problems in the MAF or in follow-up operations, should be thoroughly investigated.

People Reinstated in the Census

Another group of people excluded from the A.C.E. processing were residents of housing units that were temporarily removed from the census data processing in summer 2000 as part of the ad hoc operation to reduce duplication from the MAF. This operation identified 6 million people as potential duplicates whose records were temporarily deleted from the census. After further examination, 3.6 million of them were confirmed deletions, and 2.4 million were reinstated, but too late for inclusion in the A.C.E. These 2.4 million reinstated people contributed to reducing the net undercount when the dual-systems estimate from the A.C.E. was compared with the census count. They were about equally likely to be found among historically better-counted groups as among historically worse-counted groups, so they did not affect differences in net undercount rates.

DEMOGRAPHIC ANALYSIS

The Census Bureau's initial population estimates obtained through demographic analysis—a technique that uses birth, death, and Medicare records and estimates of net immigration to build an estimate of the population—were lower than the estimates from the census and the A.C.E. This result suggests that both the census and the A.C.E. overcounted the population. The panel finds, however, that there are serious questions about the demographic analysis, especially with regard to the methods for estimating the components of net immigration. The panel concludes that because of the uncertainties about the accuracy of the estimates of immigrants (especially the undocumented alien component) and emigrants, compounded by the difficulties of classifying people by race, demographic analysis should not be used as a standard for evaluation at this time.

NEXT STEPS

Looking to the Census Bureau's program for further evaluation of the census, the A.C.E., and demographic analysis, we urge the Bureau to devote resources to completing planned studies on as fast a schedule as practicable. The information from the 2000 evaluations is needed not only to assess the 2000 census, but also to plan for 2010.

Important aspects of census operations that we have identified for timely evaluation (some of which will be addressed in the evaluations to be released in mid-October) include:

- the completeness of coverage of the group quarters population and the effects of address list development and enumeration procedures on coverage of this population;

- the quality of the MAF and the contribution (of both good and erroneous addresses) of the Local Update of Census Addresses Program and other sources;

- sources of addresses of people deleted from and reinstated in the census;

- reasons for larger numbers of people requiring imputation to complete their census records, such as possible problems with follow-up operations; and

- evaluations of the computerized routines used for imputation.

In addition, as soon as practicable, the important demographic and socioeconomic information collected in the census long form (sent to a one-sixth sample of households) should be evaluated.

The A.C.E. operations and results were analyzed extensively by the Census Bureau prior to March 2001, but those studies left important unanswered questions, such as about the quality of the matching. The Bureau is completing additional studies that will be released in mid-October. Further research that should be conducted on the A.C.E. includes evaluation of the population strata used for estimation and sensitivity analysis of the components of the process (e.g., matching, treatment of people who moved between Census Day and the A.C.E. interview day) to help establish error bounds for the dual-systems estimates.

The Census Bureau is conducting additional evaluations of components of demographic analysis for release in mid-October. Further work is needed—particularly to improve estimates of immigration and emigration—if the results of demographic analysis are to be useful for census coverage evaluation. We urge the Bureau to increase its resources for demographic analysis. It should lead a research effort by appropriate federal agencies and outside experts to develop improved methods and sources of data for estimating legal and illegal immigrants in surveys and administrative records as input to demographic analysis and for other uses.

1

Introduction

In forming a new nation after the American Revolution, the U.S. Constitution mandated the conduct of a census of population to permit peaceful reallocation of political power among the states every 10 years. From the first census in 1790, which counted 3.9 million people, the content and operation of the census, and often the use of the results, have been a source of debate (see Anderson, 1988; Anderson and Fienberg, 2001b). The 2000 census, which counted 281.4 million people, is no exception.

The dominant point of contention regarding the 2000 census has been which set of numbers to use as the official population counts for states or small areas: the totals from the census enumeration process or the results of a procedure that uses sample-based statistical techniques to adjust those totals for the estimated net undercount. Throughout the 1990s, the issue of sample-based adjustment was debated by researchers and policy makers and contested in courtrooms (see Brown et al., 1999; Freedman, 1991; Freedman and Navidi, 1992). Those debates shaped the planning of the 2000 census and set the stage for crucial decisions on the use of adjusted census data in three major applications.

The first of these major application decisions was whether sampling could be used to adjust the state counts used to fulfill the primary constitutional mandate of the census: the reapportionment of the U.S. House of Representatives. That decision was made by the U.S. Supreme Court in January 1999, when the court ruled that existing law (in Title 13 of the U.S. Code) prohibits the use of sampling in producing population counts for reapportionment. Accordingly, the U.S. Census Bureau revised its plan for the 2000 census—which had included the possibility of that use—and the apportionment totals delivered to the president on December 28, 2000, were derived from the basic enumeration.[1]

The Supreme Court's ruling did not preclude use of sampling to adjust census data for other purposes; consequently, the Bureau carried out its planned

---

[1] The population counts for purposes of congressional reapportionment include residents of the 50 states and the District of Columbia as of April 1, 2000, comprising citizens, legal aliens (except for visitors or staff of foreign embassies), and undocumented aliens. U.S. merchant personnel on ships and federal and civilian employees overseas (who are assigned to their state of residence) are included in reapportionment counts but not in census data for other uses.

Accuracy and Coverage Evaluation (A.C.E.) Program in summer 2000. The A.C.E. matched the results of a survey of people residing in a set of randomly selected blocks to the set of census enumerations from those blocks and used the statistical method of dual-systems estimation to produce population estimates that could be used to adjust the census data.[2]

Redistricting—the redrawing of boundaries of congressional and other legislative districts to reflect population shifts—was the focus of the second major application decision regarding sample-based adjustment. The Census Bureau faced a legally mandated deadline of April 1, 2001, to release population counts at the block level for redistricting purposes. On March 1, the Census Bureau recommended to the U.S. Secretary of Commerce that unadjusted counts from the enumeration process should be the official data for redistricting; the secretary adopted the Bureau's recommendation on March 6. The Bureau's recommendation not to adjust the block-level counts was driven by the lack of time to resolve its concerns over the accuracy of disparate population estimates derived from the census, the A.C.E., and demographic analysis (a technique that constructs a national population estimate based on birth, death, and Medicare records, and estimates of net immigration).

The third major application decision on adjustment of the 2000 census is expected to occur on or about October 15, 2001, when the Bureau issues its recommendation on whether to adjust census data that are used to allocate state and federal funds and for other purposes. The Bureau has been conducting additional evaluations since March of the census, the A.C.E., and demographic analysis. It is at this juncture, between two critical decision points in the release of 2000 census data, that the Panel to Review the 2000 Census offers preliminary assessments of the census and A.C.E. processes.

CHARGE TO THE PANEL

Given the importance of the many uses of census data and the need to have an independent assessment of the quality of the 2000 census operations and results, the Census Bureau in 1998 asked the Committee on National Statistics (CNSTAT) of the National Research Council to convene a Panel to Review the 2000 Census. The panel has a broad charge to review the statistical methods of the 2000 census, particularly the use of the A.C.E. and dual-systems estimation, and other census procedures that may affect the completeness and quality of the data. A sister CNSTAT Panel on Research on Future Census Methods was convened in 1999 to begin consideration of the Census Bureau's planning process for the 2010 census (see National Research Council, 2000a).

The panel has conducted several activities to date to carry out its charge. The panel held three open workshops on topics related to the A.C.E. and the

---

[2]See the Glossary for definitions of such technical terms as dual-systems estimation.

possible adjustment of census counts, in October 1999, February 2000, and October 2000 (National Research Council, 2001a, 2001b, 2001c). Individual panel members and staff also discussed aspects of the census, the A.C.E., and demographic analysis with other experts in the field.

Panel members and staff made observation visits in 1999 and 2000 to selected census data capture centers, regional census offices, regional A.C.E. offices, and local census offices around the country. (The panel chair and staff previously observed operations in the 1998 Columbia, South Carolina, and Sacramento, California, dress rehearsal sites.) The purpose of the trips was to familiarize the panel with census and A.C.E. operations.

Because of the importance of the Master Address File (MAF) to a complete census and because of new procedures used for input to the 2000 MAF by localities, the panel commissioned a review of the 2000 Local Update of Census Addresses (LUCA) Program by a working group of six representatives of governments that participated in the program. The group conducted a survey of 101 governments that participated in LUCA, completed over a dozen in-depth case studies of LUCA participation, and analyzed data on LUCA participation and the MAF provided by the Census Bureau (LUCA Working Group, 2001).

Panel members and staff reviewed the extensive documentation and evaluation results made available by the Census Bureau in support of its March 1, 2001, recommendation not to adjust the data for redistricting.[3] The panel also conducted extensive analyses of microdata that the Bureau made available to the panel, the 2000 Census Monitoring Board, and the U.S. House of Representatives Subcommittee on the Census (see "Census Oversight," below). These data not only informed the panel about the operations of the A.C.E., but also provided a window (from the census enumerations in the A.C.E. sample blocks) into operational aspects of the census itself.

This is the panel's third report. A letter report, released in May 1999, commented on aspects of the proposed sample and post-stratification design for the A.C.E. (National Research Council, 1999a). A second letter report, released in November 2000, commented on the process and evaluations that the Census Bureau planned to follow for its March 2001 decision on whether to provide adjusted or unadjusted data for legislative redistricting (National Research Council, 2000b). We expect to issue a third letter report after the Bureau makes a recommendation on adjustment of census data for such purposes as fund allocation (see Part I). The panel is charged to issue a final report in September 2002.

---

[3]These documents, archived at http://www.census.gov/dmd/www/EscapRep.html, include a report from the Census Bureau's Executive Steering Committee for A.C.E. Policy (2001a) and 19 memoranda in the "B" series, many of which are cited in this report.

CENSUS OVERSIGHT: A BRIEF REVIEW

Our panel is not the only group charged with reviewing the 2000 census. Indeed, this census has been conducted in an atmosphere of unprecedented attention and oversight, not only during the actual enumeration, but also throughout the decade leading up to 2000.

1991–1996

Several oversight mechanisms were established early in the decade for reviewing 2000 census plans in response to concerns about the 1990 census: its high cost and yet its failure to reduce the net undercount or to narrow the difference between net undercount rates for minorities and the white population from what was measured in the 1980 census. The net undercount of the population, measured by demographic analysis, increased from 1.2 percent (2.8 million people) in 1980 to 1.9 percent (4.7 million people) in 1990. Net undercount rates for blacks increased from 4.5 percent in 1980 to 5.7 percent in 1990; net undercount rates for nonblacks increased from 0.8 percent in 1980 to 1.3 percent in 1990 (National Research Council, 1995:Table 2-1).

The Secretary of Commerce in late 1991 established a 2000 Census Advisory Committee, consisting of over 30 representatives from a wide range of associations representing business, labor, minority groups, data users, scientific professions, state and local governments, and others. This committee met several times a year over the decade (and continues to meet on planning for the 2010 census). Also meeting regularly during the 1990s on 2000 census issues were the Bureau's long-established Advisory Committee of Professional Associations and advisory committees for minority groups (Citro, 2000a).

Two Committee on National Statistics panels were established in 1992 to address 2000 census planning. One panel was convened at the behest of Congress to consider data requirements and alternative designs for 2000 (National Research Council, 1995); the other panel was convened at the Census Bureau's request to consider detailed methodology (National Research Council, 1994). Subsequently, a third CNSTAT panel was organized in 1996 to comment periodically on the Bureau's maturing plans for 2000; this panel issued its final report in 1999 (National Research Council, 1999b).

The Bureau reviewed the results of its research and testing with all of these groups and others, such as the U.S. General Accounting Office and the Department of Commerce Inspector General's Office. The Bureau's research covered a wide array of topics, including alternative methods to improve the response rate of households to mail questionnaires, simplify the short and long forms, and measure coverage of the population.

By February 1996 the Bureau had decided on a plan for the 2000 census that maximized the use of statistical sample-based techniques to conduct the enumeration and adjust the population data for measured net undercount. To reduce the costs and time needed to complete the enumeration and the adjustment, the Bureau intended to follow up households that did not mail back a questionnaire on a sample basis instead of revisiting every nonresponding household. (This procedure was termed sampling for nonresponse follow-up, or SNRFU.) To be able to produce one set of adjusted population counts by the December 31, 2000, deadline for providing state population totals for congressional reapportionment, the Bureau planned an Integrated Coverage Measurement (ICM) Program. Under this "one-number census" plan, the Bureau would conduct a large survey of 750,000 households, match the survey responses with census records, and have the results ready to produce adjusted estimates by the mandated deadline. The plan using SNRFU and ICM was first tested in the field in the 1995 test census conducted at three sites (Wright, 2000).

1997–2001

Views on the merits of the Bureau's 2000 census plan in Congress and the executive branch divided along partisan lines: the Clinton Administration and House Democrats generally supported the use of sampling while House Republicans generally opposed its use (see McMillen, 1998). Conflict between the two sides resulted in a delay of funds with which to conduct the 1998 dress rehearsal. In fall 1997 compromise legislation stipulated that unadjusted data would be released from the 2000 census in addition to any adjusted data. It also provided for expedited judicial review of the legality of the use of sampling for the census and established a 2000 Census Monitoring Board to consist of four members appointed by House and Senate Republican leaders and four members appointed by President Clinton in consultation with House and Senate Democratic leaders. The Monitoring Board was proposed as a way to address the concerns of some in Congress that the administration might manipulate the census data for political gain.[4] With this mechanism in place, there was agreement that the dress rehearsal and other necessary census planning activities would be fully funded and that the dress rehearsal in one of the planned sites would be conducted without the use of either SNRFU or ICM. The House of Representatives also established a Subcommittee on the Census in the Committee on Government Reform and Oversight, which began census oversight activities in early 1998.[5]

---

[4]The congressional and presidential appointees each have their own budgets and staffs and are charged to report periodically to Congress through September 2001 (see U.S. Census Monitoring Board Presidential Members, 2001a, 2001b; U.S. Census Monitoring Board Congressional Members, 2001).

[5]The subcommittee is slated to go out of existence at the end of 2001.

The Census Bureau consequently adjusted its planning to allow for two possible census designs—one based on SNRFU and ICM, the other implementing follow-up on a 100 percent basis and using a postenumeration survey to evaluate coverage. The Bureau implemented each design in a dress rehearsal in spring 1998: the rehearsal in Sacramento, California, used SNRFU and ICM; the one in Columbia, South Carolina, and surrounding counties, used traditional census methods with a postenumeration survey. A third dress rehearsal in Menominee County, Wisconsin (which includes the Menominee Indian Reservation), was a hybrid using 100 percent nonresponse follow-up and ICM.

Following the January 1999 Supreme Court decision that existing law did not permit sampling for congressional reapportionment but did not rule out its use for other purposes, the Census Bureau again revised its plans. The final design for the 2000 enumeration was announced by Director Kenneth Prewitt at a press conference in February 1999, little more than a year before Census Day on April 1, 2000. That design was to follow up nonresponding households on a 100 percent basis and to deliver the enumerated counts—unadjusted for coverage errors—to the President by December 31, 2000, for use in reapportioning congressional seats. The design also included the Accuracy and Coverage Evaluation (A.C.E.) Program, in which 300,000 households would be interviewed in about 11,000 block clusters and their records matched with census records in those block clusters. Adjusted estimates, constructed by applying dual-systems estimation to the matched data, would be developed on a schedule that could permit releasing adjusted block data to all states by the statutory deadline of April 1, 2001, for use in congressional redistricting.

After intense debate, Congress approved this design and provided the full amount of funding requested by the Census Bureau. The amount—over $7 billion—exceeded that spent in any previous census even after adjustment for inflation and the increased U.S. population. The 2000 census design was carried out largely as planned; spending totaled about $300 million less than the amount budgeted.

AVAILABILITY OF INFORMATION

Throughout the 2000 census planning process and particularly in the period 1998–2001, the Census Bureau has shared its plans, research results, and other information with the unusually large array of oversight groups described above and with the broader scientific and stakeholder communities. The Bureau provided extensive documentation of the design and operational procedures planned for the A.C.E. at the first two open workshops sponsored by our panel (see "Charge to the Panel," above). At a third open workshop of our panel, the Bureau provided a full explication of the decision process and kinds of evaluations it planned to complete by March 2001. These evaluations were needed for the Executive Steering Committee for A.C.E. Policy (ES-CAP), comprised of senior Bureau staff, to recommend to the director—and the director in turn to recommend to the Secretary of Commerce—whether to release adjusted or unadjusted block data for redistricting.[6]

The Census Bureau also facilitated arrangements for staff and members of its oversight groups—including our panel, our sister Panel on Research on Future Census Methods, the full 2000 Census Monitoring Board, Republican and Democratic staffs of the House subcommittee, and the 2000 Census Advisory Committee—to observe census operations in the field during spring-summer 2000 at locations around the country. In addition, the Census Bureau director testified frequently before the House subcommittee throughout the conduct of the census, and the Bureau responded to numerous requests for information on census operations as they unfolded.

Beginning January 19, 2001, the Census Bureau took the unprecedented step of providing advance access to extensive source data, including A.C.E. microdata, to its major oversight groups—our panel, the 2000 Census Monitoring Board, and the House subcommittee. The intent was to enable these groups to become familiar with the files that would form the basis of the evaluations to be reviewed by ESCAP. The data were made available under a memorandum of understanding not to make public any information that would identify individuals.[7] It was also agreed that no summaries would be made public until ESCAP had announced its recommendation and released its report and supporting evaluations publicly on the Bureau's Internet web site (`http://www.census.gov/dmd/www/EscapRep.html`).

Overall, the thoroughness with which the Census Bureau has documented every step of its procedures and the amount of information the Bureau has shared with our panel and others are noteworthy and deserving of high praise. In its conduct of the 2000 census and the A.C.E. Program, the Census Bureau has reacted positively in its willingness to accept scientific and public review and criticism in the interests of the best possible outcome for the census.

MARCH ADJUSTMENT DECISION

The March 1, 2001, decision by the Census Bureau not to recommend adjustment of the census counts for purposes of legislative redistricting was surprising to many in light of the evolution of the census design over the decade

---

[6]The Clinton Administration had issued a regulation that delegated the authority for the adjustment decision from the Secretary of Commerce to the director of the Census Bureau; the Bush Administration reversed that action, returning the authority to the secretary.

[7]The microdata are only available for analysis at a secure site at Census Bureau headquarters. Persons designated by each group to have access to the microdata were sworn in as special Census employees for that purpose.

of the 1990s and particularly due to the more prominent role of the A.C.E. relative to the analogous 1990 Post-Enumeration Survey (PES). Also, public statements by Census Bureau officials before the census was completed stressed the limitations on the ability to count everyone in the nation through field procedures and the likelihood that statistical adjustment would improve the estimates of the population for important purposes.[8]

Census Bureau's Decision Process

The Census Bureau reached its conclusion not to adjust after carefully following the decision process it had specified, which was publicly explained at the panel's workshop in October 2000. All of the evaluations that the Bureau proposed to conduct were completed and reviewed by ESCAP. Given the time constraints, these evaluations could not be exhaustive, but included detailed assessments of A.C.E. operations, supplemented by more limited assessments of census operations and comparisons of adjusted and unadjusted census counts for different levels of geography.[9] It was hoped that these assessments, which largely addressed how well operations were performed, would provide sufficient information to conclude that adjusted counts did (or did not) represent an improvement over the counts from the census process. In addition, the Census Bureau planned to take account of population estimates from demographic analysis, which have historically provided a comparison standard for the census.

What, then, were the reasons for the decision not to adjust? An important reason cited by the ESCAP report was the inconsistencies between the population estimates from the census, the A.C.E., and demographic analysis; those inconsistencies could not be resolved or explained with the available evaluation data within the time available for the decision.

As shown in Table 1-1, the A.C.E. estimated that the overall net undercount dropped from 1.6 percent of the population in 1990 as measured by the Post-Enumeration Survey to 1.2 percent of the population in 2000 and that the net undercount for blacks dropped from 4.4 percent in 1990 to 2.1 percent in

---

[8]For example, Census Bureau Director Kenneth Prewitt wrote: "The Census Bureau has determined that the A.C.E. is operationally and technically feasible and expects, barring unforeseen operational difficulties that would have a significant effect on the quality of the data, that these corrected data will be more accurate than the uncorrected data for their intended purposes" (Prewitt, 2000:2).

[9]The A.C.E. evaluations covered rates of noninterviews in the independent P-sample and missing data in the P-sample and the census-based E-sample; quality control of the matching process; the extent of imputation required for unresolved match and enumeration status; inconsistent assignment of sample cases to estimation groups in the two samples; and variance due to sampling and imputation error in the dual-systems estimates. The census evaluations covered mail return rates; quality assurance of enumerators' field work; results of unduplication operations; and extent of missing data. Comparisons with 1990 census data were included when feasible. Documentation of these studies is provided in the "B" memoranda on the Census Bureau's web site.

TABLE 1-1 Alternative Estimates of Percentage Net
Undercount of the Population, April 2000 and 1990

| | 2000 | | | 1990 | |
| | Demographic Analysis | | | Demographic | |
Category	Base	Alternate	A.C.E.	Analysis	PES
Total population	−0.65	0.32	1.15	1.85	1.58
Black	2.80	3.51	2.06	5.68	4.43
Male	5.10	5.81	2.37	8.49	4.90
Female	0.63	1.32	1.78	3.01	4.01
Nonblack	−1.19	−0.17	1.02	1.29	1.18
Male	−0.93	0.17	1.40	1.97	1.52
Female	−1.44	−0.50	0.64	0.63	0.85
Difference, black-nonblack	3.99	3.67	1.04	4.39	3.25

NOTES: All estimates include the household and group quarters population. Net undercount
rates are calculated as the estimate (from demographic analysis, A.C.E., or PES) minus the
census count divided by the estimate. The census count of the population in 2000 was 281.4
million; the census count in 1990 was 248.7 million. The census count by race in 2000 varies
depending on the treatment of people who reported more than one race. The net undercount
estimates shown for 2000 are an average of estimates calculated using two different tabulations
of the census by race (see Chapter 5).

Minus sign (−) indicates a net overcount of the population.

For 2000 demographic analysis net undercount rates, "base" uses the original estimate
that includes an allowance for 6 million undocumented immigrants; "alternate" uses an
estimate that arbitrarily doubles the flow of undocumented immigrants between 1990 and
2000, allowing for 8.7 million undocumented immigrants total (see Chapter 5).

SOURCE: Robinson (2001a:Table 6).

2000. The A.C.E. also estimated marked reductions in net undercount rates
from 1990 for children under age 18, people who rent their homes, Hispanics,
Asians, and American Indians on reservations (see Chapter 6).

The reductions in net undercount are heartening, although there is a puzzling aspect to them that the ESCAP report did not discuss: because estimates
for key components of the dual-systems estimation formula were similar in
the A.C.E. and the 1990 Post-Enumeration Survey, the net undercount should
have been similar in both years, other things equal. However, the Census
Bureau's initial estimate from demographic analysis indicated that the 2000
census resulted in a slight (0.7%) net *overcount* of the population and that the
A.C.E. overstated the population by even more. Even when the Bureau adjusted the demographic analysis estimate upward to allow for a larger number
of undocumented immigrants than were part of the base estimate, the net undercount in 2000 was only 0.3 percent of the population. Demographic analysis
agreed with the A.C.E. in estimating a reduction in net undercount for children.
Demographic analysis also estimated that black and nonblack net undercount
rates differed by about 3.7–4.0 percentage points, compared with only 1.0 percentage point as measured by the A.C.E. (see Chapter 5).

The ESCAP report did cite several areas of concern about A.C.E. operations that might have affected dual-systems estimation. It questioned the level of "balancing error" that may have occurred in a procedure called targeted extended search. (Balancing error is when different criteria, such as different areas of search, are used in processing the independent survey and the sample of census enumerations—see Chapter 6.) It also questioned the level of "synthetic error" that may have occurred for dual-systems estimates of population groups called post-strata. (Synthetic error occurs when the people included in a post-stratum—who are intended to have the same likelihood of being included in the census or the A.C.E.—are in fact not sufficiently similar in this respect.) The report also considered late additions to the census and cases of people for whom minimal information was obtained in the field (who required imputation to complete their census records). Neither of these groups could be included in the A.C.E. There were substantially more such people in 2000 than in 1990, but the report concluded that they did not likely affect the dual-systems estimates.[10]

The Census Bureau had always planned a longer term evaluation program, in addition to the short-term evaluations that were feasible to carry out before March 1, 2001. Given its conclusion that the accuracy of the census, the A.C.E., and demographic analysis population estimates could not be definitively established, the Bureau has expedited several evaluations on the longer term agenda and is carrying out additional evaluations to help reach its planned decision by October 15 on whether to recommend adjustment of census population estimates for such purposes as fund allocation. Release of these evaluations is expected to accompany the decision.

Panel's Assessment

The panel, in its letter report issued November 2000 (National Research Council, 2000b:2), commented on the Census Bureau's evaluation process for the March 2001 decision as follows:

> The planned analyses appear to cover all of the evaluations that can reasonably be expected to be completed within the time available. Furthermore, they appear to be sufficiently comprehensive that they will likely provide support for a reasonably confident decision on adjustment in March.
>
> However, since the numbers themselves, which are, of course, critical to the evaluation process, are not yet available, it is not possible at this time to comment on what the adjustment decision should be nor to conclude definitively that the planned short-term evaluations will be adequate to support the decision.

---

[10]A lawsuit brought by the state of Utah is challenging the use of some kinds of imputed census records for purposes of congressional reapportionment (see http://www.attorneygeneral.utah.gov).

As it turned out, the Bureau concluded that the evaluation studies did *not* provide sufficient information to decide that adjusted counts would be clearly preferable to unadjusted counts for redistricting. Although not mentioned by the Census Bureau, reaching a conclusion on this point is more difficult when the adjustments to be made for population groups are generally small.[11]

The panel does not necessarily agree with the weight that the Bureau gave to each factor in its decision: specifically, we conclude that demographic analysis estimates are sufficiently uncertain that they should not be used as a standard for evaluation at this time (see Chapter 5). Nonetheless, we believe that the Bureau followed a reasonable process. We also believe that its decision not to recommend adjusting the census data in March was justifiable, given its conclusion that additional evaluations of the quality of the A.C.E.—and of the census itself—were needed to resolve its concerns.

The fact that the Bureau did not recommend adjusting the census counts to be provided for redistricting does not carry any implications for the usefulness of statistical adjustment methods based on dual-systems estimation. In particular, the panel views it as an open question whether adjusted counts would constitute an improvement over unadjusted counts for such purposes as fund allocation. The panel will assess the Census Bureau's October decision on the basis of the evidence available at that time (see Part I).

SCOPE AND LIMITATIONS OF THIS INTERIM REPORT

This interim report provides a preliminary assessment of census and A.C.E. operations, briefly reviews the Bureau's demographic analysis, and examines the puzzle from the reduction in net undercount measured by the A.C.E. The report does not address the superiority of one or the other set of population counts (the census or the A.C.E. estimates) for particular uses of the data.

The information available to the panel in preparing this report is extensive but does not make it possible to draw definite conclusions about the quality of the census operations or the quality of the resulting data. This report reviews the available information to identify areas for further research and to provide background for subsequent reports of the panel. The panel may revise its interim assessments when new information becomes available.

This report has eight chapters (including this introduction), a glossary, and three appendixes. Chapter 2 considers evaluation issues, including the multiple uses of census data (which complicate the task of evaluation), sources of error in the census (from which no data collection or estimation effort can be completely free), and types of evaluation. Chapter 3 provides background information on 2000 census operations, noting important differences from the

---

[11]A small (or zero) net undercount for the population as a whole is not a reason for or against adjustment because net undercounts can mask sizable gross errors of omissions and erroneously included enumerations. The issue is how the balance between these components of error differs among population groups and geographic areas, resulting in different net undercount rates.

procedures used in 1990. (Appendix A provides a more detailed description.) Chapter 4 provides the panel's initial assessment of census operations. (Appendix B provides detailed results from an analysis of mail return rates in 1990 and 2000.)

Chapter 5 reviews demographic analysis and the issues surrounding the demographic estimates for 2000. Chapter 6 provides background information on the population coverage estimates from the A.C.E., the method of dual-systems estimation, and the A.C.E. operations, including important differences from the procedures used in the 1990 PES (Appendix C provides a more detailed description of the A.C.E. operations). Chapter 7 provides the panel's initial assessment of the A.C.E. operations.

Finally, Chapter 8 examines the characteristics of two groups of people who could not be included in the A.C.E. They are people whose census records were available too late for A.C.E. processing and people who required imputation to complete their census records. These groups, especially the second, account for the puzzling aspects in the A.C.E. and PES results noted above.

The panel looks forward to continuing its evaluation of the census and the A.C.E., as additional information becomes available that can support firmer conclusions about the quality of the adjusted and unadjusted census data and their appropriate use.

The panel notes that the census obtained a wide range of socioeconomic data on the long form (which was sent to about one in six households). These data are also important to assess, given the use of long-form estimates for allocation of billions of dollars of federal funds to states and localities and for other important policy purposes. Processing of the 2000 long-form data has not been completed; the panel expects to assess those data in its final report, as part of the panel's final assessment of the 2000 census.

2

Evaluation Issues

Conducting a population census of the United States is a task of awesome difficulty; it requires massive effort—in a short amount of time—to enumerate and collect data on over 280 million residents at their precise geographic location, striving always to count every resident once and only once. In order to meet this challenge, the decennial census-taking process has evolved into an extremely complex set of operations and components, some of which have been integral parts of the process for decades and others of which were introduced in 2000 as the newest and possibly best means of improving the count.

Evaluating a decennial census is a similarly daunting mission, requiring careful scrutiny of every procedure and careful assessment of the effect of each procedure on the quality of the resulting data. The ultimate benchmark against which the results of a census could be compared—namely, an unambiguously true count of the population—is as unknown and elusive to census evaluators as it is to census collectors. Thus, the task of rendering a summary judgment on the quality of a particular decennial census is a very complicated undertaking.

The overall charge of the Panel to Review the 2000 Census is to assist the Census Bureau in evaluating the 2000 census, and this report constitutes the panel's preliminary findings. Hence, the panel believes that it is appropriate to begin this report by explaining the manner in which it conceptualizes its primary objective—that is, describing how it defines the job of evaluating the decennial census. In this chapter we discuss two general principles that shape our approach to the problem: the necessity of assessing data quality in the context in which the data are used and the inevitability of error in the decennial census. We then outline a basic program for evaluating the 2000 census. This program is necessarily ambitious, and this interim report is decidedly *not* intended to be a full realization of that program. Rather, this chapter illustrates the panel's general orientation toward census evaluation and provides the context for the panel's own work and its recommendations for evaluation to the Census Bureau.

CENSUS DATA IN CONTEXT

The result of a decennial census is a collection of data products, which can generally be classified into two broad categories: basic population counts and summaries of the characteristics of areas or groups.[1] Collectively, these data products are used for a wide variety of public and private needs; they are examined in a myriad of contexts and interpreted in many different ways.[2] Proper evaluation of a census demands assessment of the quality and usefulness of its results in the context in which those results are actually used.

The first type of census data product—population counts for the nation as a whole and for subnational areas—satisfies the constitutional mandate for the census by providing the state-level counts required to reapportion the U.S. House of Representatives. Likewise, small-area population counts are the essential building blocks used for redistricting within states and localities. Basic population counts, sometimes differentiated by demographic group, are crucial for a variety of other uses, including:

- calibration of data from other collection and survey programs, such as the Current Population Survey, the Vital Statistics of the United States, and the Uniform Crime Reports;

- determination of eligibility for federal and state government funding programs;

- comparison and ranking of areas (such as cities and metropolitan areas) for such purposes as advertising, marketing, and public information; and

- benchmarking of intercensal population estimates.

Census count data are used to estimate both the level (raw count) and the share (proportion) of total population across different geographic areas; they are also used to compute change over time for either levels or shares.

The second type of census data product—local area or group characteristics—includes the various counts and averages that result from detailed cross-classification by geographic, demographic, and socioeconomic variables, particularly those collected on the decennial census long form. Examples of these characteristics include per capita income by census tract and state-level counts by demographic group, educational level, and employment type. Data sets of this type form the cornerstone of basic and applied socioeconomic research.

---

[1]A third type of data product not considered in this categorization are public-use microdata sample (PUMS) files, which are sampled individual records from census files (using appropriate safeguards to protect confidentiality and privacy); these files are used to support a wide range of academic research.

[2]See National Research Council (1985:Ch.2) and National Research Council (1995:Ch.1, Apps.C, D, E, F, G, H, and M) for more detailed discussions of census data use.

They play central roles in the evaluation of equal employment opportunity and other programs, and they are used in fund allocation formulas.

Both census data types are vital ingredients for general planning, analysis, and decision making by both governmental and nongovernmental (commercial) entities of all sizes. State and local governments rely on these data for such purposes as assigning personnel to police and fire precincts, identifying the areas of a city in greatest need of service facilities, and conducting traffic planning studies. Likewise, business plans and decisions depend on census count and characteristics data: applications include locating retail outlets, comparing the market potential of different cities, and assessing the availability of needed occupational skills in different labor market areas. Both census data types are essential to many academic and private-sector researchers whose work depends on charting population differences and their changes over time.

There is no single, dominant use of census data. The significance of this fact for census evaluation is that there is no single, dominant metric against which census results can be compared in order to unequivocally determine that they are either good or bad. For example, a census could provide outstanding count data but subpar characteristics data: this could happen if serious problems occurred with the census long form. The data from such a census would be perfectly adequate for some uses but would fail to satisfy others. Similarly, the representation of the data as levels or shares, or the level of geographic aggregation, might affect one's judgment of the quality of the data. For instance, a purely hypothetical census that—for some reason—did an excellent job of collecting information from males but not from females could still produce reasonably accurate inferences when the data are presented as shares across different geographic areas, but would suffer badly when used as count data. Similarly, changes in census processes could improve the precision of counts while hurting the use of the same data to represent changes in counts over time. For example, the change to allow multiple responses to race and ethnicity questions in the 2000 census may make it possible to capture data on more focused demographic groups, but complicate inferences about the relative sizes of minority groups relative to past censuses. A comprehensive evaluation of a census must, therefore, strive to interpret census results in the context of all of their possible uses.

ERROR

At the most basic level, an ideal census evaluation would measure the differences between census-based counts or estimates and their associated true values. An estimated count greater than the true value would be considered a net overcount, and an estimated count less than the truth would be a net undercount. These differences between estimates and (unknown) truth are *errors*, in the statistical sense. Despite the word's colloquial meaning, these errors are not necessarily an indication that a mistake has been made.

Another measure of error would be the sum of the deviations from the true values for a population group, which would be the gross coverage error, comprising gross overcount and gross undercount. Gross error is a useful quality indicator since it may indicate problems that are not obvious from a measure of net error. For example, net coverage error could be zero for the total population, but there could be large gross errors of omissions and erroneous enumerations. To the extent that these two types of error differ among population groups, there could be different net undercounts for population groups even when total net error is zero. Moreover, even when gross omissions and erroneous enumerations balance, examination of them could help identify sources of error that would be useful to address by changing enumeration procedures or other aspects of the census.

Any evaluation of a decennial census must necessarily attempt to get some reading of the level of various types of error in the census, even though those errors cannot be computed directly. Census evaluations must confront a commonsense but nevertheless critical reality: error is an inevitable part of the census, and perfection—the absence of all error—is an unrealistic and unattainable standard for evaluation. The sources of census error are numerous, and many are simply uncontrollable. In this light, census evaluators must be aware of potential sources of error, gauge their potential effects, and develop strategies to measure and (when possible) minimize errors. We do not attempt in this section an exhaustive study of each of these topics, but intend only to provide a general flavor of the problems related to census error.

Sources of Error

Errors in the census can generally be categorized as one of two broad types. First, they may result from problems of coverage—that is, each address does not appear once and only once in the Census Bureau's address list, and each individual is not included once and only once in the enumeration. Second, errors may arise due to problems of response, in that responses on a collected questionnaire may be incomplete or inaccurate.[3]

Examples of potential errors in coverage are numerous; one natural source of such errors is the list of mailing addresses used by the Census Bureau to deliver census questionnaires. This list, the Master Address File (MAF) in the 2000 census, was constructed in order to be as thorough as possible. The dynamic nature of the U.S. population and their living arrangements make it all but impossible for the list to be completely accurate: it is difficult to fully capture additions and deletions to the list that result from construction of new

---

[3]This is a nonexhaustive categorization; other types of error do occur in the census. For instance, the census long form is only distributed to a sample (17%) of the population and so estimates based on the long form—like all survey results—are subject to sampling error. The statistical procedure used to weight long-form responses to make them comparable to short-form counts—iterative proportional fitting—is also subject to small amounts of error.

residences, demolition of former residences, and restructuring of existing residences. Identifying all residences in remote rural areas and in multi-unit structures is also a major challenge. Many individuals have more than one home (examples include "snowbirds" from cold-weather states with winter homes in Florida or the Southwest and children in joint custody arrangements), while many others are homeless most or all of the time. In the 2000 census, the Master Address File was built in part with sources that were not used in previous censuses, such as the Delivery Sequence File used by the U.S. Postal Service to coordinate its mail carriers and the direct addition of new addresses from local and tribal governments. The intent was to make the MAF as complete as possible and improve coverage; however, these sources are not guaranteed to be complete, and they may have inadvertently added duplicate addresses to the final address list. All of these complications—representing possible gaps or overages in the address list—may result in either undercounts or overcounts.

Errors in response are similarly numerous and impossible to avoid. Many people simply do not fully cooperate in filling out census forms; this is a particular concern for the census long form, parts of which some respondents may believe violate their privacy or confidentiality.[4] Some households and individuals do not respond to all the questions on the questionnaire; there may also be some degree of intentional misresponse. Of course, not all of the census response errors result from the actions of respondents; some error is also introduced—often unintentionally but sometimes deliberately—by members of the massive corps of temporary census field workers assigned to follow up on nonresponding residents. Although steps are taken to prevent the fabrication of a census response by filling in information for a housing unit without actually visiting it and conducting an interview—a practice known as curbstoning—this practice remains a well-documented source of survey error. Another source of census response error is confusion over the questionnaire itself; language difficulties may deter some respondents, while others may not understand who should and should not be included, such as students on temporary visas or away at college.

Consequences of Error

The potential effect of different levels of census error is difficult to quantify succinctly, primarily because the effects of error depend greatly on the use to which census data are put and on the fineness with which the data are aggregated geographically.[5] To date, the focus of research on the consequences of census error has been on their effect on three major uses of census data: reapportionment of the U.S. House of Representatives (as mandated in the U.S.

---

[4]See National Research Council (1995:App.L) for more details on census long-form response rates.

[5]For a more comprehensive discussion of the effects of census errors on various applications, see National Research Council (1985:Ch.2), on which we draw here.

Constitution), legislative redistricting, and formula allocation programs. In all these cases, high levels of net undercount or overcount can have major consequences, but there is no easy way to determine a threshold beyond which the level of error in a census is somehow unacceptable.

Concern over the possible effect of census coverage error on congressional reapportionment—and, more specifically, the effect of competing statistical adjustments to try to correct for said error—has fueled debate over census methodology for years. Although the U.S. Supreme Court's 1999 decision prohibited the use of sampling-based census estimates for reapportionment, the potential effects of error and adjustment on apportionment are still viable concerns, given the prominence of reapportionment as a use of census data. In studies related to the 1990 census, census data adjusted to reflect estimated net undercount produced different results when input into the "method of equal proportions" formula used for reapportionment than did unadjusted counts; specifically, one or two seats would have shifted between states if adjusted counts had been used. The sensitivity of the apportionment formula to small shifts in population counts was cited by the then Commerce Secretary Robert Mosbacher in his decision not to adjust the 1990 census. The change in political clout that can result from a shift of even one seat defies estimation; moreover, the mere fact that different levels of census error and adjustment strategies can alter apportionment opens the door to the unfounded but damaging assertion that the census can be manipulated to produce a desired political effect.

The potential effect of census error on legislative redistricting is particularly hard to assess, given the intensely political nature of the process. The shrewdness of a mapmaker in piecing together blocks into districts arguably has more effect on any perceived bias in the district than do block-level census errors. However, it is certainly possible that high levels of error in the census could have major effects on districts within states. For instance, errors in the census might affect the urban-rural balance within a state, and any resulting district map could dilute the vote of urban residents at the expense of rural residents—or vice versa. Such outcomes would depend on the average size of the districts, the differential undercoverage rates of major population groups, the proportionate distribution among areas of these population groups, and the number of contiguous districts with high rates of census undercoverage.

The large amount of federal funds distributed per year to states and localities on the basis of population counts or characteristics—about $180 billion—raises the potential for considerable effects from census errors. However, the large number of complicated (and, at times, undocumented) formulas makes it extremely difficult to carry out a comprehensive analysis. The research to date on a small subset of programs suggests two basic effects. First, the effects on allocations are larger for programs that distribute funds on a per capita basis than for programs that allocate shares of a fixed total, since in the latter situation, it is not total net undercoverage that determines additional funds, but differential undercoverage. Second, when formulas are based on factors in addition to population counts, such as per capita income, errors in census coverage often have less effect on fund distribution than the errors in the other factors (see National Research Council, 1995:Ch.2; Steffey, 1997).

Methods to Measure Error

Because true values for population counts for geographic areas are never available, estimates of the level of error in those data must necessarily be carried out indirectly. The most common measures of census error are based on external validation: comparison values from other (partly or completely independent) sources are obtained and used as substitutes for the true values, and census errors are then approximated. For the 2000 census, such comparison values either are or will be available from a host of sources: the Accuracy and Coverage Evaluation (A.C.E.) Program; demographic analysis; the Census 2000 Supplementary Survey (the pilot American Community Survey); other household surveys, such as the Current Population Survey; and administrative records such as those collected by the Internal Revenue Service. It is important to note, however, that the use of these comparison values does not guarantee accurate approximations of census error. All of these comparison values are themselves subject to error that is only partially understood, and it is possible that they are more subject to error than are the census data to which they are compared. Still, external validation can provide useful insights.

Another method is to scrutinize and study individual components of the census process for their potential effect on census undercoverage or overcoverage. For instance, when there are unresponsive households, census enumerators collect information on those households from proxies, such as neighbors or landlords. Since these proxy responses may contain inaccurate or incomplete data, the rate of proxy responses in the census is an important barometer of census response error. Similarly, such operations as the "Be Counted" Program (which made census forms available in public places) and the effort to enumerate people in soup kitchens and homeless shelters may mistakenly duplicate people already included in the mailout/mailback component of the 2000 census. Careful attention to each individual component of the decennial census process produces a long list of measures that, when viewed as a whole, can inform a judgment on census error. Such a list can also be helpful in crafting strategies—such as techniques to impute for nonresponse—to try to curb census error.

AN EVALUATION PROGRAM

Bearing the preceding concepts in mind, we now outline some primary steps of a comprehensive census evaluation program. This sketch will evolve as the panel continues its investigations and discussions. Over its lifetime, the panel will undertake as much of this evaluation program as its resources permit. In many cases, though, the Census Bureau must play a major role in compiling and analyzing relevant evaluation data from the confidential census records and voluminous ancillary data sets (e.g., performance records for census operations). Accordingly, the panel awaits results from the Bureau's own evaluation program and reports. The panel urges the Census Bureau to continue its efforts to provide complete documentation, supporting data, and evaluation results to the research community.

Assessments of Primary Components

A central part of the panel's evaluation will be an examination of the major components of the 2000 census and their subcomponents. These major components include, but are not necessarily limited to, the following (each of which is described more fully in Chapter 3 and, subsequently, in Appendix A):

(1) development of the Master Address File, including: updates from the Postal Service Delivery Sequence File, block canvassing, and the Local Update of Census Addresses Program; special efforts to list group quarters and special places; and operations to filter duplicate addresses;

(2) delivery and return of the census questionnaires by mail or in person by census enumerators, including: the procedures for identifying geographic areas in which different enumeration strategies would be used; analysis of respondent cooperation in areas enumerated through the mailout/mailback and update/leave operations; and analysis of mail response and return rates for both the short and the long forms;

(3) conduct of auxiliary operations, such as advertising and local outreach, to enhance mail response and follow-up cooperation;

(4) field follow-up of addresses that failed to report; and

(5) data processing, including the optical scanning and reading of questionnaires and the techniques used to impute missing or erroneous responses.

For each of these components and their constituent procedures, there are five major questions for which answers are needed:

• What sorts of error (either undercount or overcount) might be induced by the procedure, and what evidence exists as to the actual level of error the procedure added to the 2000 census?

- In what ways did the procedures differ from those used in the 1990 or earlier censuses? In particular, what effects did new additions to the census process have on the level of census error?

- Were the procedures completed in a timely fashion?

- Did any evidence of systematic problems arise during their implementation?

- What parts of the procedure, if any, should be changed in order to improve the 2010 and later censuses?

Assessment of External Validity Measures

Demographic analysis, the Accuracy and Coverage Evaluation (A.C.E.) Program, and possibly the Census 2000 Supplementary Survey are the primary external measures for comparison with 2000 census estimates to gauge the overall level of error. Accordingly, the quality of these sources of information must be assessed prior to their use. Particular attention must be paid to the types of error intrinsic to these measures, to their underpinning assumptions and their validity, and to the possible interpretations of discrepancies between these measures and census counts. Since these external validity measures are the result of a complex set of operations and procedures—like the census itself—the effectiveness of those procedures should be subjected to the same scrutiny as the census process, as outlined in the preceding section.

Assessment of Types of Errors

Using external validation, a crucial task is to assess the amount of net undercount and gross coverage error for various demographic groups at various levels of geographic aggregation. An important question is whether any patterns of net undercount are affected when the census results examined are used as levels (counts), as shares (proportions), or as changes in counts or shares. It is also important to assess the error in estimates on the basis of the characteristics information collected on the census long form and how that error varies with level of geographic aggregation. One technique for this latter analysis is external validation from administrative records and other sources; another is a detailed component error analysis, attempting to sort out errors due to such sources as proxy response, imputation for item nonresponse, and sampling error.

Geographic Patterning of Error and Systematic Bias

The census data need to be carefully examined to identify patterns or clusters of either net undercount or net overcount, both to inform data users and to consider remedies for future censuses. Such patterns, if they correspond to areas that share common characteristics (such as demographic composition or level of income), may be indicative of a census process that is biased for or against those types of areas. Should any such patterns emerge, they should be checked against the results of previous censuses as a confirmatory measure.

SUMMARY

Evaluation of a decennial census is not an easy task, and it does not lend itself to snap summary judgments. That is, it is both futile and unfair to try to render verdicts like a "good census" or a "bad census," a "perfect census" or a "failed census." A thorough evaluation of a census must measure the quality of all of its various outputs, interpreting them in the context of their many possible uses; it must examine all procedures for the types of error they may introduce and use appropriate techniques to estimate the total level of error in the census. In this chapter the panel has sketched out its basic objectives and guidelines; in the remainder of this interim report, we begin this program of evaluation.

3

Census Operations: Overview

The process of conducting the 2000 decennial census involved a complex set of operations, with five primary components:

(1) develop the Master Address File (MAF), a list of addresses of all housing units in the country (along with a roster of dormitories, nursing homes, and other special places where people live in group quarters);[1]

(2) mail or hand deliver census questionnaires to each address on the MAF, asking households to fill them out and return them by mail, and enumerate households in selected areas in person;

(3) carry out such processes as advertising and outreach, with the intent of boosting mail response and follow-up cooperation;

(4) follow up those addresses that failed to report and implement other field-based checks and coverage improvement procedures; and

(5) process the data through the steps of data capture, unduplication, editing and imputation, and tabulation.

This set of components is an outline of the census enumeration process. It does not include the generation of demographic analysis estimates of overall patterns of census coverage (see Chapter 5); the Accuracy and Coverage Evaluation (A.C.E.) Program (see Chapters 6 and 7); or other evaluations and experiments by the Census Bureau (see National Research Council, 1999b, 2000a).

Table 3-1 lists the basic components in the census, summarizing the challenges for each component, innovative procedures used in 2000 to meet these challenges, and the possible benefits and risks from the 2000 innovations relative to the procedures used in 1990. The overarching challenge was to complete as accurate a count of people and housing units in the United States as possible. Ideally, the census would correctly include all of the population and

---

[1]Special places can also include separate residences (e.g., a warden's home in a prison complex).

TABLE 3-1 Operational Components and Challenges for the 2000 Census

Component	Challenges	2000 Solutions	Possible Benefits/Risks Compared with 1990
(1) Develop MAF for mailback universe (99% of population in 2000); develop list of special places for enumerating people in group quarters (dormitories, nursing homes, etc.)	Create list with fewest possible omissions and fewest possible duplicates or other erroneous addresses; assign (geocode) addresses correctly to census geographic units	Begin with 1990 list for most addresses; use multiple sources to update and correct (Postal Service list, field canvassing, local input, updating during enumeration, computer checking to reduce duplication)	❑ Multiple sources could reduce omissions (benefit), but increase duplication (risk) ❑ Local review could vary in extent and completeness (risk) ❑ Unduplication procedures (including the unplanned summer 2000 operation) could be incomplete (risk)
(2) Deliver questionnaires to each address on the list for households to fill out and mail back (enumerate rural households directly)	Obtain highest possible mail response and return rates through delivery procedures [see also (3)]	Use enumerators instead of U.S. Postal Service to reach non-city-style addresses; make multiple mailings (e.g., advance letter; use shortened user-friendly questionnaire; provide options to respond by telephone or the Internet; allow people to pick up "Be Counted" forms if they failed to receive a mailing	❑ Redesigned questionnaires and multiple mailings could boost mail response (benefit) ❑ Space for only 6 people on the questionnaire (7 in 1990) could affect count of large households (risk) ❑ Widespread availability of "Be Counted" forms could increase duplication (risk)
(3) Before and throughout census operations, conduct outreach and advertising programs to boost mail response rate and cooperation with follow-up enumerators	Reach and motivate general public and, especially, traditionally hard-to-count groups to fill out their census form	Run extensive Census in Schools Program; pay for advertising, including ads targeted to minority groups; hire partnership specialists; partner with local governments, businesses, and others for special outreach efforts; challenge communities to meet or exceed their 1990 mail response rate	❑ Much more extensive advertising and outreach could stem the decline in mail response rates that occurred from 1970 to 1990 (benefit) ❑ Partnership efforts could vary in effectiveness (particularly because Census Bureau could provide materials and limited staff help but not funding) (risk)

(4) Follow-up activities			
Send enumerators to follow up addresses for which no questionnaire is returned	Obtain accurately completed questionnaire (or designation of address as vacant or nonresidential) from every address not responding in a timely manner	Recruit more enumerators than are expected to be needed so that follow-up can be completed in a timely manner; pay higher area-adjusted wages to attract and keep good people	☐ More timely completion of follow-up could increase data quality and facilitate coverage evaluation (benefit) ☐ Push to complete enumeration could increase duplications and other errors (risk)
Send smaller, second wave of enumerators to recheck addresses designated as vacant or delete, enumerate late additions to MAF, check "Be Counted" and telephone forms, and enumerate lost or blank forms, so as to improve coverage	Carry out coverage improvement field checks accurately and on a timely basis	Limit rechecks of vacant units to those not classified as such in two previous operations; drop several 1990 operations: local review of preliminary housing counts, field reinterview of questionnaires with minimal information, and parolee and probationer coverage program	☐ Targeted coverage operations could reduce erroneous enumerations (benefit) at small risk of increased omissions ☐ Reduced follow-up for incomplete questionnaires could increase use of computerized statistical imputation techniques (neutral or risk)
(5) Process the questionnaires through data capture, coverage edit, unduplication, imputation for missing data, and tabulation	Carry out all data processing operations with a high degree of accuracy in a timely manner	Hire contractors to capture the data, using optical character recognition; identify forms with insufficient information about household members for telephone follow-up; unduplicate people and addresses [see (1)]; edit answers and impute values for missing answers; release data products in various formats (e.g., Internet)	☐ More centralization of computer processing and greater use of computerized editing could reduce errors and variability (benefit) ☐ Unduplication efforts could be incomplete (risk) ☐ Greater use of imputation could or could not effectively replace field work (neutral or risk)

miss none of the population. More practically, the goal for 2000 was to reduce the measured net undercount below previously observed levels for the total population and important population groups. In addition, the census had to be completed within statutory deadlines and within budget.

This chapter briefly describes the five major components of the 2000 census, emphasizing key differences from the 1990 census procedures. This overview provides background for the assessments in Chapters 4 through 8. Additional details on census procedures are in Appendix A, which contains full descriptions of census processes in 2000 and 1990.

DEVELOPING THE MASTER ADDRESS FILE

The procedures used by the Census Bureau to develop its 2000 computerized mailing list—the MAF—differed in several important respects from those used in past censuses.[2] The major difference from 1990 was that the 2000 MAF was constructed using more sources. The expected benefit was that the MAF would be more complete. The possible risks were that the MAF would have more duplicate or erroneous addresses that were not weeded out from the final list and that the quality of the MAF would vary significantly across geographic areas. The risks were considered high because many of the new and previously untapped sources of addresses for the MAF were being used for the first time in 2000. As it turned out, the Census Bureau had to alter several parts of the MAF development process as it proceeded, in order to keep on schedule and improve the quality of the list.

Initial Development

The Census Bureau used somewhat different procedures to develop the MAF for areas believed to have predominantly city-style addresses (house number and street) than for areas believed to have predominantly rural route and post office box addresses (see Box A-1 in Appendix A). The base for the city-style portion of MAF was the final address file used in the 1990 census, which was augmented periodically by updates from U.S. Postal Service files. Additional city-style addresses were obtained through three auxiliary programs: the Local Update of Census Addresses (LUCA) Program, in which local and tribal governments reviewed the address lists for their areas;[3] block canvass, a field operation to check the entire list, which was not part of the original plans; and a new construction LUCA Program added in response to

---

[2]The Census Bureau refers to the version of the MAF that was used in the census as the Decennial Master Address File or DMAF. It is an extract of the full MAF, which includes business as well as residential addresses. Our use of the term MAF refers to the Bureau's DMAF.

[3]The Address List Improvement Act of 1994 (P.L. 103-430) made it possible for the Postal Service to share its list with the Census Bureau and for the Bureau to share the MAF with localities that signed a pledge to treat the list as confidential. Local review efforts in previous censuses were limited to review of housing unit counts for census blocks but not the individual addresses.

local concerns, in which localities could identify addresses newly constructed between January and March 2000. An intensive check by the Postal Service of its own address files produced a set of updates that were made to the MAF in early 2000 prior to mailout; questionnaires were delivered by the Postal Service in March.

The base for the non-city-style portion of the MAF was a complete block canvass, or prelist, conducted in late 1998 and early 1999. A LUCA Program for non-city-style address areas was implemented in 1999. The MAF for these areas continued to be updated in February-March 2000, as census enumerators were asked to note new entries for the MAF as they dropped off questionnaires to households.

For remote rural areas, Census Bureau enumerators developed the address list concurrently with enumerating households in person. For special places (e.g., college dormitories), the Bureau used a variety of sources to develop an address list.

Further Development

MAF was a dynamic file during the operation of the census. Not only were addresses added from each stage of census field operations, but addresses were also deleted in an effort to minimize duplicate and erroneous entries. The Census Bureau estimates that a total of about 4 million addresses were added to the MAF—2.3 million during questionnaire delivery and 1.7 million during follow-up. At the same time, the Bureau estimates that a total of about 10.4 million addresses were removed as duplicative of other addresses or nonexistent—about half were deleted on the basis of field checks and half on the basis of internal computer checks. One computer check was performed prior to non-response follow-up; another (not included in the original plans) was performed in summer 2000 (see below). The final 2000 MAF included addresses for 115.9 million occupied and vacant housing units.

Unduplication and Late Additions

An unanticipated complication arose from evaluations of MAF between January and June 2000. These evaluations, which compared MAF housing unit counts to estimates prepared from such sources as building permits, led the Census Bureau to conclude that there were probably still a sizable number of duplicate housing unit addresses on the MAF despite prior computer checks. Field verification carried out in June 2000 in a small number of localities substantiated this conclusion.

Consequently, the Bureau mounted an ad hoc operation to identify duplicate MAF addresses and associated census returns. Housing unit and person records flagged as likely duplicates were deleted from the census file and further examined. After examination, it was decided that a portion of the deleted records were likely separate housing units not already in the census, and they were restored to the census file. At the conclusion of the operation, 1.4 million housing units and 3.6 million people were permanently deleted from the census; 1 million housing units and 2.4 million people were reinstated.[4]

QUESTIONNAIRE DELIVERY AND MAIL RETURN

The 2000 census, like the 1980 and 1990 censuses, was conducted primarily by delivering questionnaires to households and asking them to mail back a completed form. Procedures differed somewhat, depending on such factors as type of addresses in an area and accessibility; in all, there were nine types of enumeration areas (see Box A-2 in Appendix A).

The two largest types of enumeration areas covered 99 percent of the household population: mailout/mailback, covering almost 82 percent of the population, in which Postal Service carriers delivered questionnaires; and update/leave/mailback (usually termed update/leave), covering almost 17 percent of the population, in which Census Bureau field staff delivered questionnaires and updated the MAF at the same time. The remaining 1 percent of the household population was enumerated in person. Separate enumeration procedures (not discussed in this report) were used for such special populations as people who frequented shelters for the homeless, residents of group quarters, and transients.[5]

The goal for the mailback universe for this phase of the census was to get a questionnaire to every housing unit on the MAF and motivate people to fill it out and mail it back (every mail return was one less address to follow up in the field). It was expected that mail response would continue to decline, as it had from 1970 to 1990, due to broad social and economic changes that have made the population more difficult to enumerate. These changes include rising numbers of new immigrants, both those who are legally in the country and those who are not, who may be less willing to fill out a census form or who may not be able to complete a form because of language difficulties; increasing amounts of junk mail, which may increase the likelihood that a household will discard its census form without opening it; and larger numbers of households with multiple residences, making it unclear which form they should mail back.[6]

The Bureau's challenge was to forestall a further decline in mail response and, if possible, increase it above the level achieved in 1990. Approaches to boost mail response in 2000 included four major activities:

---

[4]The reinstated people are often called "late additions." Although not enumerated late, they were added back to the census too late to be included in the A.C.E. (see Chapter 6).

[5]The 2000 census developed specific procedures only to enumerate the homeless population who use shelters, soup kitchens, and specifically identified nonsheltered outdoor locations.

[6]There were no instructions on the 2000 questionnaire for how to respond to forms for more than one residence.

- Redesigning the questionnaires and mailing package: The questionnaires were made more attractive and easy to fill out. They were shortened by providing space to report characteristics for six people instead of seven as in 1990. In addition, most housing items previously included on the short form were moved to the long form. The mailing package emphasized the mandatory nature of the census, and multiple mailings were made to households, including an advance letter (in mailout/mailback areas), the questionnaire, and a reminder postcard.

- Adapting enumeration procedures to special situations: This involved having nine types of enumeration areas (see Box A-2 in Appendix A).

- Allowing multiple modes for response: Households could mail back their questionnaire or provide responses by telephone; recipients of the short form could submit their form on the Internet. In addition, people could pick up a "Be Counted" form from a local site if they thought they had been missed. (To reduce the potential for duplication, the Bureau did not widely advertise the Internet submission or "Be Counted" programs.)

- Expanding advertising and outreach efforts (see "Outreach," below).

A significant achievement of the 2000 census was that it did halt the historical decline in the mail response rate. The rate (about 66%) was similar to that in 1990 (65%) and considerably higher than the Bureau had projected (61%), which reduced the burden of field follow-up. The mail return rate—a more refined measure of public cooperation than the mail response rate—was slightly lower in 2000 (about 72%) than in 1990 (74%). However, for long forms, the mail return rate in 2000 was only about 58 percent, compared with about 72 percent for short forms, a much wider difference than occurred in 1990; see Box 3-1 for details.

Note that questionnaires counted as "mail" returns in the 2000 census include responses from the multiple modes. Of 76 million "mail" returns, about 66,000 were Internet returns, 605,000 were "Be Counted" forms, and 200,000 were telephone responses.

OUTREACH

The Census Bureau engaged in large-scale advertising and outreach efforts for 2000. For the first time, the census budget included funds for a paid advertising campaign ($167 million). (In previous censuses, the Advertising Council arranged for advertising firms to develop ads and air them on a pro bono, public service basis.) The advertising ran from October 1999 through May 2000 and included separate phases to alert people to the importance of the upcoming census, encourage them to fill out the forms when delivered, and motivate

BOX 3-1
Mail Response and Return Rates

Definitions and Uses

The *mail response rate* is defined as the number of households returning a questionnaire by mail divided by the total number of questionnaires sent out in mailback areas. Achieving a high mail response rate is important for the cost and efficiency of the census because every returned questionnaire is one less household for an enumerator to follow up in the field.

The *mail return rate* is defined as the number of households returning a questionnaire by mail divided by the number of occupied households that were sent questionnaires in the mailback areas. This rate is an indicator of public cooperation. Achieving a high mail return rate (at least to the level of 1990) is important because of evidence from 1990 that mail returns are more complete than enumerator-obtained returns.

In 2000, because of the alternative modes by which households could fill out their forms, the numerator of both "mail" responses and "mail" returns included responses submitted on the Internet, over the telephone, and on "Be Counted" forms. The denominator of the mail response rate included all addresses on the April 1, 2000, version of the MAF, covering both mailout/mailback and update/leave areas. The denominator of the mail return rate excluded addresses on the MAF that field follow-up determined were vacant, nonresidential, or nonexistent.

Rates, 1970–2000 Censuses

	Census			
	1970	1980	1990	2000
Mail response rate	78%	75%	65%	66%
Mail return rate	87%	81%	74%	70–72%[a]

Source for 1970–1990 rates: National Research Council (1995:Table 3.1, App. A). Mail response and return rates are not strictly comparable across censuses because of differences in procedures used to compile the address list, percentage of the population included in the mailback universe (about 60% in 1970 and 95% or more in 1980–2000), and time allowed for mailback.

Differences in Mail Return Rates: Short and Long Forms

Return rates of long forms are typically below the return rates of short forms. This difference widened substantially in 2000.

	Census			
	1970	1980	1990	2000[a]
Short-form rate:	87.8%	81.6%	74.9%	72%
Long-form rate:	85.5%	80.1%	70.4%	58%

[a] Overall preliminary mail return rates have been cited as 72 percent and 70 percent; if 70 percent is correct, then 72 percent and 58 percent are approximately correct for the short-form and long-form rates. Rates may change when the Census Bureau completes its evaluation of mail response.

people who had not returned a form to cooperate with the follow-up enumerators. Ads were placed on TV (including an ad during the 2000 Super Bowl), radio, newspapers, and other media, using multiple languages. Using information from market research, the ads stressed the benefits to people and their communities from the census, such as better targeting of government funds to needy areas for schools, day care, and other services.

In addition to the ad campaign, the Census Bureau hired partnership and outreach specialists in local census offices, who worked with community and public interest groups to develop special initiatives to encourage participation in the census. The Bureau signed partnership agreements with more than 30,000 organizations, including federal agencies, state and local governments, business firms, nonprofit groups, and others. A special program was developed to put materials on the census in local schools to inform school children about the benefits of the census and motivate them to encourage their adult relatives to participate.

FIELD FOLLOW-UP

Because not all households will mail back a form, and because many addresses to which questionnaires are delivered will turn out to be vacant or nonresidential, the 2000 census—like previous censuses—included a large field follow-up operation (see Appendix A). More than 500 local census offices (LCOs) were set up across the country (reporting to 12 regional census centers). The LCOs were responsible for hiring the temporary enumerators and crew leaders to conduct follow-up operations. In update/leave areas, enumerators were hired to deliver questionnaires prior to Census Day and to return to follow up nonresponding households. LCOs also carried out operations to enumerate special populations.

Anticipating possible difficulties in hiring and also the possibility that the mail response rate would decline from 1990, LCOs were authorized to recruit aggressively in advance of Census Day, hire more enumerators than they thought would be needed, permit part-time work schedules, and pay above-minimum wages (which differed according to prevailing area wages). Most offices were successful in meeting their hiring goals before the first follow-up operations began in mid-April 2000.

Follow-up operations were carried out in two separate stages. The first stage was nonresponse follow-up (NRFU), designed to obtain a questionnaire from every nonresponding unit in the mailback universe or to determine that an address was vacant or nonresidential. The NRFU operation involved visiting 45 million addresses. It began in late April 2000 and was completed in late June, a week ahead of schedule (unlike 1990, when NRFU fell considerably behind schedule). The second stage was coverage improvement follow-up

(CIFU), which occurred in June-August and included specific operations designed to check and supplement NRFU. The CIFU workload included 8.7 million addresses. Several operations included in the 1990 CIFU were dropped for 2000.

Timely completion of NRFU was expected to help population coverage, given evidence from previous censuses that returns obtained earlier in the process are more accurate than late returns (see Chapter 4). Similarly, focusing the 2000 CIFU effort on selected operations was expected to reduce erroneous enumerations in comparison with 1990. The possible downside risk was that pressure on field staff could lead to rushed and less accurate work.

DATA PROCESSING

Data processing for the 2000 census was a continuing, high-volume series of operations that began with the capture of raw responses and will end with the production of voluminous data products for the user community that will be available in 2001–2003. Important innovations for 2000 included the use of outside vendors for major data processing components; the use of optical mark and character recognition technology for data capture; and greater reliance on computer routines to supply missing information, in place of field checks. The challenge for each phase of data processing was to keep on schedule, follow procedures carefully, and minimize last-minute revisions to planned procedures that could affect quality.

Several data processing operations in 2000 differed in important ways from those in 1990:

- Data capture: The return address on mailback questionnaires directed them to one of four data capture centers—the Bureau's National Processing Center in Jeffersonville, Indiana, and three centers run by contractors. Every questionnaire had a bar code that was scanned to record its receipt. The questionnaires were then imaged electronically, checkbox data items were read by optical mark recognition (OMR), and write-in character-based data items were read by optical character recognition (OCR). Clerks keyed data from images if the OMR/OCR technology could not make sense of the questionnaire answers. Images of the long-form items were set aside temporarily to permit the fastest possible processing of short-form data. (In 1990, in contrast, many questionnaires were sent to local offices for check-in, clerical review, and field follow-up, if necessary, to complete the population count and characteristics of the household. Data capture was performed using a microfilm-based system first developed for the 1960 census.)

- Coverage edit and telephone follow-up: After data capture, the questionnaires were reviewed by computer to identify returns that required a reinterview by telephone. About 2.3 million cases were in the telephone follow-up workload, including: returns that reported a higher total count of household members than the number of members for which individual information (e.g., age, race, sex) was provided; returns that did not report a household count and provided information for exactly six people (the limit of the space provided on the questionnaire); returns that reported household counts of seven people or more; and returns of four or more people that contained nonrelatives of the household head. The purpose of the operation was to reduce undercounting of people in large households and nonfamily households. (Telephone follow-up was also used in the 1990 census, but, unlike 2000, the 1990 operation addressed missing characteristics as well as coverage problems and included a field follow-up effort when telephone follow-up was not successful.)

- Unduplication of households and people: Two major, computer-based unduplication operations were carried out subsequent to field follow-up. One operation was the special effort in summer 2000 to reduce duplication of housing unit addresses in the MAF (see "Unduplication and Late Additions," above). The other operation, which was planned from the outset, used the primary selection algorithm (PSA) to unduplicate multiple returns for the same address.

  The purpose of the PSA was to determine which households and people to include in the census when more than one questionnaire was returned with the same census address identification number. Such duplication could occur, for example, when a respondent mailed back a census form after the cutoff date for determining the NRFU workload and the enumerator then obtained a second form from the household. In all, 9 percent of census housing units had two returns and 0.4 percent had three or more returns. In most instances, the PSA discarded duplicate household returns or extra vacant returns; less often, the PSA found additional people to assign to a basic return or identified more than one household at an address.

- Editing and imputation: It is standard census practice to use editing techniques to reconcile inconsistent or anomalous answers for a person or household and to use imputation routines to provide values for missing responses. In 2000, all editing and imputation were computer-based; there was no clerical editing of the questionnaires as in 1990 and past censuses. In instances when it was not possible to perform an edit that used other information for the same person or household, imputation was performed with "hot deck" methods that made use of information for other, similar people and households in the immediate neighborhood (see Box A-3 in Appendix A).

One kind of imputation involved substituting the record of another person or an entire household: 5.8 million people required such whole person imputation in 2000, amounting to 2.1 percent of the household population count. (In 1990, only 1.9 million people, or 0.8 percent of the household population, were imputed in this way.) Whole person imputations in 2000 included: cases for which there was no information about the number of people living at that address or their characteristics (0.4% of the household population); cases for which household size was known but not the characteristics of the members (0.8% of the household population); and cases for which no information was provided for the individual, although other household members had reported data (0.9% of the household population).

Editing and imputation rates for missing values for individual short-form content items, such as age, race, sex, and housing tenure, were low—ranging from 1.1 percent to 4.3 percent. (These rates exclude wholly imputed people.) In many instances, it was possible to fill in an answer from other information for the person or household, so that rates of hot-deck imputation for short-form items were lower still. Information about editing and imputation rates for long-form content items is not yet available.

4

Census Operations: Assessment

In this chapter we present our initial overall assessment of the 2000 census. We consider broadly how well the census design and operations were carried out and to what extent six major innovations for 2000 were successful:[1]

(1) use of multiple sources to develop the Master Address File (MAF) in general, and, specifically, the Local Update of Census Addresses (LUCA) Program;

(2) improvements in the questionnaire and mailing strategy to encourage household response;

(3) use of paid advertising and more extensive outreach to encourage response;

(4) advance hiring and higher wages for enumerators to ensure timely follow-up of nonresponding households;

(5) use of contractors and improved technology for data capture and other operations; and

(6) greater reliance on computers for processing incomplete responses.

We also consider briefly the completeness of coverage of the population achieved in the 2000 census, in total and for important population groups, and two outcomes of census operations as they relate to coverage: mail return rates and imputations of whole persons. Details of population coverage are discussed in subsequent chapters. We are not able at this time to assess the quality of the census data for characteristics of the population. There is potentially a serious problem for the quality of the long-form information because of substantially lower mail return rates for long forms than short forms.

---

[1]We do not assess a seventh major innovation: the expanded use of the Internet for release of data products to users. There has not been enough time yet for users to assess the usefulness and ease of accessing the 2000 census data through such mechanisms as the Census Bureau's American FactFinder interface (http://factfinder.census.gov).

OVERALL DESIGN AND EXECUTION

Our general assessment from the evidence available at this time is that the 2000 census was well executed in many respects. All statutory deadlines for data release were met, and most of the individual operations were completed on or ahead of schedule. Strategies for obtaining public cooperation in completing and mailing back their census forms succeeded in keeping mail response rates at the levels attained in 1990. This outcome represents an important achievement given the large decline in mail response rates from the 1980 census to the 1990 census.

Few instances occurred in 2000 when operations had to be modified in major ways after Census Day. In contrast, the 1990 census experienced serious and unexpected problems in executing such key operations as nonresponse follow-up, and the Census Bureau had to return to Congress to obtain additional funding to complete all needed operations.

One unexpected modification in summer 2000 was the special operation to minimize duplicate housing unit addresses in the Master Address File. This operation deleted 3.6 million people from the census who duplicated another enumeration and reinstated 2.4 million people who were initially believed to be duplicates. It was mounted quickly when the need for it became apparent and completed with little or no apparent adverse effect on other operations.[2] Another late change in plans, made early in 2000, was to set aside data capture of long-form information in order to keep short-form processing on schedule.

Most innovations for 2000 appeared effective, but some exhibited problems in implementation that deserve attention. In particular, the MAF development process was problematic in several respects as discussed below. Also, in comparison with 1990, the 2000 census had increased numbers of people who required imputation. Some of the increase was likely due to two design features of 2000: the use of a shorter questionnaire with space to record characteristics for six instead of seven household members, and the use of telephone follow-up, not supplemented by field work, to contact households whose returns appeared to be incomplete (see Chapter 3). However, some of the increase in people requiring imputation is not readily explained; it may have been due to errors in MAF, problems in follow-up operations, or other factors. More evaluation is needed of the sources and quality of census imputations, as well as of people reinstated in the census due to the special MAF unduplication operation.

On balance, though, the 2000 census appears to have been well carried out, particularly in view of the problems that hampered planning and preparations. The basic design was not finally determined until winter 1998–1999,

---

[2]Neither the reinstated people described here nor the imputations discussed in the next paragraph are included in the Accuracy and Coverage Evaluation (A.C.E.) Program. The large numbers of such people in 2000 complicate the interpretation of the A.C.E. results when those results are compared with the 1990 Post-Enumeration Survey (see Chapters 7 and 8).

little more than a year from Census Day. Census managers faced uncertainties about funding, which impeded staffing and resolution of specific elements of such operations as coverage improvement (see Waite et al., 2001). After full funding was obtained for the final agreed-upon design, the Bureau executed the census and the Accuracy and Coverage Evaluation (A.C.E.) operations in a controlled manner. Control was maintained even though—of necessity—specific procedures for several operations were only finalized very late. Likewise, many data processing systems were implemented almost as soon as they were completed, without benefit of advance testing. The relatively smooth operation of the census was facilitated by generous funding and the dedication and energy of Census Bureau staff.

MULTIPLE SOURCES FOR MAF

With the bulk of the population enumerated by mailout/mailback and update/leave/mailback techniques, the quality of the 2000 address list was essential to the completeness and accuracy of population coverage. The Census Bureau early in the 1990s made a decision to partner with other organizations and use multiple sources to develop the MAF. Contributing to the 2000 MAF were the 1990 address list augmented by updates from the U.S. Postal Service (in mailout/mailback areas), a full block canvass by Census Bureau staff, input from localities that participated in LUCA, and census field operations.

The goal of using multiple sources to build as complete a list as possible was a worthy one. Because many of the procedures were new, implementation was not always smooth. The decision to conduct a complete, instead of targeted, block canvass was made late in the decade and required additional funding to implement; an even later decision was to provide localities in city-style-address areas an opportunity to add addresses for units newly constructed in January-March 2000. Original plans for a sequential series of steps in the LUCA Program, involving back-and-forth checking with localities, had to be combined under pressures of time, and many LUCA components experienced delays; see Table 4-1. Questionnaire labeling had to occur before the Bureau had the opportunity to check most of the addresses supplied by LUCA participants. Local review of the address list for special places (group quarters) was delayed, and errors in assigning special places to geographic areas apparently occurred. Except for the stage of appealing to the U.S. Office of Management and Budget, localities were not given additional time for their review.

The Bureau recognized early on that the MAF was at risk of including duplicate and other erroneous addresses. The risk of omitting valid addresses was also present, but MAF procedures were expected to reduce the level of omissions from previous censuses. An increased risk of including duplicate addresses in the 2000 MAF resulted not only from the planned use of multiple

TABLE 4-1 Original and Actual Timelines for the Local Update of Census Addresses (LUCA) Program

Planned Dates	Actual Dates	Activity
LUCA98[a]		
November 1997	February 1998	Census Bureau sent invitation letters to eligible localities
April-August 1998	May 1998-March 1999	Bureau sent initial materials (address list, maps) to participants
May-December 1998	May 1998-June 1999	LUCA participants conducted initial review of materials from Bureau
Not part of original plan	January-May 1999	Bureau conducted full (instead of targeted) block canvassing
May-October 1999	July-December 1999	Bureau verified participants' addresses in the field (reconciliation) (original plan was to send results to localities to obtain feedback before sending final determination materials)
March-November 1999	October 1999-February 2000	Bureau sent detailed feedback/final determination materials to participants
Original deadline, January 14	November 1999-April 3, 2000	LUCA participants filed appeals (addresses were visited in coverage improvement follow-up)
April-August 1998	December 1999-April 2000	Special Places LUCA (Bureau did not complete Special Places list until November 1999)
Added operation	January-March 2000	Participating localities submitted new construction addresses (addresses were visited in coverage improvement follow-up)
LUCA99[b]		
July 1998-February 1999	July 1998-February 1999	Census Bureau field staff listed addresses
September-October 1998	September-October 1998	Bureau sent invitation letters to eligible localities
January-April 1999	January-August 1999	Bureau sent initial materials (block counts, maps) to participants
January-April 1999	January-October 1999	LUCA participants conducted review of initial materials from Bureau
March-May 1999	May-October 1999	Bureau verified participants' block counts in the field (reconciliation)
March-June 1999	September 1999-February 2000	Bureau sent detailed feedback/final determination materials to participants
Original deadline, January 14	October 1999-April 3, 2000	LUCA participants filed appeals for specific addresses
January-April 1999	December 1999-April 2000	Special Places LUCA

[a] This program was conducted in areas with mostly city-style addresses.

[b] This program was conducted in areas with mostly rural route and post office box addresses.

SOURCE: Adapted from LUCA Working Group (2001:Figure 1).

sources, but also from the operational problems just reviewed. To minimize duplication, the Bureau used a combination of field checking and internal consistency checks of the MAF file (see Chapter 3).

We are unclear on how to assess the overall success of the MAF development process at this time. On the plus side, despite the various implementation problems noted, all elements of the MAF development process were completed, and delays in component operations did not appear to affect other census operations, such as mailout, field follow-up, and data processing. With regard to accuracy, we believe it likely that the MAF contains more duplicate addresses than were detected in the various checking operations. In particular, some of the people reinstated in the census may in fact duplicate other enumerations, even though the evidence was not strong enough to weed them out during the special MAF unduplication operation. Similarly, duplicates and other errors in the MAF may have contributed to the increased number of people in 2000 compared with 1990 who required imputation to complete their census records. Yet the MAF may have omitted some valid addresses as well, and we do not yet know the balance between overcounting and undercounting errors. Further, whether errors in the MAF contributed more or less to population coverage errors than omissions or erroneous inclusions of people in otherwise correctly enumerated households remains to be established from analysis of the A.C.E. and other sources. Finally, there may be significant variability in the accuracy of the MAF across geographic areas due to the LUCA Program (see below) and other factors. All of these aspects of MAF need evaluation.

PARTICIPATION IN LUCA

Preliminary data show variable patterns of participation in the Local Update of Census Addresses (LUCA) Program. Of 39,051 counties, places, and minor civil divisions that were eligible for either or both LUCA98 (conducted in city-style-address areas) or LUCA99 (conducted in areas with large numbers of rural route and post office box addresses), 25 percent participated fully in one or both programs. By full participation, we mean that they informed the Census Bureau of needed changes to the address list for their area (LUCA Working Group, 2001:Ch.2).[3]

---

[3]It is not straightforward to determine participation in LUCA from the available data. In addition to full participants, 7 percent of eligible governments received Census Bureau materials and were coded as returning them to the Bureau without comment. Some of these governments may have been satisfied with the MAF for their areas, but, more likely, they did not have time or resources to conduct a full review. Also, participation by a county could mean that it reviewed the MAF for the entire county or only for selected jurisdictions in the county.

The substantial variation in LUCA participation is shown in Table 4-2. Factors that relate to participation include:

- geographic region—jurisdictions in the Pacific and Mountain states participated at a higher rate than jurisdictions in other parts of the country;

- population size—jurisdictions with larger populations participated at a higher rate than those with smaller populations;

- type of government—places and counties participated at higher rates than minor civil divisions; and

- type of program—areas eligible for LUCA98 or both LUCA98 and LUCA99 participated at a higher rate than areas eligible only for LUCA99.

In addition, a multivariate regression analysis found that, among counties and places that signed up to participate in LUCA, the 1990 census net undercount rate was a strong predictor that a jurisdiction would participate fully. Case studies also identified instances in which a vigorous coordination effort by a state or regional government facilitated participation by local jurisdictions.

The governments that participated in LUCA appeared to cover a higher proportion of the nation's housing stock than the proportion of participating governments to eligible governments would suggest. From preliminary data, places that participated fully in LUCA98 accounted for 67 percent of the 1990 housing stock in eligible places, even though they included only 48 percent of eligible places.[4] Even though coverage was higher for housing than for governments, which would be expected given the greater propensity of larger-size areas to participate, substantial portions of the MAF were not accorded local review.

There has not been a full accounting of the contribution of LUCA to MAF. As a rough indicator of order of magnitude, fully participating places among those eligible for LUCA98 submitted 3.7 million additional addresses, of which the Census Bureau initially accepted 2.1 million before appeals; those 2.1 million addresses represented 5 percent of the housing stock of participating places. These places also submitted corrections and deletions. What is not known is what LUCA contributed uniquely—that is, the number and proportion of added addresses that were missed by other Census Bureau address updating operations and that resulted in added (nonduplicative) census enumerations. A thorough assessment of the LUCA Program is needed, including not only the effects of LUCA on the completeness of the census count in participating areas, but also the possible effects on the counts in other areas from not having had a LUCA review.

---

[4]See LUCA Working Group (2001:Ch.2). Data are not available to permit constructing estimates for all eligible jurisdictions or for the two programs (LUCA98 and LUCA99) combined.

TABLE 4-2 Participation of Local Governments in the 2000 Local Update of Census Addresses (LUCA) Program

Category	LUCA98 Only		LUCA99 Only		Both LUCA98 and LUCA99				Total Number Eligible	Percent Participated in One or Both
	Number Eligible	Percent Participated[a]	Number Eligible	Percent Participated[b]	Number Eligible	Percent Participated in				
						LUCA98 Only	LUCA99 Only	LUCA98 and 99		
Total	9,044	41.6	21,760	14.2	8,247	17.7	7.6	12.0	39,051	25.4
Geographic Division										
New England	518	41.5	1,047	6.7	66	12.1	3.0	1.5	1,631	18.1
Middle Atlantic	2,034	43.3	2,133	16.2	662	19.2	7.0	12.7	4,829	30.7
East North Central	3,944	35.0	3,187	10.6	3,483	15.4	5.3	5.1	10,614	24.6
West North Central	548	40.3	9,437	13.3	1,414	17.4	10.7	19.1	11,399	18.8
South Atlantic	697	52.7	1,681	24.1	585	18.1	11.5	21.4	2,963	36.1
East South Central	411	35.5	1,046	11.0	427	14.8	7.3	11.7	1,884	21.5
West South Central	241	37.8	1,914	14.1	886	13.5	9.8	14.0	3,041	22.7
Mountain	113	68.1	966	23.7	328	35.7	6.4	22.3	1,407	36.7
Pacific	538	72.1	349	20.1	396	33.6	9.6	21.0	1,283	55.5
Population Size (1998 est.)										
1,000 or fewer	1,743	26.0	15,100	12.1	1,436	14.2	10.5	6.3	18,279	14.8
1,001–10,000	4,550	40.9	6,080	18.9	4,044	17.8	6.6	11.7	14,674	30.4
10,001–50,000	2,157	50.2	563	21.1	1,827	17.6	8.1	12.6	4,547	41.8
50,001–100,000	364	64.7	17	23.5	444	19.6	7.4	16.9	825	52.7
100,001–1,000,000	217	58.5	0	—	469	25.2	6.4	23.2	686	56.0
1,000,001 or more	13	69.2	0	—	27	25.9	7.4	44.4	40	75.0
Government Type										
County	122	46.7	982	17.1	1,956	10.3	9.3	10.6	3,060	26.7
Minor civil division	3,624	29.8	9,887	7.7	3,082	13.7	4.2	5.2	16,593	15.4
Place	5,298	49.6	10,891	19.8	3,209	25.9	9.9	19.4	19,398	33.8

NOTES: Not all regions have minor civil divisions. The analysis excludes 340 American Indian Reservations, 12 Alaska Native areas, 78 county-level municipios of Puerto Rico, and 3 places for which 1998 population estimates could not be determined.

[a] Participation in LUCA98 is defined as the local government returning at least one action record (addition, deletion, or correction) to the Census Bureau after reviewing the Master Address File for its area.

[b] Participation in LUCA99 is defined as the government challenging at least one block count provided by the Census Bureau for its area.

SOURCE: Tabulations by panel staff from preliminary U.S. Census Bureau data (LUCA98 and LUCA99 spreadsheets, June 2000), modified by assigning county codes to minor civil division and place records and augmenting the file with 1998 population estimates and variables from the Census Bureau's 1990 Data for Census 2000 Planning (1990 Planning Database, on CD-ROM) (see LUCA Working Group, 2001:Tables 2-2, 2-3).

REDESIGNED QUESTIONNAIRE AND MAILING STRATEGY

The Census Bureau redesigned the census questionnaire and mailing strategy for 2000 as part of its effort to encourage the public to fill out questionnaires and return them in the mail (or over the Internet or the telephone; see Chapter 3). The Bureau budgeted for a decline in the mail response rate to 61 percent in 2000 (from the 65 percent rate achieved in 1990), but its stated goal was to keep the response rate at least as high as in 1990.

Maintaining the 1990 mail response rate was key to the Bureau's ability to complete nonresponse follow-up on time and within budget. Estimates produced in conjunction with the 1990 census were that each 1 percentage point decline in the mail response rate would increase census costs by 0.67 percent (National Research Council, 1995:48). In addition, evidence from the 1990 census, confirmed by analysis of 2000 data (see below), indicated that mail returns, on balance, were more complete in coverage and content than returns obtained in the field.[5]

The changes to the 2000 questionnaire and mailings were based on extensive research carried out in the early 1990s. In one test, mail response to a user-friendly "booklet" form of the type used in 2000 was 3.4 percentage points higher than response to the type of form used in 1990; the difference in response rates for areas that were hard to enumerate in 1990 was even greater, 7.6 percentage points (Dillman et al., 1993). Adoption of optical scanning technology for data capture made it possible to create a more visually appealing questionnaire in 2000.

The results of another experiment suggested that the use of more mailings could substantially increase response. Individually, it appeared that sending an advance letter (used for the first time in 2000) increased response by 6 percentage points, sending a reminder postcard (used both in 1990 and 2000) increased response by 8 percentage points, and sending a second questionnaire to nonrespondents (not used) increased response by 10–11 percentage points. Another test demonstrated that stressing the mandatory nature of filling out the questionnaire on the mailing envelope (implemented in 2000) was effective in encouraging response, while emphasizing the benefits of the data or their confidentiality was not particularly effective (National Research Council, 1995:120-121).

The 2000 census was successful in achieving the goal of stemming the historic decline in mail response rates. The rate achieved was about 66 percent.[6] This accomplishment was of major importance for the success of the census in terms of timely, cost-effective completion of operations. It seems likely that the changes to the questionnaire and mailing package and the use of an advance

---

[5]See Box 3-1 in Chapter 3 for definitions of mail response and return rates and rates for 1970–2000.

[6]The Census Bureau is in the process of evaluating 2000 mail response and return rates; percentages cited in the text should be treated as approximate.

letter—despite or perhaps even because of the publicity due to the addressing error in the letter (see Appendix A)—contributed to maintaining the response rate, although how large a role these elements played in this achievement is not yet known.

One disappointment of the initiatives to encourage response in 2000 (which also included expanded advertising and outreach—see below) was that they did not stem a steep decline in the response of households that received the long form: the long-form mail response rate was 13 percentage points below the rate for short forms (67% and 54%). Similarly, the long-form mail return rate (based on occupied, not total, addresses) was 14 percentage points below the short-form rate (72% and 58%). This difference was double the difference that the Bureau expected (U.S. General Accounting Office, 2000b:5), and far larger than differences between long-form and short-form return rates seen in previous censuses (see Box 3-1 in Chapter 3).[7]

The low return rate for long forms could well have serious effects on the quality of the long-form data. The reason is the difficulty of obtaining long-form information in follow-up. While enumerators visit all nonresponding households, evidence from the 1990 census indicates that, very often, they succeed in obtaining responses only to the short-form questions from the households in the long-form sample and not also the additional information on the long form (National Research Council, 1995:App.L).

A second disappointment of the 2000 census mailing strategy was that the plan to mail a second questionnaire to nonresponding households had to be discarded (see Appendix A). At the time of the dress rehearsal, vendors said they could not turn around the address list for a targeted second mailing on the schedule required. In addition, experience in the dress rehearsal suggested that mailing a second questionnaire to every address would generate adverse publicity and increase the number of duplicate returns that would need to be weeded out from the census count.

PAID ADVERTISING AND PARTNERSHIPS

An important element of the Census Bureau's strategy in 2000 to reverse the historical decline in mail response rates and to encourage nonrespondents to cooperate with follow-up enumerators was to advertise more extensively and expand local outreach efforts well beyond what was done in the 1990 census. An integral part of the advertising strategy was to pay for ads instead of securing them on a pro bono basis. Advertising and outreach efforts began in fall 1999 and continued through May 2000.

---

[7]One of the Bureau's questionnaire experiments in the early 1990s, using an appealing form and multiple mailings, presaged this outcome: it found an 11 percentage point difference between short-form and long-form response rates (Treat, 1993). It was expected, however, that the publicity in a census environment would narrow this difference.

The advertising campaign appeared very visible and appealing, and we believe that it very likely contributed to maintaining the response rate in 2000 at the 1990 level. However, data are not yet available with which to evaluate the extent of its contribution, either overall or for specific population groups to whom ads were targeted. Although it may not be possible to link specific ads or the overall campaign to response in any direct way, evaluation studies should be pursued to explore this question.

Similarly, partnerships with local communities for outreach seemed more numerous and vigorous than in 1990. It might be useful to conduct case studies of outreach efforts in specific communities, even if it is likely not possible to evaluate their contribution to mail response or the success of follow-up overall.

Also, it could be useful to analyze variations in the extent of partnerships in different communities. While the Census Bureau offered opportunities for outreach partnerships nationwide, some localities were more supportive and put forth more resources than others. (The Census Bureau provided materials and limited staff support but not direct funding.) Variation in the presence and effectiveness of outreach partnerships (just as variation in participation in the LUCA Program) could have helped reduce variability in population coverage to the extent that outreach was more effective in traditionally hard-to-count areas. Alternatively, such variation could have led to greater variability in population coverage across geographic areas than in previous censuses, which is of concern for uses of census data that involve population shares (e.g., allocation of federal funds—see Chapter 2).

AGGRESSIVE RECRUITMENT OF ENUMERATORS

Just as critical to the success of the census as developing the MAF and encouraging mail response was the follow-up effort to visit nonresponding households and either obtain an enumeration or determine that the address was a vacant unit or should not have been included in the MAF. Nonresponse follow-up was a major problem in the 1990 census because the mail response rate not only dropped below the rate in 1980, but also dropped several percentage points below the budgeted rate. The Bureau had to seek additional funding, scramble to hire enough enumerators, and stretch out the effort much longer than planned. In contrast, in 2000, fears of a tight labor market that could make it difficult to hire short-term staff led the Bureau to plan aggressive recruitment of field staff from the outset. Generous funding made it possible for the Bureau to implement its plans, which included directing local offices to recruit twice as many enumerators as they expected to need at competitive wages (see Chapter 3).

The Bureau's recruitment strategy seems to have been very successful. Most local offices had little or no problems meeting their staffing goals, and nonresponse follow-up was completed slightly ahead of schedule—a major achievement of the 2000 census. A midstream assessment of nonresponse follow-up concluded that it was going well in most offices (U.S. General Accounting Office, 2000b).

It is possible that the success in completing nonresponse follow-up on time, and, similarly, in fielding a more focused coverage improvement follow-up effort than in 1990, contributed to reduction in measured net undercount. In 1990, questionnaires with later check-in dates (the date of entering the Census Bureau's processing system) were more likely to include erroneous enumerations than were returns checked-in earlier. Specifically, the percentage of erroneous enumerations increased from 2.8 percent for questionnaires checked-in through April 1990 (largely mail returns), to 6.6 percent, 13.8 percent, 18.8 percent, and 28.4 percent, respectively, for those checked in during May, June, July, and August or later (largely, enumerator-obtained returns) (Ericksen et al., 1991:Table 2).

Although the correlation between timing of receipt and accurate coverage of household members on a questionnaire may be spurious, there are several plausible reasons to support such a relationship. For example, people who moved between Census Day and follow-up could well be double-counted—at both their Census Day residence and their new residence (e.g., snowbirds in transit from a southern winter residence to a northern summer residence or college students in transit between home and dormitory around spring or summer vacation).[8] More generally, the later a household was enumerated, the less accurately the respondent might have described the household membership as of Census Day.

Given the delays in nonresponse follow-up in 1990, it appears that as much as 28 percent of the workload was completed in June or later, when erroneous enumeration rates were 14 percent or higher. We do not have information on the relationship of erroneous enumerations to the timing of enumeration in the 2000 census. However, we do know that nonresponse follow-up was completed by the end of June. Some returns were obtained through coverage improvement follow-up in July and August, but these represented a small percentage of the total. (Most coverage improvement work involved quality checks on already received returns rather than new enumerations—see Appendix A.) Hence, although we cannot be sure, it is possible that the speedier completion of nonresponse follow-up in 2000 contributed to reduction in net undercount.

It is also possible, however, that the drive to complete nonresponse follow-up on schedule led to coverage errors that were not corrected in the second wave of coverage improvement follow-up. In support of this possibility, at the end of all follow-up operations, there were more people requiring imputation

---

[8]Duplicate enumerations of snowbirds and other people with multiple residences may have increased in 2000 because of the lack of instructions on the questionnaire for how such people should respond to multiple forms.

to complete their census records in 2000 (5.8 million or 2.1% of the household population) than in 1990 (1.9 million or 0.8% of the household population). Some of this increase was not unexpected because follow-up of large households and other households that were thought to be incomplete was handled by telephone, without field work, but some of the increase in people requiring imputation is not yet explained (see Chapter 8).

USE OF CONTRACTORS AND IMPROVED TECHNOLOGY

A major innovation for the 2000 census was the use of outside contractors and improved technology for key operations. Three outside vendors were contracted for data capture using imaging and optical mark and character recognition, supplemented by clerical keying; the Census Bureau's National Processing Center at Jeffersonville, Indiana, was the fourth data capture center. Also, outside vendors were used to provide telephone questionnaire assistance and to carry out telephone follow-up for questionnaires that were identified as possibly incomplete in coverage (e.g., households that reported more members than the number for which they answered individual questions—see Chapter 3).

Outside contracting for data capture was essential to handle the workload, given that almost all questionnaires were checked in at one of the four processing centers. By contrast, in 1990, most questionnaires went first to local offices for check-in and editing, and no use was made of contractors for data capture or other major operations.

In testing data capture operations in early 2000, some problems were identified in the accuracy of the optical mark/character recognition, and changes were made to improve the accuracy rate and reduce the number of questionnaires that had to be keyed or rekeyed from images by clerks (U.S. General Accounting Office, 2000a). Data capture systems were redesigned to separate capture of short-form data from long-form data. This change was made on the basis of operational tests of keying from images, which demonstrated that keying could not occur fast enough to handle short-form and long-form data at the same time and keep to the overall schedule (U.S. General Accounting Office, 2000b).

Evaluations of the accuracy and efficiency of contractor data capture and other operations are under way. Little hard evidence is yet available, but it appears that the contractors performed well and that the Census Bureau was able to retain appropriate oversight and management control of contractors' work. The Bureau reported that overall rates of accuracy of optical character recognition (99%) and keying from image (97%) exceeded performance standards. There were no apparent data processing delays that affected field or other operations, except that long-form questions were set aside to ensure that short-form processing stayed on schedule.

INCREASED USE OF COMPUTERS

The 2000 census used computers whenever possible to replace tasks that were previously performed in part by clerks or enumerators. Notably, questionnaires went directly to one of the four data processing centers for data capture instead of being processed by clerks in local census offices, as occurred for much of the workload in 1990. Editing and imputation of individual records to supply values for missing responses to specific questions or reconcile inconsistent answers were handled entirely by computer; there was no clerical editing or effort to revisit households to obtain more content information as occurred for some of the workload in 1990. Mail returns that appeared to be missing information for some household members were followed up by telephone, but in contrast to 1990, there was no field follow-up when telephone follow-up was unsuccessful except for follow-up of completely blank returns (see Appendix A). After completion of all follow-up procedures, sophisticated computer routines were used, as in previous censuses, to complete the census records for households and people that had minimal information. These imputation routines used records from neighboring households or people who matched as closely as possible whatever information was available for the household or individual requiring imputation (see Chapter 8).

The advantages expected from greater computerization of data processing included savings in cost and time to complete the data records. Also, it was expected that computer systems for editing and imputation would be better controlled and less error-prone than clerical operations.

The 2000 census computer systems for data processing appear to have worked well. Although programming of systems was delayed because of the delays in determining the final census design, there appear to have been little adverse effects on the timing of other operations. Computer problems did delay the implementation of the coverage edit and telephone follow-up operation by a month.

Data are not yet available for evaluating the quality of computer-based editing and imputation. The rates of missing data for individual short-form items, such as age and sex, are known and were low (1%–4%). Moreover, it was often possible to infer a missing value from other information on the household's own questionnaire instead of having to use information from neighboring households. Imaging of forms helped in this regard, as names were captured along with responses to questions (see Appendix A).

The Bureau's editing and imputation routines for missing and inconsistent data items have been increasingly refined over several decades of computer processing of censuses and household surveys, although few studies have been performed of the errors introduced by imputation. With the likely exception of race/ethnicity data, examination of published tables from the 1990 census of the distributions of individual items before and after imputation shows little effect of the imputations, particularly for short-form items for which rates of missing data are low (see U.S. Census Bureau, 1992b). Assuming that the Bureau maintained good quality control of editing and imputation specifications and implementation in 2000, the use of computer routines to provide values for specific missing short-form items would have had little adverse effect on data quality. The resulting data products will be more complete and therefore useful for a broader range of purposes.

The Bureau has also used computerized imputation routines for several censuses to supply data records for households and people with minimal information. In general, such a procedure is likely preferable to deleting the person or household, given that there is good reason to believe the person or household exists and should be included. In 2000, there were considerably more such people than in 1990, which helps explain some puzzling findings about population coverage in the two censuses (see below). For this reason, the performance of the computerized imputation routines for whole person imputations should be carefully evaluated to determine if the imputations were appropriate.

POPULATION COVERAGE

The evidence from the A.C.E. indicates that the 2000 census, compared with previous censuses, succeeded in its primary goals to reduce net undercount and to narrow the differences between net undercount rates for historically less-well-counted and better-counted groups (see Chapter 6). Not all planned analyses of the A.C.E. have yet been completed—particularly studies of balancing error and matching error—so we must reserve judgment about the accuracy of particular A.C.E. results. Nonetheless, the overall patterns of net undercount in the A.C.E. for major groups accord with knowledge from previous censuses: while differences in net undercount rates were narrowed, the rates remained somewhat higher for such groups as minorities in comparison with non-Hispanic whites, renters in comparison with owners, men in comparison with women, and younger people in comparison with older people.

Estimates of the population from demographic analysis indicate that the census either had a net *overcount* of the total population or had a net undercount considerably smaller than that measured by the A.C.E. The different demographic estimates result from different assumptions about net undocumented immigration (see Chapter 5). The demographic analysis results corroborate the A.C.E. findings of reduced net undercount for children. They also show a difference in net undercount rates for blacks and others—indeed, a larger difference than that measured in A.C.E. The uncertainties about estimates of immigrants and the categorization of the population by race lead us to conclude that the available demographic estimates should not be a standard for evaluating the census or the A.C.E.

Until additional evaluations under way at the Census Bureau are completed, we cannot endorse either the census or the A.C.E. estimates of the total population. Nonetheless, it seems clear that net undercount was reduced in 2000—from about 4.0 million people in 1990 (1.6% of the population) to about 3.3 million people (1.2% of the population), or possibly less.[9] It is also clear that counting errors occurred in both directions: the census missed people who should have been counted and duplicated or included other people who should not have been counted. Indeed, a puzzle from the A.C.E. was that rates of erroneous enumerations and missed people were not dissimilar from the rates in the 1990 Post-Enumeration Survey (PES), which should result in similar estimates of net undercount, other things equal. Yet the A.C.E. measured lower net undercount (see Chapter 7).

One aspect of population coverage in 2000 for which no evaluation data are available is the completeness of enumeration of people in group quarters. Almost 3 percent of the population counted in 2000 resided in such group settings as college dormitories, nursing homes, prisons, military barracks, migrant worker dormitories, and others. Group quarters residents were excluded from the A.C.E. estimation because of problems in developing dual-systems estimates for them in the 1990 PES due to their high rates of short-term mobility (see Killion, 1997; see also Chapter 6).[10] The Bureau planned more intensive enumeration procedures for group quarters in 2000 (e.g., advance visits to special places and additional training for field staff), expecting that enumeration would be more accurate than dual-systems estimation for this population. However, scattered evidence suggests that the enumeration of group quarters residents was not as well controlled as the enumeration of the household population.

The development of the address list for special places (e.g., dormitories) was not integrated with the MAF until late in the process, and census data users have reported that dormitory and prison populations were assigned to incorrect geographic locations in some instances, usually to a neighboring area (see Anderson and Fienberg, 2001a). Our observation of field offices suggests varying levels of cooperation from administrators of special places, which could have impeded complete enumeration. We cannot assess coverage for group quarters residents until the Census Bureau completes its evaluations, including an assessment of whether the A.C.E. properly treated group quarters enumerations in developing dual-systems estimates for the household population.

---

[9]The estimates in the text are from the PES and the A.C.E., respectively. Demographic analysis estimated a slightly higher net undercount in 1990 (1.9% of the population), but a lower net undercount in 2000 (0.3% of the population) or, possibly, a small net overcount (Robinson, 2001a:App. Tables 1, 3).

[10]The PES estimation included noninstitutionalized group quarters residents but not inmates of institutions.

COVERAGE-RELATED FACTORS

In endeavoring to understand changes in population coverage patterns between 1990 and 2000 by comparing the A.C.E. and PES estimates, we analyzed two census operational outcomes for which data were available: mail returns and people who could not be included in the A.C.E. (or PES) because they lacked sufficient reported information for matching or because their census records were available too late to be processed. Our preliminary mail return rate analysis did not shed much light on changes in coverage patterns; it is summarized below and detailed in Appendix B. Our analysis of people not included in the A.C.E. was more informative; it is briefly described below and discussed in detail in Chapter 8.

Mail Return Rates

Our interest in mail return rates stemmed from 1990 research showing that, in the census context, a mail return filled out by a household member tends to be more complete in coverage (and content) than an enumerator-obtained return. Analysis of 2000 A.C.E. data largely confirmed the 1990 findings: mail returns were somewhat less likely to omit one or more household members than were enumerator-obtained returns, and they were also less likely to include an erroneous enumeration. At the neighborhood (census tract) level, rates of household omissions and erroneous enumerations (particularly omissions) declined as the neighborhood mail return rate increased.

Because overall mail return rates were similar between 2000 and 1990, the reduction in net undercount for the total population from 1990 could not be due to mail returns. However, the distribution of mail return rates could have changed in ways that would explain the smaller differences in net undercount rates between usually hard-to-count and easier-to-count groups in 2000 compared with 1990. For instance, targeted advertising and outreach might have increased mail return rates for renters while the rates for owners fell off slightly from 1990 levels.

Regression analysis of mail return rates for 1990 and 2000 for census tracts characterized by such variables as percentage minorities or renters in 1990 (2000 variables were not available) did not support our supposition (see Appendix B). Much the same variables explained mail return rates in both 1990 and 2000,[11] and the available demographic and socioeconomic variables failed to explain differences in mail return rates for census tracts between 1990 and 2000. Census tracts that experienced unusually large increases or decreases

---

[11]A 1990 hard-to-count score constructed by the Census Bureau and the 1990 percentage net undercount, percentage people in multi-unit structures, and percentage people who were not high school graduates had large negative effects on mail return rates not only in 1990 but also in 2000; the 1990 percentage population over age 65 had a strong positive effect in both years.

in mail return rates did show a tendency to cluster geographically. Research on particular characteristics of such clusters, including any distinctive features of outreach and other census operations, could be useful to identify factors that particularly help or hinder mail response.

Imputations and Late Additions

We were puzzled by the reduction in net undercount measured in the A.C.E. because the rates of omissions and erroneous enumerations in the A.C.E. were generally as high or higher as the rates in the 1990 PES. We identified a major reason for this result—namely, the considerably larger number of people in 2000 than in 1990 who could not be included in coverage evaluation but who were part of the total census count that is compared to the dual-systems estimate from the A.C.E. (or the PES) to calculate net undercount.

The people who could not be included in the A.C.E. comprised two groups: (1) people reinstated in the census from the special MAF unduplication operation and (2) people who lacked sufficient information for matching and so required imputation to complete their census records (whole person imputations). Only a small number of people in 1990 were enumerated too late to be included in the PES, so the much larger number of reinstated people in 2000 (2.4 million) contributed to reducing the net undercount. Such people were about equally likely to be found among historically better-counted groups as among historically worse-counted groups, so they did not affect differences in net undercount rates. In contrast, people requiring imputation were not only a much larger group in 2000 (5.8 million) than in 1990 (1.9 million), but they were also disproportionately found among minorities, renters, and children, thus accounting in large part for the reduction in differential net undercount for these groups relative to non-Hispanic whites, owners, and older people. We discuss the types of people requiring imputation, as well as the people reinstated in the census, and the possible implications for the quality of census operations from their larger numbers, in Chapter 8.

CONCLUSIONS

Overall, we conclude that the census was well executed in many respects, particularly given the difficulties of changes in the overall design and other problems encountered in the years leading up to 2000. Many innovations appeared to be effective. These included: (1) contracting for data operations and use of improved data capture technology, (2) use of a redesigned questionnaire and mailing strategy, (3) paid advertising and expanded outreach, and (4) aggressive recruitment of enumerators. Greater reliance on computers for data editing and imputation requires evaluation of the effects on data quality.

The concept behind the development of the MAF—namely, to make use of multiple sources, some for the first time—makes sense. However, there were problems in execution that may have increased duplicate and other erroneous enumerations and contributed to the larger number of people in 2000 who required imputation to complete their census records.

An achievement was to maintain the overall mail response rate at the 1990 level. A disappointment was that long-form response rates were considerably lower than short-form rates. Another achievement was the reduction in measured net undercount from 1990 levels, overall and for historically less-well-counted groups. The larger numbers of people requiring imputation largely explained these reductions, which otherwise are not compatible with the estimated rates of omissions and erroneous enumerations in the A.C.E.

Our analyses of these topics are limited by the available data. Consequently, our conclusions are preliminary and incomplete. The Census Bureau has under way a comprehensive set of evaluations, which should provide information for a definitive assessment of population coverage and data quality and of design and operational features of the 2000 census that most affected coverage and quality (U.S. Census Bureau, 2000). An important tool for evaluation of the effects of census operations should be the Bureau's planned Master Trace Sample—essentially a compilation of major census databases for a systematic sample of addresses to permit tracing each step of the operations (see National Research Council, 2000a).

Some evaluations in the Bureau's planned program were moved up in priority and other evaluations were added last spring when the Bureau realized that the available assessments of the A.C.E., demographic analysis, and the census were not adequate to permit a decision to use A.C.E. estimates to adjust the census counts for legislative redistricting. These evaluations cover components of demographic analysis, several kinds of possible error in the A.C.E., enumeration procedures for and coverage of the group quarters population, whole person imputations, and people reinstated in the census from the MAF unduplication. The results of the Bureau's work over the last 6 months will be released when the Bureau makes a decision around mid-October on whether to adjust population estimates for fund allocation and other purposes. We will review these evaluations at that time.

NEXT STEPS

Looking to the Census Bureau's longer range evaluation program, we urge the Bureau to devote resources to completing planned studies on as fast a schedule as practicable. Even when the results of the last 6 months' work are released, there will not be answers to many of the questions about the census, particularly which operations and design features had the greatest effects on coverage and data quality. Further, the information from the 2000 evaluations is needed for planning the 2010 census.

Important aspects of census operations that we have identified for timely evaluation include:[12]

- Group quarters: The completeness of coverage of the group quarters population and the effects of address list development and enumeration procedures on coverage should be assessed.

- MAF and LUCA: The quality of the MAF and the part played by LUCA and other sources of addresses in identifying good addresses, as well as in adding erroneous addresses, should be examined. In particular, the sources of addresses of people deleted from and reinstated in the census from the special MAF unduplication operation should be determined. It could be useful to conduct field work to estimate the extent of duplicate enumerations remaining among the reinstated people (see Chapter 8).

- Whole person imputations: Reasons for larger numbers of people requiring imputation to complete their census records should be sought, such as possible problems with the coverage edit and telephone follow-up and coverage improvement follow-up operations. Evaluations of the computerized routines used for imputation should be conducted (see Chapter 8).

In addition, early completion of the Master Trace Sample should be a priority to permit tracing through the effects of each step of the census operations for a sample of addresses. Finally, as soon as practicable, the demographic and socioeconomic information collected in the long form should be thoroughly evaluated.

Looking ahead to the 2010 census, the Census Bureau has made an early start on design and preparation. Its current plans include a major effort to reengineer MAF and the associated TIGER system of assigning addresses to geographic areas;[13] the use of a new American Community Survey (ACS) to provide long-form information on an annual basis;[14] and the implementation of a simplified short-form-only census in 2010 that makes maximum use of improved technology for enumeration and data capture (see Miskura et al., 2001; Waite et al., 2001). Our sister Panel on Research on Future Census Methods is charged to review the 2000 census evaluation results and the Bureau's evolving plans for 2010 to recommend appropriate research and testing that will lead to a successful 2010 design (see National Research Council, 2000a). That

---

[12]Some of these topics will be covered in the evaluations to be released in mid-October; however, additional studies may be required. Priorities for research on demographic analysis and the A.C.E. are addressed in Chapters 5 and 7, respectively.

[13]TIGER stands for Topologically Integrated Geographic Encoding and Referencing System.

[14]When fully implemented in 2003, the ACS will survey 250,000 households each month, or 3 million households per year, using a mailout questionnaire similar to the 2000 long form, a targeted second questionnaire mailing to encourage response, telephone follow-up for nonresponse, and field follow-up of one-third of remaining nonrespondents. As a separate sample-based survey with a permanent staff, the ACS is expected to provide better quality long-form-type information than it appears possible to obtain in the census (see National Research Council, 2000c:Ch.4).

panel is currently reviewing such topics as MAF reengineering, ACS estimation issues, and administrative computer systems for operations management.

We are not charged specifically to recommend changes to the census design for 2010. Based on our evaluations of 2000 operations to date, we do offer two suggestions for consideration.

- First, the Bureau's plans for the MAF for 2010 include continuation of a LUCA-type program. Implementation of LUCA for the 2000 MAF was difficult and participation was variable. The report of the LUCA Working Group suggests that participation can perhaps be most effective when it is coordinated for localities by a state or regional agency, such as a metropolitan association of governments. We suggest that the Census Bureau review its experience with LUCA partnerships in 2000 and consult with state and local governments to determine partnership strategies for 2010 that are likely to work well for both the Bureau and its LUCA partners.

- Second, we endorse the recommendations of two prior Committee on National Statistics panels that serious consideration should be given to moving Census Day to an earlier date than April 1, preferably to the middle of a month (National Research Council, 1994:38-40; 1999b:43-44). Changing Census Day could well improve the accuracy of enumeration of several groups of the population. These include: people moving into a new rental apartment or home, which is more likely to occur at the beginning than the middle of a month; college students, who may be less likely to be on spring break at an earlier date and less likely to have ended their spring semester when nonresponse follow-up is in progress; and snowbirds who may be less likely to be in transit at an earlier date. In addition, more time in which to evaluate the census, the A.C.E., and demographic analysis could make it possible to reach a decision about whether to adjust the census data for legislative redistricting without the uncertainties that affected the Bureau's decision last March.[15]

Moving Census Day would require changing Title 13 of the U.S. Code, which specifies key delivery dates in terms of months after Census Day rather than a specific day (e.g., 12 months after Census Day for delivery of redistricting data). A possibility is to change Title 13 to specify the current delivery dates of December 31 of the census year for reapportionment counts and April 1 of the following year for redistricting counts, while giving the Census Bureau the authority to change Census Day should the Bureau conclude that such a change would facilitate the enumeration. Work to change Title 13 should begin soon if the Bureau is to have the option of moving Census Day in 2010.

---

[15]Changing Census Day could have some effect on the time series of estimates from the census, depending on how the new and old dates relate to seasonal patterns of residence.

5

Demographic Analysis

We begin our assessment of population coverage in the 2000 census by reviewing demographic analysis (DA), which has been used extensively by the Census Bureau for coverage evaluation of past population censuses. Demographic analysis was also advanced by the Bureau as a benchmark against which not only the census counts, but also the survey-based Accuracy and Coverage Evaluation (A.C.E.) estimates could be compared. Given the role of DA in contributing to the Census Bureau's March 2001 recommendation not to adjust the census data for redistricting, we believe it important to assess the strengths and weaknesses of this tool for census coverage evaluation. In subsequent chapters, we examine the A.C.E. methods and results and the effects on population coverage of people requiring imputation and people reinstated in the census too late to be included in the A.C.E. processing.

METHODOLOGY: OVERVIEW

The methodology of demographic analysis uses aggregate data from administrative records, supplemented by census and survey results, to estimate the total population by age, sex, and race (two categories—black and all other). Since 1970, estimates have been constructed separately for people under age 65 and aged 65 and older (see Robinson, 2001a:App.A; National Research Council, 1985:133-139, 148-151).

Estimates of the population under age 65 are constructed for single-year birth cohorts by sex and race. The procedure uses the number of births as the starting point (e.g., estimates of people aged 60 in 2000 begin with the number of births in 1940), subtracts deaths, and adds estimates of net immigration in each year to the estimation year.[1] Birth and death data are from vital statistics records collected by the states in a common format and forwarded to the federal government. (All states and the District of Columbia have been part of the vital statistics registration system since about 1933.) Corrections are made for

---

[1] In practice, the DA estimate for a census year (2000) usually begins with the DA estimate for the previous census year (1990), updated with estimates of births, deaths, and net immigration in the decade between the two years.

TABLE 5-1 Total Population Counts for 2000

| Source | Population (in millions) | Difference from Census Count | |
		No. (in millions)	Percent
Census count	281.4		
DA base estimate	279.6	−1.8	−0.65
DA alternate estimate	282.3	0.9	0.32
A.C.E. estimate	284.7	3.3	1.15

NOTE: See text for discussion.
SOURCE: Robinson (2001a:Table 3).

underregistration of births, using the results of birth registration studies adjusted by interpolation and extrapolation (the latest study covered 1964–1968). Administrative data from the Immigration and Naturalization Service are used to estimate legal immigration, but they must be adjusted to fill in gaps for undocumented (illegal) immigration and emigration.

For the population aged 65 and over, estimates are constructed from Medicare enrollment statistics. The Medicare data are adjusted for those not enrolled, who were estimated to be 3.7 percent of people aged 65 and over in 2000.

THE 2000 ESTIMATES

The Census Bureau's concerns about differences in the census, DA, and A.C.E. estimates of the total population are illustrated by the several different figures available for 2000 shown in Table 5-1. The *census count* is that reported for April 2000, including household and group quarters residents in the United States. The *DA base estimate* is that developed by demographic analysis as described above, which, at the time of the census, was the Census Bureau's initial and best estimate of the "true" population to be used as a measure for evaluating overall census coverage. The *DA alternate estimate* is that developed by the Census Bureau in early 2001, which incorporated a higher allowance for net undocumented immigration than that included in the DA base estimate. The *A.C.E. estimate* is that developed by dual-systems estimation for the household population from the results of matching census enumerations and an independent postenumeration survey in a sample of blocks. For comparability with DA and the census count, the A.C.E. estimate is augmented by approximately 7.5 million people to cover residents of group quarters and people enumerated in other special operations not included in A.C.E. (e.g., the remote Alaska enumeration).[2]

---

[2]There is also a *postcensal estimate* for 2000, which is the 1990 census count (not adjusted for net undercount) carried forward with data on births, deaths, and net immigration. We do not discuss the Census Bureau's postcensal estimates program in this report.

Thus, we can summarize the data in Table 5-1. The DA base estimate for 2000 of 279.6 million is 1.8 million lower than the census count of 281.4 million, implying a net *overcount* in the census of 0.7 percent. However, the A.C.E. estimate is 284.7 million, which implies a net *undercount* in the census of 3.3 million (1.2%). There is a need then to reconcile a difference of 5.1 million between the two estimates—base DA and A.C.E.—to come to closure in choosing the "best" estimate for evaluating the census count of the U.S. population in 2000.[3] The alternative DA estimate developed by the Census Bureau reduces the difference from the A.C.E. estimate somewhat, but not entirely (the difference decreases from 5.1 million to 2.4 million).

By age and sex, coverage patterns estimated by DA are broadly similar between 1990 and 2000 in that women were better counted then men, and older people were better counted than younger people. The 1990 PES and 2000 A.C.E. also show these patterns. However, the 2000 DA net undercount estimates are much lower than the 1990 DA estimates, even when the 2000 DA population estimates are adjusted to allow for a greater number of undocumented immigrants than originally estimated; see Table 5-2.

UNCERTAINTY IN IMMIGRATION ESTIMATES

The main area of uncertainty in the DA estimate of the total population lies with the immigration component, especially the number of undocumented immigrants. Other components, such as emigrants and some categories of legal immigrants, also add to the margin of error.

The DA base estimate assumes that there are about 6.0 million undocumented immigrants living in the United States under age 65—3.3 million from the 1990 DA estimate plus a net increase during the 1990s of 2.7 million.[4] The estimated net increase during the decade essentially represents an extrapolation of net undocumented immigration derived from estimates that mainly reflect changes between 1992 and 1996. Considering a number of factors, Census Bureau researchers believe that 6 million is a reasonable lower-bound estimate of the number of undocumented immigrants at the time of the 2000 census (Robinson, 2001a). For purposes of comparative analysis, the Census Bureau simply assumed a doubling of net undocumented immigration over the decade, to 8.7 million (bringing the total population to 282.3 million. This alternate estimate (see Table 5-1) implies a census undercount of 0.9 million, or 0.3 percent, still far below the 3.3 million (1.2%) indicated by the A.C.E.

---

[3]In 1990, in contrast, the DA estimated a higher net undercount than that estimated by the Post-Enumeration Survey (PES). The DA estimate of the net undercount was 1.9 percent; that of the PES was 1.6 percent.

[4]For people age 65 and over the adjustment for Medicare underregistration presumably includes undocumented immigrants. See Robinson (1991) for a discussion of the Medicare adjustments for the 1990 DA estimates.

TABLE 5-2 Net Census Undercount, by Sex and Age, as Measured by Demographic Analysis and Post-Enumeration Surveys, 1990 and 2000 (in percent)

| | 1990 | | 2000 | | |
| | Demographic | | Demographic Analysis[a] | | |
Category	Analysis	PES	Base	Alternate	A.C.E.
Male					
Total	2.79	1.93	−0.13	0.91	1.51
0–17 years	2.16	3.17	−0.51	0.27	1.53
18–29 years	2.15	3.16	−2.57	0.34	3.45
30–49 years	3.83	1.85	1.28	2.26	1.81
50 years and over	2.72	−0.57	0.15	0.29	−0.24
Female					
Total	0.94	1.25	−1.16	−0.25	0.79
0–17 years	2.43	3.20	0.06	0.87	1.54
18–29 years	0.64	2.81	−3.07	−0.66	2.11
30–49 years	0.50	0.88	−0.91	0.04	0.95
50 years and over	0.24	−1.20	−1.43	−1.28	−0.76
Total	1.85	1.58	−0.65	0.32	1.15

NOTES: Minus sign (−) indicates a net overcount of the population. Net undercount is the difference between the estimate (A.C.E., PES, or demographic analysis) and the census divided by the estimate. Total population includes household and group quarters populations; the census count of group quarters is added to the A.C.E. for comparability with DA.

   [a] Base is the originally produced DA estimate which includes an allowance for 6 million undocumented immigrants; alternate is a DA estimate that arbitrarily doubles the flow of undocumented immigrants between 1990 and 2000, allowing for 8.7 million undocumented immigrants total.

SOURCE: Robinson (2001a:Tables A, 5).

There are no direct, comparative measures for evaluating the net immigration component, especially the undocumented component, of DA. At present, a "residual" process is used to estimate the number of undocumented immigrants: that is, an estimate of the expected number of foreign-born people legally residing in the country is derived from reported data on legal immigration, and this figure is compared with the number of foreign-born people reported in the census long-form sample or, more recently, in the Current Population Survey (CPS).[5] The difference between the two represents the number of undocumented immigrants included in the census (or CPS). The computations are carried out in some detail by country (or region) of birth and year of entry, which is believed to add to the validity to the estimates. (Data on country of birth and year of immigration are now included regularly in the CPS so that the computations can be carried out more frequently, perhaps adding some stability in the estimates over time.)

---

   [5]The census long-form sample included about 17–18 million households in 1990 and 2000; the CPS includes about 50,000 households each month.

There has been much speculation about the adequacy of the immigration component used in the DA estimates. Passel (2001) argues that data now available support a significantly higher estimate of undocumented immigrants in the population in 2000 than that used by the Bureau. Specifically, looking at the March 2000 CPS foreign-born estimates, Passel concludes that one can easily support an estimate of undocumented immigrants of 7 million, which is 1 million higher than the DA base estimate. Furthermore, using 2000 census and A.C.E. data to adjust the March 2000 CPS would support even higher estimates of undocumented immigrants—perhaps in the 8–9 million range. Some recent work by Warren (2001), released by the Immigration and Naturalization Service, supports an estimate of 6.5 to 7.5 million undocumented immigrants in the United States at the time of the census—higher than the DA base estimate but lower than Passel's high estimates. Recently released data from the Census 2000 Supplementary Survey supports Passel's higher estimates of 8–9 million undocumented immigrants in the United States in 2000.[6]

Passel's research also suggests that the Census Bureau understated two components of legal immigration: foreign-born people living in the country legally with temporary visas (e.g., foreign-born students and guest high-tech workers) and Mexicans living in the United States as legal residents. According to Passel, both of these groups increased in number during the 1990s more than indicated by data on legal admissions. Reasonable estimates for these two groups would add about another 750,000 people to the estimates. Furthermore, there are indications that the Bureau's allowances for net emigration may have overstated the number of immigrants who left the country during the 1990s.[7]

In response, the Census Bureau has suggested that these higher estimates of legal and illegal immigrants imply that the proportions of foreign-born people in the U.S. population—particularly Hispanics—are much higher than are reasonable based on past history. Bureau researchers are currently looking at detailed information from the 2000 census long form and the Census 2000 Supplementary Survey on country of birth, year of immigration, and other characteristics to try to resolve competing estimates of legal and illegal immigrants.

This discussion is not intended to answer the question of the quality of the DA estimate, but rather to point out the problem of fine-tuning and interpreting the DA estimate in light of the uncertainty associated with estimates of the immigration (legal and illegal) components. As already noted, there are no precise tools for evaluating the accuracy of DA. Rather, one uses analyses of such

---

[6]The Census 2000 Supplementary Survey included 700,000 households, of which about 58,000 households were surveyed each month in 2000 by mail with telephone and personal follow-up using a questionnaire similar to the long form. It is intended to provide the basis for a transition from the census long form to the planned American Community Survey, which will sample 250,000 households each month beginning in 2003.

[7]Administrative data on emigration represent only a very small fraction of emigrants and are, themselves, of uncertain quality. The method for estimating emigration is essentially an extrapolation of previous trends.

TABLE 5-3 Net Census Undercount by Race, as Measured by Demographic Analysis and A.C.E., 2000 (in percent)

| | Demographic Analysis | | | | |
| | Base Estimate[a] | | Alternate Estimate[b] | | |
Category	Model 1[c]	Model 2[d]	Model 1[c]	Model 2[d]	A.C.E.[e]
Total Population	−0.65	−0.65	0.32	0.32	1.15
Black	4.67	0.93	5.36	1.65	2.06
Male	6.94	3.26	7.64	3.98	2.37
Female	2.52	−1.27	3.20	−0.56	1.78
Nonblack	−1.48	−0.90	−0.45	0.12	1.02
Male	−1.21	−0.65	−0.11	0.44	1.40
Female	−1.74	−1.14	−0.79	−0.20	0.64
Black-nonblack difference	6.15	1.83	5.81	1.53	1.04

NOTES: Minus sign (−) indicates a net overcount of the population. Net undercount is the difference between the estimate (A.C.E. or demographic analysis) and the census divided by the estimate. Total population includes household and group quarters populations; the census count of group quarters is added to the A.C.E. for comparability with DA.

[a] Base is the originally produced demographic analysis (DA) estimate that includes an allowance for 6 million undocumented immigrants.
[b] Alternate is a DA estimate that arbitrarily doubles the flow of undocumented immigrants between 1990 and 2000, allowing for 8.7 million undocumented immigrants total.
[c] Model 1 compares the 2000 DA estimates for blacks with 2000 census tabulations for people who only reported black race.
[d] Model 2 compares the 2000 DA estimates for blacks with census 2000 tabulations for people who reported black whether or not they reported any other race.
[e] The A.C.E. estimates are the average of Model 1 and Model 2, which differ by no more than 0.3 percent.
SOURCE: Robinson (2001a:Table 6).

data as country of origin of the foreign born, year of entry, and citizenship—to name the most important variables—to arrive at some estimate. The question then is whether the overall DA estimates can be used as a gold standard for measuring census coverage and the adequacy of surveys such as the A.C.E., given the continuing high level of uncertainty of a major component.

It should be noted that a similar problem arose in 1980 when the DA estimate was initially about the same as the 1980 census count. Further analysis suggested that the DA estimate failed to allow for significant numbers of undocumented immigrants in the country (then estimated at about 3 million). The DA estimates were revised to incorporate the estimate of 3 million undocumented immigrants, which then became part of the base DA for later periods.

In summary, the DA estimate of total population is subject to a high degree of uncertainty and its strength for comparative analysis is not clear. What seem to be needed are data and measuring instruments to evaluate DA, preferably before census or other survey results become available. At the moment, it seems that the DA estimate, which is supposed to help analyze and measure overall census and survey coverage, is increasingly dependent on the census and survey results to establish its own validity and provide the basis for adjustments to the estimates.

ESTIMATES BY RACE

The total population estimate is only one aspect, although a major one, of DA analyses. There are other relevant, informative estimates, such as the estimates by race. As stated above, DA estimates are prepared for blacks and nonblacks separately.[8] Race in DA largely reflects the race assigned in the particular administrative record at the time of the event (birth, death, etc.). Thus, the comparison of the DA estimate with the census—the net undercount—will be affected if people who are classified as a particular race in DA—such as black—report a different race in the census.

In 2000 the measure of the net black undercount is affected and made more complicated by the multiple race classification instruction ("mark one or more") used in 2000. As a result, the 2000 tabulations do not include a "black" race category that is comparable with either previous censuses or the DA estimate. Rather, tabulations for the black population for 2000 can be made in one of two ways: as the number of people reporting only black as their race or as that number plus the number of people reporting black in combination with one or more other races.

To deal with this problem in measuring black net undercount as reflected in DA, the Census Bureau developed two estimates, representing the range of the two tabulations indicated above. Using the DA base estimate, the black net undercount ranges from 4.7 percent based on those reporting black only in the census to 0.9 percent when black in combination with other races is included in the count of blacks—a fairly wide range with the truth somewhere in between. Note that using the Bureau's alternate DA estimate (i.e., an estimate with 8.7 million instead of 6.0 million undocumented immigrants) serves only to slightly raise the overall level of the estimated black net undercount; the wide range remains unchanged; see Table 5-3.

Another inconsistency in the race comparison arises from the millions of people—mainly Hispanic—who report their race as "other race-not specified" in the census. To make the census counts consistent with the historical race categories used in DA estimation, these people need to be redistributed to the standard race categories. In 1990 there were about 10 million people in the "other race-not specified" category who were reassigned to a specific race category. A similar modification was made in 2000; approximately 15 million people were so reclassified.

---

[8]Administrative records do not yet provide a basis for developing demographic estimates for Hispanics or other race groups.

TABLE 5-4 Sex Ratios (Men per 100 Women) from the Census, Demographic Analysis, A.C.E., and PES, 1990 and 2000

	1990			2000		
	Demographic Analysis	PES	Census	Demographic Analysis[a]	A.C.E.[b]	Census[b]
Black						
Total	95.16	90.44	89.59	94.90	91.05	90.59
0–17 years	102.42	102.37	102.42	102.73	103.30	103.31
18–29 years	99.27	92.13	93.99	100.22	94.10	93.99
30–49 years	95.92	89.00	86.17	96.47	89.66	88.53
50 or more years	78.33	72.08	71.49	76.94	73.51	73.47
Nonblack						
Total	97.19	96.54	95.89	97.66	97.88	97.15
0–17 years	105.23	105.51	105.51	104.95	105.50	105.53
18–29 years	104.94	104.57	103.78	104.81	106.89	105.27
30–49 years	102.00	100.34	99.59	101.94	101.36	100.59
50 or more years	80.79	79.86	79.38	84.17	83.54	83.10

[a] The 2000 demographic analysis sex ratios are those for the base estimate, which is the originally produced demographic analysis estimate for 2000 that includes an allowance for 6 million undocumented immigrants (the base estimate sex ratios differ by less than 0.4 percent in every instance and less than 0.1 percent in most instances from sex ratios computed for the alternate estimate, which arbitrarily doubles the flow of undocumented immigrants between 1990 and 2000, to 8.7 million undocumented immigrants total).

[b] Sex ratios for the A.C.E. and the 2000 census are based on Model 1, which categorizes blacks as people who only reported black race. (Sex ratios computed under "Model 2," which categorizes blacks as people who reported black whether or not they reported any other race, differ by less than 1.0 in every instance and less than 0.1 in most instances from the Model 1 sex ratios.)

SOURCE: Robinson (2001a:Table 8).

Traditionally, the DA breakdown of black and nonblack populations has been intended to provide a contrast between net undercount rates in prevailing majority and minority populations. A question about the usefulness of DA estimates is whether the black-nonblack dichotomy is still relevant to capture this contrast. The black population represents a smaller proportion of the minority population than in the past (about 40% in 2000 compared with over 50% in 1970). Correspondingly, the nonblack population is currently estimated at about 20 percent minority, and this percentage will probably increase with the passage of time. The black population is a growing fraction of the national population, and DA estimates of net undercount in the black population remain a vitally important product. However, research on a more refined indicator of summary demographic undercount than black-nonblack is needed.

OTHER ESTIMATES

Another component of DA analysis worth noting is the DA estimates of sex ratios, that is, the number of males per 100 females. For blacks, DA shows

TABLE 5-5 Comparisons of
Population Estimates for Children

	Census Count/DA Estimate	
Age Group	2000	1990
Under 5 years	0.972	0.963
5–9 years	0.997	0.965
10–14 years	1.025	0.988
Total under 10 years	0.985	0.964
Total under 15 years	0.998	0.972

SOURCE: Data from U.S. Census Bureau.

consistently significantly higher sex ratios at ages 18–29 and 30–49 than shown in the 2000 census or the A.C.E., for which sex ratios for blacks at these ages are similar and below what one would expect. In other words, both the 2000 census and the A.C.E. show net undercounts of black males relative to females at these ages, continuing a pattern exhibited in earlier censuses; see Table 5-4. This pattern is believed to be due to the lower propensities for black men to be counted in any census or survey than black women ("correlation bias"). Sex ratios for nonblacks ages 18–29, on the other hand, are somewhat higher in the A.C.E. than in DA, which was not the case in 1990.

Yet another component that can shed some light on the comparison of DA with the census are the estimates for people under age 15. The DA estimates at these ages are less affected by the uncertainties associated with the immigration component, especially undocumented immigrants. Table 5-5 shows the ratios of census to DA estimates for 1990 and 2000 (base estimate) for age groups under age 15. If one assumes that DA is fairly reliable at these younger ages, either the 2000 census had higher coverage at these ages than in 1990 or there was more overcounting (duplication) than in the 1990 census.

CONCLUSIONS

Demographic analysis has strengths as well as weaknesses in its processes and underlying assumptions for developing estimates of the expected total population for groups. For 2000, it would appear that the demographic estimates are weakest, or at least most uncertain, for two elements of major importance: total population for use in measuring overall net undercount and differential undercount for blacks and nonblacks. The DA estimates of sex ratios by race and of younger ages are informative, but limited in usefulness for measuring the comparative coverage of the three data sets—census, A.C.E., and DA.

We conclude that there are enough uncertainties about the estimates of net immigration, compounded by the difficulties of classifying people by race, so that demographic analysis should not be used as a standard for evaluating the census or the A.C.E. at this time. At present, the Census Bureau has under way extensive reanalysis and evaluation of the components of DA to help inform its upcoming decision about whether to adjust census population estimates that are used for fund allocation and other important purposes.

Looking to the future, we urge the Bureau to expand its resources that are regularly devoted to estimating components of population change, particularly immigration (including the illegal component) and emigration. Resources are also needed for estimating uncertainty in the demographic population estimates. Finally, we urge the Census Bureau to lead a research effort by appropriate federal agencies and outside experts to develop improved methods and sources of data for estimating legal and illegal immigrants in surveys and administrative records as input to demographic analysis and for other uses.

6

Accuracy and Coverage Evaluation: Overview

The Accuracy and Coverage Evaluation (A.C.E.) Program was designed for two purposes: to be the primary source of information about the completeness of coverage in the 2000 census for population groups,[1] and to provide the basis for recommending adjustment of the census counts for estimated net undercount if the Census Bureau determined that adjusted estimates were more accurate than unadjusted counts for important uses of the data. The design and implementation of the A.C.E. were based on over 20 years of experience at the Census Bureau with dual-systems estimation of the population, using a sample of census records and a sample of records from a separate postcensus survey.

This chapter first summarizes key results from the A.C.E. for 2000, comparing them with results from the 1990 Post-Enumeration Survey (PES) and drawing implications for population coverage in the two censuses. It then gives an overview of dual-systems estimation, which uses results from the A.C.E. and the census to estimate the population. The final section describes the design and operational procedures for the A.C.E. (Appendix C provides a more detailed description) and summarizes important differences from the 1990 PES. The next chapter presents the panel's assessment of what is known about the quality of the A.C.E. operations.

COVERAGE PATTERNS, 2000 AND 1990

Table 6-1 shows net undercount rates and the associated 90 percent confidence intervals from the 2000 A.C.E. and the 1990 PES for race/ethnicity domains, age and sex, and housing tenure.[2] (Separate population estimates

---

[1]Demographic analysis (see Chapter 5) is another source for evaluating census population coverage; however, demographic analysis is limited to population estimates for age, sex, and black-nonblack population groups for the nation as a whole.

[2]The 90 percent confidence interval is the estimate (e.g., net undercount for Hispanics) plus or minus 1.645 times the standard error of the estimate. Standard errors were estimated by the Census Bureau (see Davis, 2001; see also Appendix C).

TABLE 6-1 Net Undercount for Major Groups, 2000 A.C.E. and 1990 PES (in percent)

	2000 A.C.E.		1990 PES	
	Net Undercount	90% Confidence Interval	Net Undercount	90% Confidence Interval
Total Population	1.18	(0.97 , 1.39)	1.61	(1.28 , 1.94)
Race/Ethnicity Domain				
American Indian and Alaska Native on Reservation	4.74	(2.77 , 6.71)	12.22	(3.52 , 20.92)
American Indian and Alaska Native off Reservation	3.28	(1.09 , 5.47)	N.A.	N.A.
Hispanic Origin (any race)	2.85	(2.22 , 3.48)	4.99	(3.64 , 6.34)
Black or African American (not Hispanic)	2.17	(1.59 , 2.75)	4.57	(3.67 , 5.47)
Native Hawaiian, Other Pacific Islander (not Hispanic)	4.60	(0.04 , 9.16)	N.A.	N.A.
Asian (not Hispanic; includes Pacific Islander in 1990)	0.96	(−0.09 , 2.01)	2.36	(0.07 , 4.65)
White or Some Other Race (not Hispanic)	0.67	(0.44 , 0.90)	0.68	(0.32 , 1.04)
Age and Sex				
Under 18 years	1.54	(1.23 , 1.85)	3.18	(2.70 , 3.66)
18 to 29 years				
Male	3.77	(3.24 , 4.30)	3.30	(2.41 , 4.19)
Female	2.23	(1.75 , 2.71)	2.83	(2.06 , 3.60)
30 to 49 years				
Male	1.86	(1.55 , 2.17)	1.89	(1.36 , 2.42)
Female	0.96	(0.68 , 1.24)	0.88	(0.47 , 1.29)
50 years and over				
Male	−0.25	(−0.55 , +0.05)	−0.59	(−1.15 , −0.03)
Female	−0.79	(−1.07 , −0.51)	−1.24	(−1.72 , −0.76)
Housing Tenure				
In owner-occupied housing units	0.44	(0.21 , 0.67)	0.04	(−0.31 , 0.39)
In nonowner-occupied housing units	2.75	(2.32 , 3.18)	4.51	(3.80 , 5.22)

NOTES: Net undercount is the difference between the estimate (A.C.E. or PES) and the census, divided by the estimate. Minus sign (−) indicates a net overcount. For 2000, total population is the household population; for 1990, it is the household population plus the noninstitutional group quarters population (see Appendix C). The 90% confidence interval is the estimate plus or minus 1.645 times the standard error of the estimate. See Table 6-2 for definitions of race/ethnicity domains in 2000. N.A.: not available (not estimated).

SOURCE: Hogan (2001a:Tables 2a, 2b).

were produced for many more groups—called post-strata—than are summarized here; see "A.C.E. Operations," below.[3]) The A.C.E. estimates apply to the household population; they exclude people in institutional and noninstitutional group quarters (e.g., dormitories, prisons, nursing homes, group homes), for whom coverage is not estimated and who therefore, by default, are assumed to have zero net undercount.[4] People living in remote Alaska and people enumerated in shelters are also not included in the A.C.E. The PES estimates include people in noninstitutional group quarters, but there are no separate estimates for them.

Overall, the population was undercounted by 1.2 percent in 2000 as estimated by the A.C.E., less than the net undercount rate of 1.6 percent estimated for 1990 by the PES. The 2000 and 1990 estimates of net undercount show similar patterns, in that net undercount rates are significantly higher in both censuses for most minority groups than they are for the white or some other races (not Hispanic) category. However, the 2000 net undercount rates for Hispanics and non-Hispanic blacks are significantly lower than the rates in 1990: for 2000 they are estimated as 2.9 percent and 2.2 percent, respectively, compared with estimates from 1990 of 5 percent and 4.6 percent, respectively. The net undercount rates for the white or other races category are the same in both censuses, 0.7 percent.

By age and sex, net undercount rates in 2000, as in 1990, were higher for men than women. Net undercount rates were also higher in both censuses for younger people than for those aged 50 and over, for whom there is a small estimated net overcount. The most pronounced difference in net undercount rates by age between 1990 and 2000 is for children under age 18, for whom the rate is significantly lower in 2000 (1.5%) than it was in 1990 (3.2%).

By housing tenure, people who rent continued to be undercounted at a higher rate than people who own their homes, but the net undercount rate for renters is significantly lower in 2000 compared with 1990. For owners, the net undercount rate is estimated at less than 0.5 percent in both censuses; for renters, the estimated net undercount rate is 2.8 percent in 2000, compared with 4.5 percent in 1990.

---

[3]In census terminology, the racial and ethnic groupings used in defining post-strata are called domains. They are carefully defined in a hierarchical manner (due to the option to report more than one race; see Table 6-2), and may differ from colloquial definitions of a particular racial/ethnic group.

[4]This assumption needs evaluation since people in group quarters are estimated to be 2.8 percent of the total population (see Chapter 4).

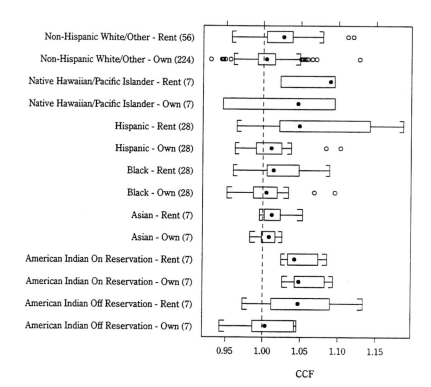

FIGURE 6-1 Post-stratum coverage correction factors (CCF) by domain and tenure, 2000 A.C.E.

NOTES: The number in parentheses following a label indicates the number of post-stratum groups belonging to that domain/tenure classification (see Table 6-2 for definitions of individual post-strata). Coverage correction factors are the dual-systems estimate of the population divided by the census count. For each box on the plot, the black dot indicates the median of the observations. The end-points of the rectangular box are the 25th and 75th percentiles of the observations, so the box spans the locations of one-half of the observations. The "whiskers" extend from the end of the box to a length based on the interquartile range of the observations; observations beyond these whiskers are indicated by open circles and may be considered outliers in the distribution.

SOURCE: Tabulations by panel staff from U.S. Census Bureau, Pre-Collapsed Post-Stratum Summary File (U.S.), February 16, 2001.

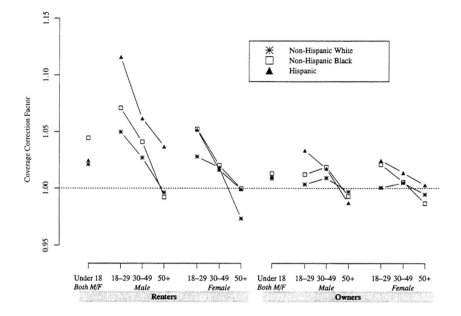

FIGURE 6-2 Coverage correction factors by race/ethnicity domain, housing tenure, and age/sex groups.

Figure 6-1 shows distributions (boxplots) of estimated census coverage correction factors from the A.C.E. for some of the strongest relationships in the estimation, namely, that for owners and renters for each of seven race/ethnicity domains.[5] While there is variation in the coverage correction factors for individual post-strata within each race/ethnicity and tenure group, renters have higher median coverage correction factors than owners in every race/ethnicity domain except for American Indians and Alaska Natives on reservations. Indeed, white renters have a higher median coverage correction factor than most minority owners.

Figure 6-2 shows aggregate coverage correction factors for age/sex groups among three race/ethnicity domains (Hispanics, non-Hispanic blacks, and non-Hispanic whites and other races) for owners and renters.[6] Higher coverage correction factors for men and young adults relative to children, older people, and women are more pronounced for renters than for owners in each

---

[5]Coverage correction factors represent the population estimated from the A.C.E. using dual-systems estimation divided by the census population. For groups estimated to have a net undercount, the coverage correction factor minus 1.0 will be slightly higher than the net undercount rate measured by taking the difference between the dual-systems estimate and the census count and dividing that difference by the dual-systems estimate (e.g., a coverage correction factor of 1.04 is equivalent to a net undercount rate of 0.038 or 3.8%).

[6]Separate coverage correction factors by sex are not available for children under age 18.

race/ethnicity category, as are differences between the non-Hispanic white and other races domain and the other two groups.

The measured reduction in the net undercount rates and associated coverage correction factors for minorities relative to the rates for the white and other races category has been cited as a major achievement of the 2000 census. Also noted has been the reduction in the net undercount rate of children relative to that for older people, as well as the reduction in the undercount rate of renters relative to that for owners (Executive Steering Committee on A.C.E. Policy, 2001a). An important question is the reason(s) for these reductions. In this chapter, we focus on the operation of the A.C.E. itself, which is necessary to understand the estimated net undercount rates and to determine whether the estimation of those rates is accurate.

DUAL-SYSTEMS ESTIMATION

The A.C.E., like its predecessors, the 1990 PES and the 1980 Post-Enumeration Program (PEP), was designed to estimate the population of the United States and population groups by dual-systems estimation (DSE). This method is closely related to a widely used statistical methodology known as capture-recapture, which was first developed for estimating wildlife populations. The methodology requires adaptation for the census context, as described in Fienberg (2000) and Hogan (1992, 2000a, 2000b).

The basic concept is that a total population estimate—the dual-systems estimate—can be developed on the basis of being able to estimate how many people who were validly included in a second, independent survey (the P-sample) were also found in the first survey (here, the census enumerations in the A.C.E. sample blocks). Not every census enumeration is correct; some are erroneous (e.g., a duplicate), so the process also involves estimating how many of the records in a sample of census enumerations in the A.C.E. blocks— the E-sample—represent correct enumerations.[7]

In general terms, the P-sample and E-sample are used to estimate two components of the formula for calculating the DSE for each of several hundred population groups, called post-strata. These components are the proportion of the population correctly included in the census, which is estimated by the P-sample match rate, and the proportion of the census records that were correctly included, which is estimated by the E-sample correct enumeration rate:

- The match rate is the weighted estimate, M, of P-sample persons who match with E-sample or other census persons, divided by the weighted estimate, P, of all valid P-sample persons (including matches and non-matches).

---

[7]The E-sample does not include every census enumeration in the A.C.E. blocks, for such reasons as subsampling of large blocks (see "A.C.E. Operations," below).

- The correct enumeration rate is the weighted estimate, CE, of E-sample persons who were correctly enumerated in the census (including matches and correct nonmatches), divided by the weighted estimate, E, of all E-sample persons (including correct and erroneous enumerations).

These components are applied in a formula for each post-stratum (ps):

$$DSE_{ps} = (C - II)_{ps} \left(\frac{CE}{E} \right)_{ps} \left(\frac{P}{M} \right)_{ps}, \tag{1}$$

where:

- DSE is the dual-systems estimate of the post-stratum total population, ps;

- $C - II$ is the census count, C, *minus* people requiring imputation and late additions to the census count, II, who are excluded from the E-sample because they cannot be matched to the P-sample;[8]

- CE/E is the weighted correct enumeration rate from the E-sample; and

- P/M is the inverse of the weighted match rate from the P-sample.

For any post-stratum, the net undercount rate (UR) is computed as:

$$UR = \frac{DSE - C}{DSE}, \tag{2}$$

and the coverage correction factor (CCF) is computed as

$$CCF = \frac{DSE}{C}, \tag{3}$$

where C is the census count, *including* people requiring imputation and late additions to the count (IIs).

The basic assumption underlying the calculation of the DSE can be stated as follows: Given independence of the P-sample survey from the census, the estimated proportion of P-sample people in a post-stratum who match to the census (M/P) is a good estimate of the estimated proportion of all people in

---

[8] II is a Census Bureau term that originally stood for "insufficient information for matching." Its meaning has evolved, and it now covers late additions to the census and people whose census records were incomplete and required imputation. In 2000, there were no late enumerations as such; however, there were 2.4 million people whose records were temporarily removed from the census file and reinstated too late to be included in the A.C.E. processing.

the post-stratum who were correctly enumerated in the census (CE/DSE). Solving for DSE in the following equation,

$$\frac{M}{P} = \frac{\left[(C - II)\left(\frac{CE}{E}\right)\right]}{DSE}, \tag{4}$$

gives equation (1) above.

Five points are worth noting about dual-systems estimation in the census context. First, if there were no IIs, that is, no census enumerations that either lacked sufficient information or were added too late to be included in the A.C.E. matching, then the coverage correction factor, CCF, would be equivalent to the correction ratio, CR. The correction ratio is the correct enumeration rate, CE/E, divided by the match rate, M/P. (The equivalence is evident by setting II equal to zero in equation (4) and solving for (DSE/C).)

Hogan (2001b) demonstrates why, in principle, the level of IIs does not bias the DSE (see also Chapter 8). However, the larger the number of IIs, the more the correction ratio will exceed the coverage correction factor. Consequently, if a census had a considerable number of IIs, examination of the correction ratio from the A.C.E. process would lead one to expect higher net undercount rates than actually result when the DSE is compared with the census count inclusive of IIs. In Chapter 8, we examine the role of IIs—people requiring imputation and late additions to the census count—who were several times more numerous in 2000 (8.2 million) than in 1990 (about 2.2 million).

Second, there is no assumption that the P-sample must be more complete than the E-sample for DSE to work; it is expected that the P-sample will miss some people who were correctly enumerated in the census, and vice versa. What is important is that the information obtained in the P-sample that is needed to determine a match or valid nonmatch be of high quality and obtained independently of the census.

Third, a key assumption in the calculation of the DSE in the census context is that the procedures used to define who is in and who is not in the census are balanced. The E-sample is used to determine how many census enumerations are correctly in the census according to specified criteria (e.g., a college student living in a dormitory should be enumerated at the college and not at his or her parental home). For the DSE model to work, the same criteria must be applied to determine how many P-sample people match to correct census enumerations (whether or not they are in the E-sample). Failure to apply the same criteria will create an error of balancing (see Chapter 7).

An important dimension of balancing involves geographic correctness. For each person, there is a defined area where he or she should have been enumerated (this is the block cluster in the A.C.E.). In searching for a match for a person in the P-sample, it is important to search all the census enumerations that are in the correct area and only those enumerations in the correct area.

Geographic balancing error occurs when the actual search area for P-sample matches is larger or smaller than that used in the E-sample to determine correct enumerations.

Fourth, the DSE is sample based, which means that it is important not only to estimate the DSE itself, but also to accurately estimate the variance in the DSE due to sampling error and other sources of variation.

Finally, if DSE results are to be used to adjust the census for undercount, the process would involve applying the coverage correction factors to the population counted in each geographic area for which adjusted counts are desired, separately for each post-stratum. This procedure assumes that the probabilities of being included (captured) in the A.C.E. or the census do not vary significantly by geographic area within post-strata.

A.C.E. OPERATIONS

Overview

Sampling and Address Listing

The 2000 A.C.E. began with a series of steps to obtain a sample of about 11,000 block clusters and 300,000 household addresses nationwide in which interviews would be conducted for the independent P-sample survey (see Appendix C; remote Alaska was not part of the A.C.E.). The steps included:

- drawing a large sample of block clusters and sending field staff to develop a complete address list for them, independent of the census Master Address File (MAF);

- reducing the sample for medium and large block clusters (those with 3 to 79 housing units and 80 or more housing units, respectively) in a manner that oversampled minority areas;

- reducing the sample for small block clusters;

- matching the addresses on the P-sample address list against the MAF addresses in the sampled block clusters to provide information for the last stage of sampling and facilitate other operations; and

- subsampling addresses within large block clusters to reduce the interviewing workload.

P-Sample Interviewing

Beginning in late April 2000, interviewers used laptop computers to obtain information for all addresses in the P-sample block clusters. The first wave of interviewing was conducted by telephone for households that provided a telephone number on their census questionnaire and for which there was a clear city-style address. Fully 29 percent of the P-sample household interviews were obtained by telephone. The second wave of interviewing, which began in mid-June and continued through August, was in person. Interviewers were instructed to strive for a household respondent, but proxy interviews from neighbors or landlords were accepted if attempts to contact the household directly proved futile. The interviewers asked about three types of household residents:

- nonmovers—those who lived in the house on Census Day and still lived there;

- outmovers—those who lived in the house on Census Day but had subsequently moved away; and

- inmovers—those who were current residents but had not lived in the house on Census Day.

People who were determined to be group quarters residents were removed from the P-sample.

Initial Matching and Targeted Extended Search

Once the P-sample survey was complete and the E-sample of census enumerations was drawn for the A.C.E. sample of block clusters, the first round of matching was conducted. The E-sample excluded certain census enumerations: group quarters residents, people reinstated in the census too late for A.C.E. processing ("late additions"), and people requiring imputation (people having only one reported short-form characteristic among name, age, sex, race, ethnicity, and household relationship).[9]

The first stage of matching was done by computer; the matching algorithm assigned a match probability score by examining the available variables (name and demographic characteristics) according to specified rules. Probability score cutoffs identified clear matches, possible matches, and nonmatches within each block cluster. (P-sample and E-sample records lacking enough reported data for A.C.E. matching and follow-up, including a name and at least two characteristics, were flagged for imputation of match or enumeration status.) P-sample records could match to census records that were not in the E-sample, such as census records excluded from the E-sample due to large block subsampling. Clerks then reviewed the possible matches and nonmatches to identify additional matches. Their work was reviewed in turn by a small staff of technicians and a yet smaller staff of analysts.

---

[9]Such census records are termed "whole person imputations" or "non-data-defined."

In selected block clusters, the clerks performed a targeted extended search (TES): they searched the blocks adjacent to the block cluster for census enumerations that matched P-sample households not already matched to an E-sample household in the block cluster. They also searched for E-sample enumerations in the surrounding blocks that had been identified as goecoding errors—that is, their addresses were incorrectly assigned to the block cluster.

Field Follow-Up and Final Matching

An important part of the A.C.E. was an operation to recheck certain cases to clarify their status. About half of P-sample nonmatched cases and most unresolved cases were followed up in the field to obtain information that would clarify their residence status (whether they resided at the address on Census Day), as well as their match status. In addition, almost all nonmatched and unresolved E-sample cases were followed up in the field to obtain information that would clarify their enumeration status (whether they were a correct, nonmatched enumeration or a duplicate or other type of erroneous enumeration). The information provided by field follow-up was used to determine a final match and enumeration status for as many P-sample and E-sample cases as possible.

Weighting and Imputation

Prior to estimation, the sampling weights for P-sample cases were adjusted to represent households that, despite best efforts, could not be interviewed. Also, a series of imputations were performed, including: imputation of values for specific missing characteristics needed for post-stratification (age, sex, race, ethnicity, and housing tenure); imputation of enumeration status for unresolved E-sample cases; imputation of residence status for unresolved P-sample cases; and imputation of match status for unresolved P-sample cases who were reported or imputed to be Census Day residents at the P-sample address.

Post-Strata Estimation

The final step in the A.C.E. process was estimation of the DSE and its associated variance for post-strata. Post-strata were prespecified to form 448 individual strata that grouped people by age, sex, race/ethnicity, housing tenure, and, in some cases, geographic region, a mail return rate for their neighborhood calculated for the A.C.E., and size of metropolitan area. Table 6-2 shows the A.C.E. post-strata. If a post-stratum had fewer than 100 nonmovers and outmovers, it was combined with another stratum; this procedure reduced the number of post-strata from 448 to 416 for the final analysis.

TABLE 6-2 Post-Strata in the 2000 A.C.E., 64 Major Groups

Race/Ethnicity Domain	Other Characteristics
1. American Indian or Alaska Native on Reservation[a]	❑ 2 groups: owner, renter
2. American Indian or Alaska Native off Reservation[b]	❑ 2 groups: owner, renter
3. Hispanic[c]	❑ 4 groups for owners: ❖ High and low mail return rate ❖ By type of metropolitan statistical area (MSA) and enumeration area ➤ Large and medium-size MSA mailout/mailback areas ➤ All other ❑ 4 groups for renters (see Hispanic owners)
4. Non-Hispanic Black[d]	❑ 4 groups for owners (see Hispanic owners) ❑ 4 groups for renters (see Hispanic owners)
5. Native Hawaiian or Pacific Islander[e]	❑ 2 groups: owner, renter
6. Non-Hispanic Asian[f]	❑ 2 groups: owner, renter
7. Non-Hispanic White or Some Other Race[g]	❑ 32 groups for owners: ❖ High and low mail return rate ❖ By region (Northeast, Midwest, South, West) ❖ By type of metropolitan statistical area and enumeration area: ➤ Large MSA, mailout/mailback areas ➤ Medium MSA, mailout/mailback areas ➤ Small MSA and non-MSA, mailout/mailback areas ➤ Other types of enumeration area (e.g., update/leave) ❑ 8 groups for renters: ❖ High and low mail return rate ❖ By type of metropolitan statistical area and enumeration area ➤ (See owner categories)

All 64 groups were classified by 7 age/sex categories (below) to form 448 post-strata; in estimation, some age/sex categories were combined (always within one of the 64 groups) to form 416 strata.

Under age 18
Men aged 18–29; women aged 18–29
Men aged 30–49; women aged 30–49
Men aged 50 years and older; women aged 50 years and older.

NOTES: Large metropolitan statistical areas (MSAs) are the largest 10 MSAs in the United States; medium MSAs are other MSAs with 500,000 or more population; small MSAs are MSAs with less than 500,000 population.

The description of race/ethnicity domains is simplified somewhat; see Haines (2000) for complete set of classification rules (see also Farber, 2001a).

[a] All people on a reservation with American Indian or Alaska Native as their single or one of multiple races.

[b] All people in Indian Country not on a reservation with American Indian or Alaska Native as their single or one of multiple races; all non-Hispanic people not in Indian Country with American Indian or Alaska Native as their single race.

[c] All Hispanic people in Indian Country not already classified in Domain 2; all Hispanic people not in Indian Country except those living in Hawaii with Native Hawaiian or Pacific Islander as their single or one of multiple races.

[d] All non-Hispanic people with Black as their only race; all non-Hispanic people with Black and American Indian or Native Alaska race not in Indian Country; all non-Hispanic people with Black and another single race group, except those living in Hawaii with Black and Native Hawaiian or Pacific Islander race.

[e] All non-Hispanic people with Native Hawaiian or Pacific Islander as their only race; all non-Hispanic people with Native Hawaiian or Pacific Islander and American Indian or Alaska Native race not in Indian Country; all non-Hispanic people with Native Hawaiian or Pacific Islander and Asian race; all people in Hawaii with Native Hawaiian or Pacific Islander as their single or one of multiple races.

[f] All non-Hispanic people with Asian as their only race; all non-Hispanic people with Asian and American Indian or Alaska Native race not in Indian Country.

[g] All non-Hispanic people with White or some other race as their only race; all non-Hispanic people with White or some other race in combination with American Indian or Alaska Native not in Indian Country; or in combination with Asian; or in combination with Native or Pacific Islander not in Hawaii; all non-Hispanic people with three or more races (excluding American Indian or Alaska Native) in Indian Country or outside of Indian Country (excluding Native Hawaiian or Pacific Islander in Hawaii).

To form the DSE, weighted estimates were developed of E-sample total cases and correct enumerations; P-sample nonmover cases, inmover cases, and outmover cases; and P-sample matched nonmover cases and outmover cases. In a procedure called PES-C that was used for most post-strata (see "Major Differences from 1990 PES," below), the match rates calculated for outmovers were applied to the estimated number of inmovers as part of developing an overall match rate for each post-stratum. Also tabulated for each post-stratum was the census count and the count of *II*s (people requiring imputation and late additions). These rates and counts permitted the calculation of the DSE, the net undercount rate, and the coverage correction factor for individual post-strata.

Major Differences from 1990 PES

The 2000 A.C.E. procedures and concepts differed in a number of respects from those incorporated in the 1990 PES (see Hogan, 2000b). This section briefly summarizes the major differences.

Universe

The A.C.E. universe excluded people living in institutions, college dormitories, and other group quarters; the PES universe included most noninstitutional group quarters. The Census Bureau decided to limit the A.C.E. to the household population because of its experience in the 1990 PES.[10]

Sample Size and Design

The 2000 A.C.E. was twice the sample size of the 1990 PES: the 2000 P-sample comprised about 300,000 housing units, compared with 165,000 housing units in the 1990 P-sample. Because of its larger overall sample size, the A.C.E. could produce reliable direct estimates for minorities and other groups with less oversampling than was used in the PES to develop post-strata estimates by means of a smoothing model. Consequently, the A.C.E. weights varied less than the PES weights, which contributed to reducing the variance of the A.C.E. estimates.

---

[10]Rates of unresolved match status were much higher for group quarters residents than for household members in the PES because of much higher rates of short-term mobility for people in group quarters (e.g., college students moving between dormitories and their parental homes, shelter residents moving from one shelter to another, migrant worker dormitory residents moving from one farm to another).

Initial Housing Unit Match

The A.C.E. included a new operation to match P-sample and January 2000 MAF housing units prior to interviewing. The purpose of the match was to facilitate such operations as large block subsampling, telephone interviewing, and matching. Although the P-sample and census address lists were linked, independence was maintained because no changes were carried over from one list to the other as a consequence of the match.

P-Sample Interviewing Technology

The A.C.E. used computer-assisted telephone and personal interviewing (CATI/CAPI) to facilitate the accuracy of the information collected and the speed of data capture and processing. The PES used paper-and-pencil techniques throughout.

Matching Technology

The A.C.E. clerical matching operation was conducted by clerks examining computerized P-sample responses and questionnaire images for census cases in the sampled block clusters. The technology was designed to be user friendly. Because of complete computerization of the operation, all matching could be done at one location, instead of seven as in 1990.

Treatment of Movers

A major change from 1990 was the treatment of movers. The goal of the 1990 PES was to visit each P-sample address and find out where the current residents usually lived as of Census Day, April 1. This procedure is called PES-B, which requires collecting Census Day address information for inmovers (people resident at the P-sample address on interview day but not on Census Day) and searching nationwide to determine if they were enumerated or missed at their reported Census Day residences.[11] The original design for Integrated Coverage Measurement for 2000 ruled out PES-B because of the plan to use sampling for nonresponse follow-up, which meant that movers might not match because their Census Day addresses did not fall into the nonresponse follow-up sample. This decision was carried over to A.C.E.

The 2000 A.C.E. had two goals: to find out who lived at each P-sample address on Census Day and determine whether they were enumerated or missed in the census at that address and to find out who lived at each P-sample address as of the A.C.E. interview day. This procedure is called PES-C; it results in

---

[11]See Marks (1978), who also described a PES-A procedure in which the goal is to visit each P-sample address to find out who lived there on Census Day.

obtaining information not only for nonmovers and inmovers, but also for out-movers (Census Day residents not resident on interview day). The PES-C procedure involved estimating the P-sample match rate for movers by match-ing outmovers.

At the same time, for most post-strata, the A.C.E. estimated the *number* of matched movers by applying the *outmover* match rate to *inmovers*. The un-derlying assumption is that inmovers would be more completely reported than outmovers. The advantage of PES-C is that the searching operation for the Census Day residence of inmovers is not required. The potential drawback is that the quality of the information collected to use in the matching for out-movers may be impaired because their information is always supplied by other people.

Targeted Extended Search Procedures

Another important change from the 1990 PES concerned the TES proce-dure for searching surrounding blocks if a search in the sampled block cluster did not turn up a match for a P-sample household and to find out if misgeocoded E-sample cases were located nearby. In 1990, one ring, or sometimes two rings, of blocks surrounding each sample block cluster were searched for ad-ditional P-sample matches and E-sample correct enumerations. The purpose was to reduce the variance and bias of the DSE estimates. For efficiency rea-sons, it was decided for the 2000 A.C.E. to target the extended search and to conduct it on a sample basis.

Definition of Post-Strata

The 448 post-strata in 2000 (reduced to 416 for estimating DSEs) were similar to the 357 post-strata that were implemented in the reestimation of the 1990 PES.[12] The 2000 post-strata included two additional race/ethnicity domains, one for American Indians and Alaska Natives not living on reserva-tions and another for Native Hawaiian and other Pacific Islanders (who had been combined with Asians in 1990). The 2000 post-strata also categorized non-Hispanic whites and other races, non-Hispanic blacks, and Hispanics by mail return rate (two categories—high and low—calculated separately for each group by tenure). Region was dropped as a stratifier except for people in the non-Hispanic white and other race category who owned their homes.

---

[12]See Thompson (1992); U.S. Census Bureau (1992a). The original 1990 estimation used 1,392 strata together with a composite estimation procedure to smooth the resulting DSEs (see Hogan, 1992).

7

Accuracy and Coverage Evaluation: Assessment

This chapter presents the panel's assessment of the Accuracy and Coverage Evaluation (A.C.E.) Program because the A.C.E. is crucial to any assessment of the census itself. We consider nine separate aspects of the A.C.E.:

- conduct and timing;

- household noninterviews in the P-sample;

- imputation for missing characteristics and unresolved residence, match, and enumeration status;

- quality of matching;

- the targeted extended search;

- post-stratification;

- variance estimates;

- final match codes and rates; and

- gross errors.

We end this chapter with our summary assessment of the A.C.E.

CONDUCT AND TIMING

Overall, the A.C.E. appears to have been well executed. Although the sample size was twice as large as that fielded in 1990, the A.C.E. was carried out on schedule and with only minor problems that necessitated rearrangement or modification of operations after they had been specified.[1] Some procedures,

---

[1]Mostly, such modifications involved accommodation to changes in the Master Address File (MAF) that occurred in the course of the census. For example, the targeted extended search (TES) procedures had to be modified to handle deletions from and additions to the MAF that were made after the determination of the TES housing unit inventory (Navarro and Olson, 2001:11).

103

such as telephone interviewing, proved more useful than had been expected. All processes, from sampling through estimation, were carried out according to well-documented specifications, with quality control procedures (e.g., reviews of the work of clerical matchers and field staff) implemented at appropriate junctures.

HOUSEHOLD NONINTERVIEWS IN THE P-SAMPLE

Because the quantity being estimated—the net undercount of the population—is very small relative to the total population (1–2%), it is essential that the P-sample survey meet high standards with regard to the completeness of reporting. A high rate of household noninterviews that required extensive adjustments to the sampling weights would be detrimental to the dual-systems estimation that is the key to the A.C.E. A high rate would not only increase variance, but also likely introduce bias due to the likelihood that nonresponding households differ from responding households in systematic ways that are important for estimation.

Interview/Noninterview Rates

Overall, the A.C.E. obtained interviews from 98.9 percent of households that were occupied on interview day. This figure compares favorably with the 98.4 percent interview rate for the 1990 Post-Enumeration Survey (PES).[2] However, the percentage of occupied households as of Census Day that were successfully interviewed in A.C.E. was somewhat lower—97 percent, meaning that a weighting adjustment had to account for the remaining 3 percent of noninterviewed households.

The lower interview rate for Census Day households is due largely to the fact that households that had been occupied entirely by outmovers at the time of the census were harder to interview than other households. This result is not surprising because the new occupants of such households may know nothing of the people who lived there before, and it may not always be possible to interview a knowledgeable neighbor or landlord. The interview rate for outmover households was 81.4 percent. Such households comprised 4 percent of Census Day occupied households in the P-sample.

Noninterview Weighting Adjustments

Two weighting adjustments were calculated so that interviewed households would represent all households that should have been interviewed: one for the A.C.E. interview day and the other for Census Day. Each of the two

---

[2]These percentages are unweighted; they are about the same as weighted percentages. Weighted percentages are not available for 1990.

weighting adjustments was calculated separately for households by type (single-family unit, apartment, other) within each individual block cluster. Mover status was not a factor for reweighting.

For Census Day, what could have been a relatively large noninterview adjustment for outmover households in a block cluster was spread over all interviewed Census Day households in the cluster for each of the three housing types. Consequently, adjustments to the weights for interviewed households were quite low, which had the benefit of minimizing the increase in the variance of A.C.E. estimates due to differences among weights: 52 percent of the weights were not adjusted at all because all occupied households in the adjustment cell were interviewed; for another 45 percent of households, the weighting adjustment was between 1.0 and 1.2 (Cantwell et al., 2001:Table 2; see also "Variance Estimates," below).

MISSING AND UNRESOLVED DATA

Another important aspect of A.C.E. data quality is the extent of missing and unresolved data in the P-sample and the E-sample and the effectiveness of imputation procedures to supply values for missing and unresolved variables. Understanding the role of imputation necessitates understanding the designation of the E-sample and the treatment of certain cases in the matching.

As noted above, the E-sample excluded whole person imputations in the census, defined as people with only one short-form characteristic (which could be name). Matching was performed on the P-sample and E-sample, using only reported information. During the course of matching, it was determined that some cases lacked enough reported data for matching and follow-up when a more stringent criterion was applied than that used to exclude whole person imputations from the E-sample. Cases in the P-sample and E-sample lacking name and at least two other short-form characteristics could not be matched. Such cases were retained in both the E- and the P-samples; in the E-sample they were coded as erroneous enumerations and in the P-sample they were not yet assigned a final match status.

After all matching and follow-up had been completed, the next step was item imputation. Missing characteristics were imputed separately for each item in the P-sample records (including those records that lacked enough reported data for matching). Imputations for missing characteristics in the E-sample records (including those records that lacked name and at least two other short-form characteristics) were obtained from those on the census data file (see Appendix A). Then, match probabilities and Census Day residence probabilities were imputed for unresolved P-sample cases, including those that were set aside in the matching, and correct enumeration probabilities were imputed for unresolved E-sample cases. E-sample cases set aside in the matching were assigned a correct enumeration probability of zero.

TABLE 7-1 Missing Data Rates for Characteristics, 2000 A.C.E. and 1990 PES P-Sample and E-Sample (weighted)

| | Percentage of People with Imputed Characteristics | | | |
| | 2000 A.C.E. | | 1990 PES | |
Characteristic	P-Sample	E-Sample	P-Sample	E-Sample
Age	2.4	2.9	0.7	2.4
Sex	1.7	0.2	0.5	1.0
Race	1.4	3.2	2.5	11.8
Hispanic Origin	2.3	3.4	N.A.	N.A.
Housing Tenure	1.9	3.6	2.3	2.5
Any of Above	5.4	10.4	N.A.	N.A.

NOTES: A.C.E. E-sample imputations were obtained from the imputations performed on the census records; PES E-sample imputations were performed specifically for the E-sample. A.C.E. E-sample "edits" (e.g., assigning age on the basis of the person's date of birth, or assigning sex from first name) are not counted as imputations here. The base for the A.C.E. P-sample imputation rates includes nonmovers, inmovers, and outmovers, including people who were subsequently removed from the sample as nonresidents on Census Day. Excluded from the base for the A.C.E. P-sample and E-sample imputation rates are people eligible for the targeted extended search who were not selected for the targeted extended search sample and who were treated as noninterviews in the final weighting. N.A., not available.

SOURCE: Cantwell et al. (2001:Tables 3b, 3c).

Missing Characteristics

Extent

Overall, the extent of missing characteristics data in the P-sample and E-sample was low, ranging between 0.2 percent and 3.6 percent for the characteristics age, sex, race, Hispanic origin, and housing tenure. Missing data rates for most characteristics were somewhat higher for the E-sample than for the P-sample. Missing data rates for the 2000 A.C.E. showed no systematic difference (up or down) from the 1990 PES; see Table 7-1.

As would be expected, missing data rates in the P-sample were higher for proxy interviews, in which someone outside the household supplied information, than for interviews with household members; see Table 7-2. By mover status, missing data rates were much higher for outmovers than for nonmovers and inmovers, which is not surprising given that 73.3 percent of interviews for outmovers were obtained from proxies, compared with only 2.9 percent and 4.8 percent of proxy interviews for nonmovers and inmovers, respectively. Even "non-proxy" interviews for outmovers may have been from household members who did not know the outmover.

For the E-sample, one can distinguish mailed back returns from returns obtained by enumerators in nonresponse follow-up, although there is not information on proxy interviews for the latter. Table 7-3 shows that missing data rates were higher for some, but not all, characteristics when the return was obtained in nonresponse follow-up than when the return was mailed back by the household.

TABLE 7-2 Percentage of 2000 A.C.E. P-Sample People with Imputed Characteristics, by Proxy Interview and Mover Status (weighted)

Characteristic	Percentage of People with Imputed Characteristics				
	Household Interview	Proxy Interview	Nonmover	Inmover	Outmover
Age	2.1	7.9	2.3	2.3	6.0
Sex	1.5	4.2	1.7	0.4	3.4
Race	1.0	8.7	1.2	1.3	8.0
Hispanic Origin	1.8	11.0	2.1	0.8	9.0
Housing Tenure	1.7	5.2	1.9	0.4	2.4
Any of Above	4.4	21.9	5.0	3.7	17.4
Percent of Total P-Sample	94.3	5.7	91.7	4.8	3.4

NOTES: See notes to Table 7-1.

SOURCE: Cantwell et al. (2001:Table 3b).

Effects of Item Imputation

Because the overall rates of missing data were low, the imputation procedures had little effect on the distribution of individual characteristics (Cantwell et al., 2001:24-26). However, imputation could misclassify people by post-strata and contribute to inconsistent post-strata classification for matching P-sample and E-sample cases (see "Post-Stratification," below). The reason is because the P-sample and E-sample imputations were performed using somewhat different procedures; also, imputation procedures for the P-sample were carried out separately for each characteristic.[3]

Unresolved Residence, Match, and Enumeration Status

Residence Status

The weighted percentage of all P-sample nonmover and outmover cases with unresolved Census Day residence status was 2.2 percent, of which 51.7 percent were cases lacking enough reported information for matching. The remaining 48.3 percent of unresolved residence cases were confirmed matches, confirmed nonmatches, and possible matches. After imputation, the percentage of cases estimated to be Census Day residents dropped slightly, from 98.2 percent of resolved cases to 97.9 percent of all cases because the imputation

---

[3] For example, tenure on the P-sample was imputed by using tenure from the previous household of the same type (e.g., single-family home) with tenure reported, while race and ethnicity were imputed when possible from the distribution of race and ethnicity of other household members or from the distribution of race and ethnicity of the previous household with these characteristics reported (see Cantwell et al., 2001).

TABLE 7-3 Percentage of 2000 A.C.E. E-Sample People with Imputed or Edited Characteristics, by Type of Return (weighted)

Characteristic	Percentage of People with Imputed or Edited Characteristics	
	Mail Return	Enumerator Return
Age		
Imputed	1.1	7.0
Edited	1.2	1.9
Sex		
Imputed	0.1	0.4
Edited	0.9	1.1
Race		
Imputed	3.2	3.2
Edited	0.0	0.0
Hispanic Origin		
Imputed	3.5	3.0
Edited	0.3	0.4
Housing Tenure		
Imputed	2.2	6.8
Edited	0.5	0.8
Any of Above		
Imputed	8.5	14.7
Imputed or edited or both	10.9	18.1
Percent of Total E-Sample	69.3	28.0

NOTES: Mail returns are those obtained before the April 18, 2000, cutoff to begin nonresponse follow-up (NRFU). Enumerator returns are those obtained during NRFU. The table excludes 2.7 percent of total E-sample (e.g., list/enumerate, rural update/enumerate, urban/update enumerate, late mail returns).

SOURCE: Tabulations by panel staff of U.S. Census Bureau, E-Sample Person Dual-System Estimation Output File, February 16, 2001; tabulations weighted using TESFINWT (see notes to Table 7-7).

procedure assigned lower residence probabilities to unresolved cases (77.4 percent overall; this figure is a correction from the original number in Cantwell et al., 2001:Table 8).[4]

To impute a residence probability, the Census Bureau classified resolved and unresolved cases by match status follow-up group, race, and tenure. The eight match status groups discriminated well: for example, residence probabilities were very low for potentially fictitious people or people said to be living elsewhere on Census Day (14%);[5] moderate for college and military age children in partially matched households (84%); and very high for cases resolved

---

[4]One would not expect there to be confirmed non-Census Day residents or unresolved cases among nonmovers and outmovers; however, it could happen because mover status was assigned prior to field follow-up work.

[5]Fictitious people are those for whom it seems clear that the data were fabricated by the respondent or enumerator (e.g., a return for Mickey Mouse.)

before follow-up (99%). The addition of race and tenure to the imputation cells did not capture much additional variability in the probability of Census Day residence (Cantwell et al., 2001:Table 8). The residence probabilities assigned to people without enough reported data for matching—84 percent overall—were based on the average of the probabilities for people in the other match status groups within each race and tenure category.

Match Status

The weighted percentage of P-sample cases with unresolved match status was only 1.2 percent.[6] This percentage compares favorably with the 1.8 percent of cases with unresolved match status in the 1990 PES. Very little was known about the A.C.E. P-sample people with unresolved match status; 98 percent of them lacked enough reported data for matching (i.e., they lacked a valid name or at least two characteristics or both).

After imputation, the percentage of matches dropped slightly, from 91.7 percent of resolved cases (matches and nonmatches) to 91.6 percent of all cases because the imputation procedure assigned lower match status probabilities to unresolved cases (84.3% overall). To impute a match status probability, the Census Bureau classified resolved and unresolved cases by mover status (nonmover, outmover), whether the person's housing unit did or did not match, and whether the person had one or more characteristics imputed or edited. These categories discriminated well: the probability of a match for nonmovers was 92 percent overall, compared with only 76 percent for outmovers overall. The lowest match probability was 52 percent for outmovers when the housing unit did not match; the highest match probability was 95 percent for nonmovers when the housing unit matched and the person had no imputed characteristics (Cantwell et al., 2001:Table 9).

Enumeration Status

The weighted percentage of E-sample cases with unresolved enumeration status was 2.6 percent, slightly higher than the comparable 2.3 percent for the 1990 PES. Most of the unresolved cases (89.4%) were nonmatches for which field follow-up could not resolve their status as a correct or erroneous enumeration; the remainder were matched cases for which field follow-up could not resolve their residence status, possible matches, and cases for which the location of the housing unit was not clear.

After imputation, the percentage of correct enumerations dropped slightly, from 95.5 percent of resolved cases (correct and erroneous enumerations) to

---

[6]The denominator for the percentage is P-sample nonmovers and outmovers who were confirmed Census Day residents or had unresolved residence status; confirmed non-Census Day residents were dropped from the P-sample at this point.

95.3 percent of all cases because the imputation procedure assigned lower correct enumeration probabilities to unresolved cases (76.2% overall). To impute a correct enumeration status probability, the Census Bureau classified resolved and unresolved cases by match status group, whether the person had one or more imputed characteristics, and race (for some match status groups). The 12 match status groups discriminated well: for example, correct enumeration probabilities were very low for potentially fictitious people (6%) and people said to be living elsewhere on Census Day (23%); moderate for college and military age children in partially matched households (88%); and very high for cases resolved before follow-up (99%). The addition of race and whether the person had imputed characteristics did not capture much additional variability in the probability of correct enumeration (Cantwell et al., 2001:Table 10).

QUALITY OF MATCHING

Although the rates of unresolved match status and enumeration status were low, there remains a question about the accuracy of the classification of match and enumeration status for cases that were "resolved" before imputation. The accuracy of the matching and associated follow-up process is critical to dual-systems estimation (DSE).

That accuracy is critical to distinguish the proportion of P-sample people who match a census record from the proportion who genuinely exist but were not enumerated in the census. If some of the nonmatched people should have been matched or should have been removed from the P-sample because they were fictitious or not a resident at the P-sample address on Census Day or for some other reason, then the estimated match rate will be too low and the estimate of the DSE will be too high.

That accuracy is also critical to distinguish the proportion of E-sample people who were correctly counted (including matches and correct nonmatches) from the proportion who were enumerated erroneously because they were duplicate, fictitious, or for some other reason. If some cases who were classified as correct (nonmatched) enumerations were in fact erroneous, then the estimated correct enumeration rate will be too high and the estimate of the DSE will be too high.

It is not possible to assess the reliability of assignment of the final match codes until the Census Bureau publishes results from evaluation studies that involve rematching and verifying samples of A.C.E. records (see Executive Steering Committee on A.C.E. Policy, 2001b). The Bureau is also looking at possible errors in assigning correct or erroneous enumeration status to E-sample cases due to the operation of the targeted extended search and the treatment of group quarters residents who should have been excluded from the sample.

Rematching studies for 1990 found some degree of clerical matching error, although analysts disagreed on its importance (National Research Council, 1999b:70-75). The results for 2000 are not yet known. The Bureau believed that the accuracy of matching would improve through greater computerization of the process and other steps in 2000, compared with 1990. The results of quality assurance operations during the matching and follow-up interviewing indicated that relatively little error was identified in assigning match and enumeration status codes (see Childers et al., 2001). Nonetheless, the degree of matching error remains to be established. As indirect indicators of the quality of the matching, we examined specific match codes and how they related to the various steps in the process.

Extent of Checking Required to Confirm Final Match Code

We looked first at final match codes and asked what proportion of the cases in each category were confirmed at the conclusion of computer matching, at the conclusion of clerical matching, or not until after field follow-up.

Confirmed Matches

Table 7-4 shows that 80.3 percent of final confirmed P-sample matches were designated as a match by the computer and did not require follow-up in the field (last row, column 1). Another 18 percent of final confirmed matches were declared a match by clerks, technicians, or analysts and did not require a field check (last row, columns 2, 3, 4). Only 1 percent of final confirmed matches were declared a match only after confirmation of their Census Day residence status in the field (column 5); only 0.8 percent of final confirmed matches were declared a match only after confirmation of their match and residence status in the field (column 6). Similar results obtained for the E-sample (not shown).

By domain and tenure group, the percentage of final confirmed matches that were declared a match by computer varied from 65 percent to 84 percent, perhaps due to difficulties with names. However, there was relatively little variation in the percentage of final confirmed matches that did not require confirmation of residence or match status in the field (97.0% to 99.2%). Given the standards for computer and clerical matching, these results suggest that one can have a high degree of confidence about the designation of a matched case.[7]

---

[7]The cutoff probability score for a computer match was set high enough, based on previous research, so that false computer matches would almost never occur.

TABLE 7-4 Percentage of 2000 A.C.E. P-Sample Matches to Census Enumerations, by Source of Final Match Code Assignment, Race/Ethnicity Domain, and Housing Tenure (weighted)

Domain and Tenure Group	No Field Check Needed				Field Check Needed for		Percent Total Matches (7)
	Computer M (1)	Computer P, Clerk M (2)	Computer NM, Clerk M (3)	Other Final M (4)	Residence Status (5)	Match and Residence (6)	
American Indian/Alaska Native on Reservation							
Owner	80.7	10.4	6.4	1.7	0.4	0.4	0.1
Renter	82.1	12.5	2.9	1.8	0.4	0.4	0.1
American Indian/Alaska Native off Reservation							
Owner	78.8	10.4	8.4	1.1	0.8	0.5	0.3
Renter	77.8	9.9	8.3	1.8	0.7	1.6	0.2
Hispanic Origin							
Owner	76.4	12.5	8.1	1.1	1.1	0.9	5.8
Renter	68.1	14.6	12.5	1.8	1.2	1.7	5.9
Black (Non-Hispanic)							
Owner	77.7	12.1	6.7	1.4	1.1	1.0	5.7
Renter	71.2	12.9	10.9	2.0	1.4	1.5	5.1
Native Hawaiian/Pacific Islander							
Owner	76.9	12.1	6.4	2.4	0.8	1.4	0.1
Renter	64.6	15.2	14.9	3.6	0.6	1.0	0.1
Asian							
Owner	72.9	14.3	8.9	1.4	1.0	1.4	2.1
Renter	66.7	16.1	12.4	1.7	1.2	1.8	1.2
White and Other Race (Non-Hispanic)							
Owner	84.2	8.2	5.7	0.6	0.9	0.4	57.5
Renter	77.9	10.3	8.6	1.0	1.2	1.0	15.8
Total	80.3	9.8	7.2	0.9	1.0	0.8	100.0

NOTES: Columns (1)–(6) in each row add to 100%; Column (7), reading down, adds to 100%. M: match; P: possible match; NM: nonmatch (confirmed Census Day resident).

SOURCE: Tabulations by panel staff of P-sample cases that went through matching, from U.S. Census Bureau, P-Sample Person Dual-System Estimation Output File, February 16, 2001. Tabulations weighted using TESFINWT; exclude TES-eligible people not in TES sample block clusters, who have zero TESFINWT.

Confirmed P-Sample Nonmatches

Assignment of confirmed nonmatch status was always based on a field check for certain types of P-sample cases (see Appendix C), amounting to 50.4 percent of the total confirmed P-sample nonmatches. There was relatively little variation in this percentage for most race/ethnicity domain and tenure groups (data not shown), although 69 percent of final confirmed nonmatches for American Indians and Alaska Natives were not declared a nonmatch until after being checked in the field, compared with only 47 percent for non-Hispanic whites and other races. How many nonmatches were correctly assigned and how many should have been identified as either matches or cases to be dropped from the P-sample (e.g., fictitious cases or people residing elsewhere on Census Day) will not be known until the Census Bureau completes its studies of matching error.

Confirmed E-Sample Correct (Nonmatched) or Erroneous Enumerations

On the E-sample side, assignment of a final code as a correct (nonmatched) enumeration was always based on a field check. Of final erroneous enumerations (4% of the total E-sample), 35 percent were declared on the basis of a field check, while 65 percent were identified by clerks as duplicates or not enough reported data and did not require confirmation in the field.

Unresolved Cases

As noted above, the E-sample had a higher percentage of cases that could not be resolved after field checking than did the P-sample: 2.6 percent and 2.2 percent, respectively. Moreover, 52.2 percent of the unresolved P-sample cases were those coded by the computer or clerks as not having enough reported data for matching. These cases were not field checked but had their residence or match status imputed.

Extent of Reassignment of Match Codes

Another cut at the issue of matching quality is how often one stage of matching changed the code assigned in an earlier stage of matching. Table 7-5 shows that such changes happened quite infrequently. Thus (see Panel A), 99.9 percent and 99.7 percent of confirmed matches assigned by the computer for the P-sample and the E-sample, respectively, remained as such in the final coding. Also, 93 percent of computer possible matches in both the P-sample and the E-sample were confirmed as such without the need for field follow-up; another 5.5–5.7 percent were confirmed as a match (or, in the case of the E-sample, as a nonmatched correct enumeration) in the field. Only 1.3–1.5

TABLE 7-5 Outcome of Computer Matching and Cases Followed Up in the Field, 2000 A.C.E. (weighted)

	P-Sample		E-Sample	
	Percent of Total	Percent of Match Group	Percent of Total	Percent of Match Group
A. Outcome of Computer Matching (Cases Included in Matching Process)	100.0		100.0	
Computer Match				
Total	72.6	100.0	69.4	100.0
Final Match		99.9		99.7
Other Code		0.1		0.3
Computer Possible Match				
Total	9.7	100.0	9.2	100.0
Final Match, no Field Check		93.0		93.0
Field-Based Final Match (P) or Correct Enumeration (E)		5.5		5.7
Final Nonmatch (P) or Erroneous Enumeration (E)		0.5		0.6
Unresolved (or Removed for P-sample)		1.0		0.7
Computer Nonmatch				
Total	17.1	100.0	19.2	100.0
Final Nonmatch (P) or Erroneous Enumeration (E)		41.4		10.8
Final Correct Enumeration (E)		N.A.		60.2
Final Match		43.9		16.1
Unresolved (or Removed for P-sample)		14.7		12.9
Computer Not Enough Reported Data for Matching				
Total	0.6		2.2	

	P-Sample		E-Sample	
B. Outcome of Cases Followed Up in the Field[a] (7.1% of Total P-Sample; 17.1% of Total E-Sample)	100.0		100.0	
Before Follow-up Code of Match	13.5	100.0	5.2	100.1
Field Match		82.3		79.6
Field Match but Unresolved Residence		14.9		13.3
Field Valid Nonmatch (P) or Correct Enumeration (E)		0.2		0.3
Field Other Code (Removed, Unresolved, Erroneous)		2.6		6.9
Before Follow-up Code of Possible Match	10.3	100.0	3.8	100.0
Field Match		82.9		82.1
Field Match but Unresolved Residence		1.9		1.9
Field Valid Nonmatch (P) or Correct Enumeration (E)		8.7		8.5
Field Other Code (Removed, Unresolved, Erroneous)		6.5		7.5
Before Follow-up Code of Nonmatch	75.6	100.0	73.3	100.0
Field Valid Nonmatch (P) or Correct Enumeration (E)		67.8		71.9
Field Removed (P) or Erroneous Enumeration (E)		1.8		11.4
Field Unresolved		27.1		15.7
Field Match		3.3		1.0
Before Follow-up Code of Found in Surrounding Block	N.A.	N.A.	14.6	100.0
Field Correct Enumeration (E)				89.9
Field Other Code				10.1
Before Follow-Up Other Code	0.6		3.1	

NOTES: P: P-sample; E: E-sample. Correct enumerations in table are those not matching to the P-sample.

[a] Cases followed up in the field included 1 percent of P-sample and E-sample before follow-up matches; 100 percent of P-sample and E-sample possible matches; 61 percent and 100 percent of P-sample and E-sample nonmatches; and 100 percent of E-sample cases found in another block.

SOURCE: Tabulations by panel staff of U.S. Census Bureau, P-Sample and E-Sample Person Dual-System Estimation Output Files, February 16, 2001. Tabulations weighted using TESFINWT. P-sample cases in the matching process included nonmovers and outmovers; TES-eligible persons who were not in TES sample block clusters were excluded.

percent of computer possible match codes were changed to a nonmatch (P-sample) or to an erroneous enumeration (E-sample) or could not be resolved in the field.

The analysts who reviewed clerical matches rarely overturned the clerks' decisions, and field follow-up most often confirmed the before-follow-up code or left the case unresolved. Thus (see Panel B), among cases identified as matches by the computer, clerks, or analysts, only 1 percent were followed up, and 80–82 percent of those were confirmed in the field. Most of the rest remained unresolved with regard to residence status. Less than 0.5 percent were turned into a nonmatch (P-sample) or into a correct (nonmatched) enumeration (E-sample). Among E-sample cases with a before-follow-up code of nonmatch (as distinct from an erroneous enumeration or unresolved case), 100 percent were followed up, and only 1 percent turned into a match after follow-up. Among P-sample cases with a before-follow-up code of nonmatch, 61 percent were checked in the field, and only 3.3 percent of them turned into a match.

TARGETED EXTENDED SEARCH

The targeted extended search (TES) operation in the A.C.E. was designed to reduce the variance and bias associated with geocoding errors (i.e., assignment of addresses to the wrong block) in the census or in the P-sample address listing. In a sample of block clusters for which there was reason to expect geocoding errors (2,177 of 6,414 such clusters), the clerical search for matches of P-sample and census enumerations and for correct E-sample enumerations was extended to one ring of blocks surrounding the A.C.E. block cluster. Sampling was designed to make the search much more efficient than in 1990 (see Appendix C).

For the P-sample, only people in households that did not match a census address (4.7% of total P-sample cases that went through matching) were searched in the ring of blocks surrounding a sampled block cluster. On the E-sample side, only people in households identified as geocoding errors (3% of total E-sample cases) were searched in the ring surrounding a sampled block cluster. Weights were assigned to the TES persons in the sampled block clusters to adjust for the sampling.[8] Correspondingly, persons that would have been eligible for TES but were not in a sampled block cluster were assigned a zero weight.

The result of the extended search was to increase the overall P-sample match rate from 87.7 percent without TES to 91.6 percent with TES, an increase of 3.8 percentage points. At the same time, the overall E-sample correct

---

[8]The weight was either 1 for the 60 percent of sampled TES persons that were selected with certainty or 4.9 for the remaining sampled TES persons.

enumeration rate was increased from 92.3 percent to 95.3 percent, an increase of 2.9 percentage points (Navarro and Olson, 2001:Table 1). Because the increase was larger for matches than for correct enumerations, the correction ratio (correct enumeration rate divided by match rate) decreased by 1.3 percentage points, from 1.053 to 1.040; such a change has the effect of reducing the estimate of the DSE and the net undercount.

TES affected the correction ratios for age and sex groups used in the post-stratification about equally (Navarro and Olson, 2001:Table V). There was somewhat more variation in the effects on the correction ratios for race and ethnicity domains. In particular, the correction ratio for American Indians and Alaska Natives on reservations was reduced by 8.4 percentage points, compared with the average reduction of 1.2 percentage points (Navarro and Olson, 2001:Table IV).

The TES had the desired effect of reducing the variance of the DSE estimates for post-strata. The reduction in the average and median coefficient of variation (the standard error of an estimate as a percent of the estimate) for post-strata was 22 percent, similar to an average reduction of 20 percent for the nationwide extended search operation in 1990 (Navarro and Olson, 2001:7).

The underlying question, however, is whether the TES operation was unbalanced, thereby introducing bias into the DSE. The larger increase in the P-sample match rate than in the E-sample correct enumeration rate suggests an imbalance. Such an imbalance may also have occurred in 1990, when the extended search increased the P-sample match rate by 4.1 percentage points and the E-sample correct enumeration rate by 2.3 percent. A follow-up study to the 1990 census was not able to determine whether balancing error had occurred (Bateman, 1991).

What could cause balancing error in the TES? Such error would result if the search area was not defined consistently for the P-sample and E-sample, so that the clerks might count as correct an enumeration outside the search area or fail to match to an enumeration inside the search area. One possible source of the observed imbalance of additional matches compared with additional correct enumerations in the TES was that the P-sample address listing could have contained errors. For example, the P-sample address list could have assigned an address to the A.C.E. block cluster when in fact it was located in the surrounding ring. When the clerk did not find a match in the A.C.E. block cluster because there was no corresponding census address, then a search for a match in the surrounding ring would likely be successful. The Census Bureau has fielded a study to determine if P-sample address geocoding errors largely explain the larger increase in the match rate compared with the erroneous enumeration rate. If they do, then there is no effect on the DSE.

Alternatively, it is possible that there was an underestimation of census housing units that were eligible for the E-sample TES. If a nonmatched E-sample address from the initial housing unit match was not found in the field, it was classified as an erroneous enumeration, when it might in fact have been located in a nearby block and therefore should have been classified as a geocoding error. Only misgeocoded E-sample cases were eligible for TES, so housing units that were miscoded as erroneous were excluded from TES. The Census Bureau has fielded a study to determine the accuracy of the identification of E-sample units that were eligible for TES. The Bureau is also studying possible discrepancies between the classification of erroneous E-sample housing units in the housing unit match and the classification of some of the people in those units during field follow-up as correct enumerations.

POST-STRATIFICATION

Post-stratification is an important aspect of dual-systems estimation. Because research suggests that the probabilities of being included in the census or in the P-sample vary by individual characteristics, it is important to classify P-sample and E-sample cases into groups or strata for which coverage probabilities are as similar as possible within the group and as different as possible from other groups. Estimation of the DSE then is performed stratum by stratum.

Counterbalancing the need for finely defined post-strata are two considerations: each post-stratum must have sufficient sample size for reliable estimates; and the characteristics used to define the post-strata should be consistently measured between the P-sample and the E-sample. As an example, a respondent to the census who is in the E-sample may have reported a household member as age 30 when a possibly different respondent for the same household in the P-sample reported that household member as age 29. The matched person, then, would contribute to the P-sample match rate for the 18-to-29-year-old post-strata and to the E-sample correct enumeration rate for the 30-to-49-year-old post-strata. Such misclassification could be consequential if the proportions misclassified were large and if the coverage probabilities varied greatly for the affected post-strata. At the same time, the Census Bureau wanted to define post-strata in a way that could be easily explained.

Taking all these considerations into account, the Bureau decided to identify a moderate number of post-strata for which direct estimates could be developed without the use of modeling (see Table 6-2 in Chapter 6). In this regard, the Bureau adhered fairly closely to the number and type of post-strata that were used for the revised 1990 estimates, for which 357 post-strata were identified.[9] Given the larger size of the A.C.E. relative to the 1990 PES, the Bureau was able to identify a somewhat larger number of post-strata in 2000 (448, collapsed to 416) than the final number in 1990.

---

[9]The revised set of 1990 post-strata were developed by analyzing census results that had become available (e.g., mail return rates, imputation rates, crowding) to determine which characteristics that could be used for post-stratification best explained variations in those results.

Several participants at a workshop in fall 1999 (National Research Council, 2001a) urged the Bureau to use modeling techniques to develop post-strata on the basis of the A.C.E. data. The model would assess the best predictors of coverage, but the Bureau decided such an approach was not feasible. It would be desirable now for the Bureau to estimate such models to determine if the A.C.E. post-stratification was optimal or reasonably so. If a different stratification scheme seemed more effective, then it could be used to develop revised dual-systems estimates for use in any adjustment of the census.

On the face of it, the A.C.E. post-stratification seems reasonable. There are certainly wide variations in estimated coverage correction factors—from 0.958 to 1.07 among the 64 post-strata groups, excluding age and sex breakdowns, and from 0.929 to 1.186 for all 416 post-strata. As noted above (see Chapter 6), both the A.C.E. and the PES estimated higher net undercount rates for minorities than whites, for renters than owners, and for children than older people; however, estimates of net undercount rates for minorities, renters, and children were significantly lower in the 2000 A.C.E. than in the 1990 PES.

There was some inconsistency of classification by post-strata between the P-sample and E-sample in the A.C.E., although whether the level of inconsistency was higher or lower than in 1990 cannot be determined because of the unavailability of data for 1990 matched cases. Overall, 4.7 percent of A.C.E. matched cases (unweighted) were misclassified as owner or renter; 5.1 percent were misclassified among age and sex groups, and 3.9 percent were misclassified among race/ethnic domains (Farber, 2001a:Table 1).

Rates of inconsistency were much higher for matched cases for which the characteristic in question was imputed than for nonimputed cases. For example, 36 percent of cases for which age or sex were imputed were classified inconsistently among age/sex post-strata, and such cases were almost half of all inconsistent cases. However, as just noted, only 5 percent of all cases were misclassified among age/sex post-strata. The percentage of inconsistent cases for specific age/sex groups ranged from 1.3 percent for children aged 0–17 to 8.8 percent for males aged 18–29.

By race/ethnicity domain, inconsistent cases as a percentage of E-sample matches ranged from 1.5 percent for American Indians and Alaska Natives on reservations to 18.3 percent for Native Hawaiians and Pacific Islanders to 35.7 percent for American Indians and Alaska Natives off reservations. By age and sex, the percentage of inconsistent cases among American Indians and Alaska Natives off reservations ranged from 54 percent for nonowner females aged 18–29 to 68 percent for nonowner males aged 50 or older. These rates of inconsistency are very high. The major factor is that a large number of non-Hispanic whites and other races in one sample (relative to the Native American population) identified themselves as American Indians or Alaska Natives off reservations in the other sample; see Table 7-6. The effect was to lower the coverage correction factor for the latter group below what it would have

TABLE 7-6 2000 A.C.E. Matched P-Sample and E-Sample Cases: Consistency of Race/Ethnicity Post-Stratification Domain (unweighted)

Race/Ethnicity Domain	E-Sample							P-Sample	
	Domain 1	Domain 2	Domain 3	Domain 4	Domain 5	Domain 6	Domain 7	Total	% Inconsistent
P-Sample									
American Indian or Alaska Native on Reservations (Domain 1)	11,009	0	34	12	0	0	118	11,173	1.5
American Indian or Alaska Native off Reservations (Domain 2)	0	2,223	59	104	0	30	793	3,209	30.7
Hispanic Origin (Domain 3)	44	136	67,985	610	42	267	4,004	73,088	7.0
Non-Hispanic Black (Domain 4)	10	119	496	65,679	6	118	1,423	67,851	3.2
Native Hawaiian or Pacific Islander (Domain 5)	0	3	31	19	1,671	204	177	2,105	20.6
Asian (Domain 6)	1	31	107	102	143	19,679	1,062	21,125	6.8
Non-Hispanic White or Other Race (Domain 7)	107	944	5,041	2,589	183	2,105	360,125	371,094	3.0
E-Sample									
Total	11,171	3,456	73,753	69,115	2,045	22,403	367,702	549,645	
% Inconsistent	1.5	35.7	7.8	5.0	18.3	12.2	2.1		3.9

NOTE: See Table 6-2 for definitions of domains.

SOURCE: Farber (2001a:Table A-3).

been had there been no inconsistency. However, the coverage correction factor would have been lower yet for American Indians and Alaska Natives off reservations if they had been merged with the non-Hispanic white and other races stratum. The reverse flow of American Indians and Alaska Natives identifying themselves as non-Hispanic whites or other races had virtually no effect on the coverage correction factor for the latter group, given its much larger proportion of the population.

VARIANCE ESTIMATES

Overall, the A.C.E. was expected to have smaller variances due to sampling error and other sources than the 1990 PES, and that expectation was borne out. The coefficient of variation for the estimated coverage correction factor for the total population was reduced from 0.2 percent in 1990 to 0.14 percent in 2000 (a reduction of 30%). The coefficients of variation for the coverage correction factors for Hispanics and non-Hispanic blacks were reduced from 0.82 percent and 0.55 percent, respectively, to 0.38 percent and 0.40 percent, respectively (Davis, 2001:Tables E-1, F-1). However, the coefficients of variation for coverage correction factors were as high as 6 percent for particular post-strata, which translates into a very large confidence interval around the estimate of the net undercount.[10]

The overall coefficient of variation was expected to be reduced by about 25 percent due to the larger sample size of the A.C.E., almost double that of the 1990 PES. In addition, better measures of population size were available during the selection of the A.C.E. block clusters than during the selection of PES clusters, and the A.C.E. sampling weights were less variable than the PES sampling weights. The 2000 TES was much better targeted and thereby more efficient than the similar operation in 1990. Overall, TES was expected to reduce the variance of the DSE, although the 2000 TES also contributed somewhat to an increase in sampling error.

Looking at size and variation in weights, Table 7-7 shows the changes in the P-sample weights, from the initial weighting that accounted for differential sampling probabilities to the intermediate weights that included household noninterview adjustments to the final weights that accounted for TES sampling. (The table also shows the distribution of E-sample initial and final weights.) At the outset, 90 percent of the initial P-sample weights were between 48 and 654 and the highest and lowest weights were 9 and 1,288; the distribution did not differ by mover status. After the household noninterview adjustment for Census Day, 90 percent of the weights were between 49 and

---

[10]The variance estimates developed by the Census Bureau likely underestimate the true variance, but the extent of underestimation is not known. The variance estimation excludes some minor sources of error (specifically, the large block subsampling and the P-sample noninterview adjustment). It also excludes most sources of nonsampling error (see Appendix C).

TABLE 7-7 Distribution of Initial, Intermediate, and Final Weights, 2000 A.C.E. P-Sample and E-Sample

Sample and Mover Status	Number of Non-Zeros	Percentile of Weight Distribution										
		0	1	5	10	25	50	75	90	95	99	100
P-Sample												
Initial Weight[a]												
Total	721,734	9	21	48	75	249	352	574	647	654	661	1,288
Nonmovers	631,914	9	21	48	76	253	366	575	647	654	661	1,288
Outmovers	24,158	9	21	48	69	226	348	541	647	654	661	1,288
Inmovers	36,623	9	21	47	67	212	343	530	647	654	661	1,288
Intermediate Weight[b]												
Total with Census Day Weight	712,442	9	22	49	78	253	379	577	654	674	733	1,619
Total with Interview Day Weight	721,426	9	21	48	76	249	366	576	651	660	705	1,701
Final Weight[c]												
Census Day Weight												
Total	640,795	9	22	50	83	273	382	581	654	678	765	5,858
Nonmovers	617,390	9	22	50	83	274	382	581	654	678	762	5,858
Outmovers	23,405	9	23	50	77	240	363	577	655	682	798	3,847
Inmovers	36,623	9	21	47	67	214	345	530	651	656	705	1,288
E-Sample												
Initial Weight[d]	712,900	9	21	39	55	212	349	564	647	654	661	2,801
Final Weight[e]	704,602	9	21	39	56	217	349	567	647	654	700	4,009

[a] P-sample initial weight, PWGHT, reflects sampling through large block subsampling; total includes removed cases

[b] P-sample intermediate weight, NIWGT, reflects household noninterview adjustment for Census Day; NIWGTI reflects household noninterview adjustment for A.C.E. interview day

[c] P-sample final weight, TESFINWT, for confirmed Census Day residents, total, nonmovers, and outmovers (reflects targeted extended search sampling); NIWGTI for inmovers

[d] E-sample initial weight, EWGHT, reflects sampling through large block subsampling

[e] E-sample final weight, TESFINWT, reflects targeted extended search sampling

SOURCE: Tabulations by panel staff of U.S. Census Bureau, P-Sample and E-Sample Person Dual-System Estimation Output Files, February 16, 2001.

674, and the highest and lowest weights were 9 and 1,619. After the TES adjustment, 90 percent of the final weights for confirmed Census Day residents were between 50 and 678, and the highest and lowest weights were 9 and 5,858 (the variation in weights was less for outmovers than nonmovers). For inmovers, there was relatively little difference between the initial sampling weights and the final weights adjusted for household noninterview on the P-sample interview day.

While the variations in final weights for the A.C.E. P-sample (and E-sample) were not small, they were considerably less than the variations in final weights for the 1990 PES. In 1990, some P-sample weights were more than 20,000, and 28 percent of the weights exceeded 700, compared with only 5 percent in the A.C.E.

FINAL MATCH CODES AND RATES

Having examined individual features of the A.C.E., we next looked at the distribution of final match codes and rates for the P-sample and E-sample. We wanted to get an overall sense of the reasonableness of the results for key population groups and in comparison with 1990.

Final Match and Enumeration Status

P-Sample Match Codes

The distribution of final match codes for the P-sample was 89.5 percent confirmed match, 7.4 percent confirmed nonmatch, 2.2 percent match or residence status unresolved, and 0.9 percent not a Census Day resident or removed for another reason (e.g., a fictitious or duplicate P-sample case). Table 7-8 shows that the percent confirmed matches by domain and tenure varied from 80 percent for black and Native Hawaiian and Pacific Islander renters to 93 percent for non-Hispanic white and other race owners; conversely, the confirmed nonmatches varied from 15.8 percent for Native Hawaiian and Pacific Islander renters to 4.9 percent for non-Hispanic white and other race owners. Those groups with higher percentages of nonmatched cases also tended to have higher percentages of unresolved cases: they varied from 1 percent for Native Hawaiian and Pacific Islander owners to 4.7 percent for black renters.

After imputation of residence and match status, the overall P-sample match rate (matches divided by matches plus nonmatches) was 91.6 percent. The match rate ranged from 82.4 percent for Native Hawaiian and Pacific Islander renters to 94.6 percent for non-Hispanic white and other race owners.

TABLE 7-8 2000 A.C.E. P-Sample Final Match Codes, and A.C.E and PES Match Rates, by Race/Ethnicity Domain and Housing Tenure (weighted)

Domain and Tenure Group	Percent Distribution of 2000 P-Sample Final Match Codes				P-Sample Match Rate[a]	
	Match	Non-match	Unresolved	Removed	2000 A.C.E.	1990 PES
American Indian/Alaska Native on Reservation						
Owner	82.9	13.2	1.6	2.4	85.43	78.13[b]
Renter	85.6	11.5	1.6	1.3	87.08	
American Indian/Alaska Native off Reservation						
Owner	88.5	9.2	1.4	0.9	90.19	—
Renter	81.2	12.6	4.3	1.9	84.65	—
Hispanic Origin						
Owner	89.0	8.3	1.7	1.0	90.79	92.81
Renter	81.7	13.2	3.9	1.2	84.48	82.45
Black (Non-Hispanic)						
Owner	87.9	8.8	2.3	1.1	90.14	89.65
Renter	80.4	13.7	4.7	1.2	83.67	82.28
Native Hawaiian/Pacific Islander						
Owner	85.8	12.2	1.0	1.0	87.36	—
Renter	80.3	15.8	2.7	1.2	82.39	—
Asian (Non-Hispanic)[c]						
Owner	90.1	6.6	2.3	1.0	92.34	93.71
Renter	84.4	10.8	3.7	1.1	87.33	84.36
White and Other Races (Non-Hispanic)						
Owner	93.0	4.9	1.4	0.8	94.60	95.64
Renter	85.5	9.8	3.7	1.0	88.37	88.62
Total	89.5	7.4	2.2	0.9	91.59	92.22

NOTE: First four columns in each row add to 100%; —, not estimated.

[a] Match rates (matches divided by the sum of matches and unmatches) are after imputation for unresolved residence and match status for the A.C.E. and after imputation of unresolved match status for the PES.

[b] Total; not available by tenure.

[c] 1990 PES match rates include Pacific Islanders.

SOURCES: A.C.E. match codes are from tabulations by panel staff of P-sample cases who went through the matching process, weighted using TESFINWT and excluding TES-eligible people not in TES sample block clusters (who have zero TESFINWT), from U.S. Census Bureau, P-Sample Person Dual-System Estimation Output File, February 16, 2001; A.C.E. and PES match rates from Davis (2001:Tables E-2, F-1, F-2).

E-Sample Match Codes

The distribution of final match codes for the E-sample was 81.7 percent matches, 11.6 percent other correct (nonmatched) enumerations, 4.0 percent erroneous enumerations, and 2.6 percent unresolved. Table 7-9 shows that the percent confirmed correct enumerations (the sum of matches plus other correct enumerations in the first two columns) by domain and tenure ranged from 87.2 percent for black renters to 95.8 percent for non-Hispanic white and other owners. The percent erroneous enumerations ranged from 3 percent for non-Hispanic white and other owners and American Indian/Alaska Native on reservation renters to 7 percent for black renters, and the percent unresolved ranged from 1.2 percent for non-Hispanic white and other race owners to about 6 percent for Hispanic and black renters.

After imputation for enumeration status, the overall E-sample correct enumeration rate (matches and other correct enumerations divided by those groups plus erroneous enumerations) was 95.3 percent. The correct enumeration rate ranged from 91.2 percent for non-Hispanic black renters to 96.7 percent for non-Hispanic white and other race owners.

Comparisons with 1990

The P-sample match rates are similar for the 2000 A.C.E. and the 1990 PES for the total population and for many race/ethnic domain and housing tenure groups (see Table 7-8). For the total population, the A.C.E. match rate is 0.6 percent lower than the PES rate; for population groups, the A.C.E. match rates are lower than the PES rates for some groups and higher for others. The E-sample correct enumeration rates are also similar between the 2000 A.C.E. and the 1990 PES (see Table 7-9). However, there is a general pattern for the A.C.E. correct enumeration rates to be somewhat higher than the corresponding PES rates. On balance, these patterns have the outcome that the A.C.E. correction ratios (calculated by dividing the correct enumeration rate by the match rate) are higher than the corresponding PES correction ratios. If other things were equal, these results would mean that the A.C.E. measured higher net undercount rates than the PES, but the reverse is true. We explore in Chapter 8 the role of people reinstated in the census (late additions) and people requiring imputation to complete their census records—who could not be included in the A.C.E. process—in explaining the reductions in net undercount from 1990 levels that were measured in A.C.E.

GROSS ERRORS

Our discussion has focused on net undercount. Some analysts also are interested in the level of gross errors in the census—that is, total omissions and total erroneous enumerations. The A.C.E. is designed to measure net undercount (or net overcount). It measures gross errors but in ways that can be misleading. Many errors that are identified by A.C.E. involve the balancing of a nonmatch on the P-sample side against an erroneous enumeration on the E-sample side—for example, when an E-sample case that should match is misgeocoded. These kinds of balancing errors are not errors for such levels

TABLE 7-9 2000 A.C.E. E-Sample Final Match Codes, and 2000 A.C.E. and 1990 PES Correct Enumeration Rates, by Race/Ethnicity Domain and Housing Tenure (weighted)

Domain and Tenure Group	Percent Distribution of 2000 E-Sample Final Match Codes				E-Sample Correct Enumeration Rate[a]	
	Match	Other Correct Enumeration	Erroneous Enumeration	Unresolved	2000 A.C.E.	1990 PES
American Indian/Alaska Native on Reservation						
Owner	77.1	17.1	3.7	2.1	95.65	91.54[b]
Renter	78.3	14.8	3.0	4.0	96.15	—
American Indian/Alaska Native off Reservation						
Owner	81.9	11.7	4.9	1.5	94.56	—
Renter	74.1	15.2	5.0	5.7	93.16	—
Hispanic Origin						
Owner	83.2	11.7	3.3	1.9	96.25	95.56
Renter	71.7	17.0	5.3	6.0	92.79	90.58
Black (Non-Hispanic)						
Owner	80.3	12.7	5.2	1.7	94.25	92.84
Renter	68.2	19.0	7.0	5.9	91.16	89.19
Native Hawaiian/Pacific Islander						
Owner	83.0	9.8	5.7	1.5	93.79	—
Renter	72.7	16.6	6.1	4.6	92.33	—
Asian (Non-Hispanic)[c]						
Owner	83.3	11.3	3.8	1.6	95.84	93.13
Renter	72.1	15.3	5.9	6.7	92.45	92.22
White and Other Races (Non-Hispanic)						
Owner	86.6	9.2	3.0	1.2	96.70	95.84
Renter	74.9	14.3	5.6	5.2	93.20	92.61
Total	81.7	11.6	4.0	2.6	95.28	94.27

NOTES: First cour columns in each row add to 100%; —, not estimated.

[a] Correct enumeration (CE) rates (matches and other correct enumerations divided by the sum of matches, other correct enumerations, and erroneous enumerations) are after imputation for unresolved enumeration status.

[b] Total; not available by tenure.

[c] 1990 correct enumeration rates include Pacific Islanders.

SOURCES: A.C.E. match codes are from tabulations by panel staff of E-sample cases, weighted using TESFINWT and excluding TES-eligible people not in TES sample block clusters (who have zero TESFINWT), from U.S. Census Bureau, E-Sample Person Dual-System Estimation Output File, February 16, 2001; A.C.E. and PES correct enumeration rates are from Davis (2001:Tables E-2, F-1, F-2).

of geography as counties, cities, and even census tracts, although they affect error at the block cluster level. Also, the classification of type of gross error in the A.C.E. is not necessarily clean. For example, A.C.E. will not classify an enumeration of a "snowbird" at the person's winter residence as duplicating an enumeration for the same person at his or her summer residence because there is no nationwide search. A.C.E. will likely classify duplicate snowbird enumerations as erroneous in the aggregate, but will not label them as duplicates.

It is important to take note of gross errors, however, because higher or lower net undercount does not relate directly to the level of gross errors. There can be a zero net undercount and a high rate of gross omissions and gross erroneous enumerations. Hence, for completeness, Table 7-10 shows gross errors in the 2000 A.C.E. and 1990 PES. The total gross errors in the A.C.E. appear to be somewhat reduced in percentage terms from the gross errors in the PES. However, the increased numbers of people requiring imputation and late additions, who may likely have had higher-than-average error rates, cloud the issue, as these people were not part of the E-sample. Also, the sizable differences between the A.C.E. and the PES in the distribution of types of gross erroneous enumerations are puzzling. For example, the A.C.E. estimates proportionately fewer duplicate enumerations than the PES. The Census Bureau is currently studying these discrepancies, which could also be due to the higher numbers of people requiring imputation and late additions who were not included in the A.C.E. processing.

CONCLUSIONS

On the basis of the evidence now available, we conclude that the A.C.E. was conducted according to well-specified and carefully controlled procedures. We also conclude that it achieved a high degree of quality in such areas as sample design, interviewing, and imputation for missing data.

There are several outstanding questions that must be addressed before it will be possible to render a final verdict on the quality of the A.C.E. procedures (see Executive Steering Committee on A.C.E. Policy, 2001b). The major outstanding questions relate to those aspects of the 2000 A.C.E. that differed markedly from the 1990 PES and were relatively untested. First, there is concern that the targeted extended search may not have been balanced (in that the search areas for P-sample and E-sample cases may not have been equivalent) and that the imbalance could have led to incorrect treatment of nonmatched E-sample cases. There is a related concern that balancing error may have occurred because some E-sample cases were coded as correct when they were in fact outside the block cluster or because not all correct enumerations in the block cluster were searched for a match to the P-sample. Second, there is a concern that group quarters enumerations, such as of college students, may not have been handled correctly in the A.C.E. Group quarters residents were

TABLE 7-10 Gross Omissions and Erroneous Enumerations, 2000 A.C.E. and 1990 PES

Erroneous Enumerations	Percent of Weighted E-Sample		Estimated Number of People (millions)	
	2000 A.C.E.	1990 PES	2000	1990
Total	4.7	5.8	12.5	16.3
(1) Insufficient Information for matching	1.8	1.2	4.8	3.4
(2) Duplicates	0.7	1.6	1.9	4.5
(3) Fictitious	0.3	0.2	0.7	0.6
(4) Geocoding Error	0.2	0.3	0.6	0.8
(5) Other Residence	1.0	2.2	2.7	6.2
(6) Imputed	0.6	0.3	1.8	0.8

Alternative Estimates of Gross Errors	2000 A.C.E. (counts in millions)		1990 PES (counts in millions)	
	Erroneous Enumerations[a]	Omissions	Erroneous Enumerations	Omissions
(1) Including All Types of Erroneous Enumerations (EEs)	12.5	15.8	16.3	20.3
(2) Excluding EEs with Insufficient Information to Match and Imputed EEs (EE types (1) and (6) above)	5.9	9.2	11.2	15.2
(3) Excluding EEs excluded in row (2) and also "geocoding errors" and "other residence" (EE types (4) and (5) above)[a]	3.1	6.4	4.4	8.4
(4) Row (3) plus an allowance for 50 percent duplication among late additions	4.3	7.6	N.A.	N.A.

NOTES: People with insufficient information who were excluded from the E-sample at the outset are not included in any of these numbers (EE category (1) above comprises additional cases found to lack enough reported data for matching). Gross omissions are calculated by adding net omissions (3.3 million people in 2000; 4 million people in 1990) to gross erroneous enumerations.

[a] The alternative estimates of erroneous enumerations in 2000 are not consistent with the information on types of erroneous enumerations above. The discrepancy is being investigated with the Census Bureau.

SOURCE: Adapted from Anderson and Fienberg (2001a:Tables 2, 3).

supposed to be excluded from the A.C.E.; error would occur if, say, enumerations of college students at their parental home were not classified as erroneous. Third, studies of the effect of the PES-C procedure on the estimates of match rates for movers and, more generally, estimates of matching error are not yet available. Finally, additional evaluations are needed to determine if the post-stratification was the most efficient possible and to assess the sensitivity of the A.C.E. results to error from particular sources, such as matching, imputation, and the PES-C procedure used for movers.

Overall, the 2000 A.C.E. showed similar, but less pronounced, patterns of net undercount than the 1990 PES. Given that P-sample match rates and E-sample erroneous enumeration rates were similar between the A.C.E. and the 1990 PES, the key question at this time is why the A.C.E. showed a reduced net undercount, overall, and for such groups as Hispanics, non-Hispanic blacks, children, and renters. Because the only other component of the DSE equation is the number of census people with insufficient information to include in the E-sample (*II*s), our attempts to resolve the undercount puzzle centered on that component of the census results. In Chapter 8, we analyze distributions of people requiring imputation and people reinstated in the census (late additions) and determine that people requiring imputation largely explain the reduced net undercount in 2000 for historically less well-counted groups.

8

Imputations and Late Additions

We turn in this chapter to examine two groups of people whose census records were excluded from the 2000 Accuracy and Coverage Evaluation (A.C.E.) Program. The first group comprises people who required imputation to complete their census records (whole person imputations).[1] They were excluded from the E-sample of census enumerations because they could not be matched to the independent P-sample, given incomplete reporting of data for them. The second group comprises people who are often referred to as "late additions." Although they were in fact enumerated in a timely fashion, their records were deleted from the census file in summer 2000 as possibly duplicating other records. After further examination, they were reinstated in the census but too late to be included in the A.C.E. process. Collectively, these two groups are referred to as "people with insufficient information," or *II*s, in the formula for estimating the population from the A.C.E. with the method of dual-systems estimation (DSE—see Chapter 6).

Every census has people with insufficient information whose records are excluded from the coverage evaluation; however, the number of such people was considerably larger in 2000 than in 1990. The total number of *II*s in 2000 was about 8.2 million people, 2.9 percent of the household population (excluding a small number of people reinstated in the census who also required imputation); the corresponding number in 1990 was about 2.2 million, 0.9 percent of the population. The people excluded from the A.C.E. break down into 5.8 million who required imputation and 2.4 million who were reinstated too late for A.C.E. processing.[2] The people excluded from the Post-Enumeration Survey (PES) break down into 1.9 million who required imputation and 0.3 million who were enumerated in coverage improvement programs too late for PES processing. (There were no truly late enumerations in 2000 and no reinstated people in 1990.)

---

[1]Another Census Bureau term for this group is "non-data defined," meaning that their census records have reported information for only one short-form characteristic (name, age, sex, race, ethnic origin, or household relationship; see Chapter 7).

[2]Some people in group quarters also required imputation to complete their census records. Of the total population, including group quarters as well as household residents, 6 million people (2.1%) required imputation in 2000; corresponding figures for 1990 and 1980 are 2 million people (0.8%) and 3.5 million people (1.5%), respectively (Love and Dalzell, 2001:Table 1).

In this chapter we first consider the role of *II*s in explaining a puzzle from our initial analysis of the 2000 A.C.E. We then examine separately the characteristics of whole person imputations and people reinstated in the census too late to be included in the A.C.E. (Appendix A provides more detail on the material in this chapter.).

A PUZZLE

Our initial analysis of the 2000 A.C.E. and the 1990 PES led us to expect similar rates of net undercount for key population groups because of similarities in the estimates for each of two components of the DSE formula, namely, the match rate estimated from the P-sample and the correct enumeration rate estimated from the E-sample (see Tables 7-8 and 7-9 in Chapter 7). Yet the A.C.E. measured marked reductions in net undercount rates from 1990 levels for such groups as minorities, renters, and children and a consequent narrowing of differential undercount rates between historically less well-counted and better-counted groups.

Illuminating the Puzzle

Table 8-1 provides information from the 2000 A.C.E. and the 1990 PES that illustrates the puzzle and a large part of the solution. The first two columns of Table 8-1 show the coverage correction factors for 2000 and 1990. The coverage correction factor is the dual-systems estimate (DSE) of the population divided by the full census count, including people requiring imputation and people reinstated in the census too late for A.C.E. processing. The coverage correction factor minus one is similar to the net undercount rate (DSE minus the full census count divided by the DSE). The coverage correction factor would be used if the census data were to be adjusted for net undercount. The second two columns of Table 8-1 are the 2000 and 1990 correction ratios. The correction ratio is the estimated correct enumeration rate divided by the estimated match rate. If there were no people with insufficient information who had to be excluded from the E-sample, the correction ratio would equal the coverage correction factor. The third and last two columns of Table 8-1 are the 2000 and 1990 percentages of all people with insufficient information (*II*s) in the census count, including people requiring imputation and people reinstated too late for A.C.E. processing. These people were not included in the E-sample but were added back to the census count when computing the coverage correction factors (see Chapter 6).

Looking at owners and renters for the non-Hispanic white and other races domain as an example, the correction ratios for 2000 are 1.022 for owners and 1.055 for renters, for a difference of 3.3 percentage points. For 1990, the correction ratios are 1.002 for owners and 1.045 for renters, for a difference of

TABLE 8-1 Coverage Correction Factors, Correction Ratios, and Percentage Insufficient Information People, by Race/Ethnicity Domain and Housing Tenure, 2000 A.C.E. and 1990 PES (weighted)

Domain and Tenure Group	Coverage Correction Factor (DSE / Census)		Correction Ratio (CE Rate / Match Rate)		Percentage Insufficient Information People (IIs)	
	2000	1990[a]	2000	1990[a]	2000	1990[a]
American Indian/Alaska Native on Reservation						
Owner	1.053	1.139	1.120	1.172	6.00	3.16
Renter	1.043	(Total)	1.104	(Total)	5.58	(Total)
American Indian/Alaska Native off Reservation						
Owner	1.016	N.A.	1.048	N.A.	3.51	N.A.
Renter	1.059	N.A.	1.101	N.A.	4.12	N.A.
Hispanic Origin						
Owner	1.013	1.019	1.060	1.030	4.61	1.03
Renter	1.045	1.080	1.098	1.099	4.96	1.56
Black (Non-Hispanic)						
Owner	1.007	1.023	1.046	1.036	3.81	1.20
Renter	1.037	1.069	1.090	1.084	4.88	1.89
Native Hawaiian/Pacific Islander						
Owner	1.028	N.A.	1.074	N.A.	4.49	N.A.
Renter	1.070	N.A.	1.121	N.A.	4.70	N.A.
Asian (Non-Hispanic)						
Owner	1.006	0.986	1.038	0.994	3.13	0.74
Renter	1.016	1.075	1.059	1.093	4.10	1.71
White and Other Races (Non-Hispanic)						
Owner	1.003	0.997	1.022	1.002	1.93	0.46
Renter	1.019	1.032	1.055	1.045	3.47	1.44
Total	1.012	1.016	1.040	1.022	2.93	0.90

NOTE: See text for discussion.

[a] Data for 1990 includes Pacific Islanders in the Asian (non-Hispanic) group.

SOURCE: Davis (2001:Tables E-2, F-1, F-2).

TABLE 8-2 Percentage Distribution of People Requiring Imputation and Late Additions to the Census in 2000, and Percentage Distribution of Total People with Insufficient Information in 1990, by Race/Ethnicity Domain and Housing Tenure

Panel A Domain and Tenure Group	Percent of Household Population, 2000			Percent of Household Population with Insufficient Information, 1990[a]
	People Requiring Imputation	Late Additions	Total with Insufficient Information	
American Indian/Alaska Native on Reservation				
Owner	5.13	0.97	6.00	3.16
Renter	4.74	0.94	5.58	(Total)
American Indian/Alaska Native off Reservation				
Owner	2.36	1.20	3.51	N.A.
Renter	3.00	1.16	4.12	N.A.
Hispanic Origin				
Owner	3.74	0.92	4.61	1.03
Renter	3.99	1.00	4.96	1.56
Black (Non-Hispanic)				
Owner	2.84	1.00	3.81	1.20
Renter	3.95	0.96	4.88	1.89
Native Hawaiian/Pacific Islander				
Owner	3.67	0.87	4.49	N.A.
Renter	3.83	0.92	4.70	N.A.
Asian (Non-Hispanic)				
Owner	2.46	0.69	3.13	0.74
Renter	3.35	0.77	4.10	1.71
White and Other Races (Non-Hispanic)				
Owner	1.24	0.71	1.93	0.46
Renter	2.38	1.12	3.47	1.44
Total Owner	1.66	0.75	2.39	0.56
Total Renter	3.08	1.05	4.10	1.55

Panel B Age/Sex Group				
Children Under Age 18	3.11	0.92	4.00	0.82
Men Aged 18–29	2.86	0.82	3.65	1.45
Women Aged 18–29	2.56	1.03	3.46	1.45
Men Aged 30–49	1.77	0.79	2.53	0.76
Women Aged 30–49	1.58	0.81	2.37	0.70
Men Aged 50 and Over	1.25	0.81	2.04	0.69
Women Aged 50 and Over	1.30	0.80	2.08	0.79
Total	2.11	0.85	2.93	0.90

NOTE: The 2000 total with insufficient information is the unduplicated sum of people requiring imputation and late additions to the census; 1990 figures include small number of late additions to the census from coverage improvement operations.

[a] Data exclude American Indians living on reservations; the Asian (Non-Hispanic) data for 1990 include Pacific Islanders.

SOURCE: Data for 2000 are from tabulations by panel staff of U.S. Census Bureau, Pre-Collapsed Post-Stratum Summary File (U.S.), February 16, 2001; data for 1990 are from Davis (2001:Tables F.1, F.2).

4.3 percentage points. If there were no people excluded from the E-sample because of insufficient information in the census, then the correction ratios would equal the coverage correction factors, with the result that the net undercount rate would be somewhat higher for white owners in 2000 than in 1990 and similar and quite high for white renters in both censuses. The differential net undercount between white owners and renters would be 3–4 percentage points. Yet the estimated coverage correction factors for 2000 are 1.003 for white owners and 1.019 for white renters, for a difference of only 1.6 percentage points; in comparison, the corresponding difference for 1990 is 3.5 percentage points. The reason for these results is that the 2000 census recorded larger percentages than did the 1990 census of white owners and renters— particularly renters—whose census records lacked sufficient information to be included in the E-sample: the percentage of *II*s for white owners increased from 0.5 percent in 1990 to 1.9 percent in 2000; the percentage of *II*s for white renters increased from 1.4 percent in 1990 to 3.5 percent in 2000.

The same patterns hold true for owners and renters in the Hispanic, non-Hispanic black, and non-Hispanic Asian domains, and for minorities, generally, compared with the non-Hispanic white and other races domain (see Table 8-1). The same patterns also hold true for children under age 18 (data not shown). The coverage correction factor for children was 1.016 in 2000 and 1.033 in 1990, indicating a reduction in their measured net undercount. However, their correction ratio was larger in 2000 than in 1990, 1.056 and 1.039, respectively. This change would have meant an increase in the net undercount for children were it not for a large increase in the number of children in the census with insufficient information who were not part of the E-sample—4.0 percent in 2000 and only 0.8 percent in 1990.

Thus, the increased percentages of people with insufficient information in the census largely appear to explain the reduction in measured net undercount from 2000 to 1990 for historically less well-counted groups. In particular, the increased percentages of people requiring imputation—as distinct from people reinstated too late for A.C.E. processing—contributed greatly to this result. As shown in Table 8-2 and Figures 8-1 and 8-2, people requiring imputation accounted for proportionally more of historically less well-counted groups, while the distribution of late additions to the census showed little variation by race/ethnicity, housing tenure, or age/sex categories.

For some groups, other factors also played a role in reducing their net undercount. For American Indians and Alaska Natives on reservations, there is not only an increase in people with insufficient information, but also a reduction in the correction ratio (see Table 8-1). It turns out that the P-sample had a smaller proportion of nonmatched cases in 2000 than in 1990 for this group, and the reduction in the nonmatch rate (or the increase in the match rate) was proportionally greater than the change in the correct enumeration rate (see Tables 7-8 and 7-9 in Chapter 7). The targeted extended search may have

136

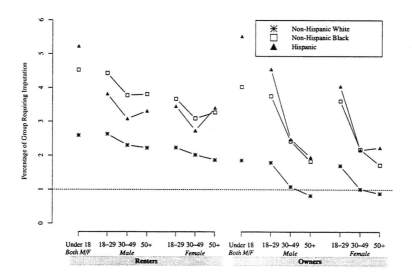

FIGURE 8-1 Persons requiring imputation by race/ethnicity domain, housing tenure, and age/sex groups (percent).

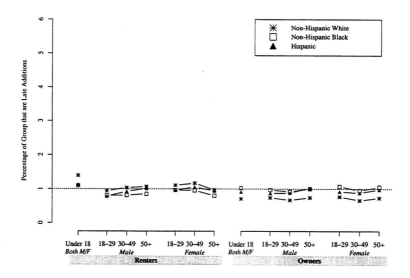

FIGURE 8-2 Late additions to the census by race/ethnicity domain, housing tenure, and age/sex groups.

been the principal cause for the increased match rate relative to the correct enumeration rate for this domain (see Navarro and Olson, 2001).

Role of *II*s in the Census and the DSE

There are two important points about people with insufficient information, whether they are people requiring imputation or people reinstated in the census too late for A.C.E. processing. First, their exclusion from the dual-systems estimation does not likely affect to any significant degree the expected value of the DSE estimate of the population (although it does affect the variance of the DSE, as well as complicating the interpretation of the A.C.E. results—see Chapter 7). Second, they do not necessarily result in poor quality census data.

With regard to the first point, if all (or some) of the census records for people with insufficient information had, instead, not required imputation and been available in time for matching, the components of the DSE formula would have changed in ways that would be expected to result in about the same level of the DSE (see Hogan, 2001b).[3] First, the base for computing the DSE—the census count minus people with insufficient information $(C - II)$—would be a higher number than that actually used in the DSE formula in 2000. Also, because more P-sample cases would have matched to the E-sample, the correction ratio would have decreased from the correction ratio that was actually estimated. The result of applying a lower correction ratio to a higher base $(C - II)$ would have been about the same DSE as the actual estimate in which a higher correction ratio was applied to a lower base. A similar result obtains even if we assume that many of the people who were excluded from the A.C.E. were duplicates or other types of erroneous enumerations (see Box 8-1).

On the second point, people with "insufficient information" do not necessarily result in poor short-form information. Almost one-third of the total *II*s in 2000 were people reinstated in the census, most of whom had complete information, although they may have included a higher-than-average proportion of duplicates. Also, imputations in many cases were carried out on the basis of knowing household size, as well as characteristics of the immediate neighborhood.

---

[3]This can be seen by reexpressing the DSE formula as: the census count, C, minus *II*s, times the correction ratio (the correct enumeration rate, CE/E, divided by the match rate, M/P). The usual expression equates the DSE to: $(C - II)$ times the correct enumeration rate times the inverse of the match rate (see Eq. 1 in Chapter 6).

BOX 8-1
Relationship of People with Insufficient Information (Imputations and Late Additions) to Dual-Systems Estimation: Illustrative Examples

A. Suppose that a post-stratum has the following characteristics:

Census count (C)	1 million
People with insufficient information in the census (II)	20,000
Match rate for P-sample (M/P)	91.6
(Weighted P-sample size is, say, 1,000,000)	
Correct enumeration rate for E-sample (CE/E)	95.3
(Weighted E-sample size is $C - II$, or 980,000)	

Then the correction ratio, CR (correct enumeration rate divided by match rate), is 1.0404, and the DSE is 1,019,600 from the following formula:

$$DSE = (C - II)(CR) = 980,000(1.0404) = 1,019,600.$$

The coverage correction factor, CCF, is 1,019,600 divided by 1 million (C) = 1.0196. The net undercount rate is $(DSE - C)/DSE$ = 1.92 percent.

B. Now suppose that all of the IIs are, instead, able to be included in the A.C.E., i.e., they do not require imputation and they are available in time for A.C.E. processing. Assume that these 20,000 people contain 15,850 matches, 3,200 other correct enumerations, and 950 erroneous enumerations (similar to the A.C.E. E-sample). Then the P-sample match rate is [15,850 + (0.916)(1,000,000)] /1,000,000 = 93.185, which is a higher match rate than shown above. The recalculated E-sample correct enumeration rate is the same at 95.3. Now the correction ratio is 1.0227 and the DSE is:

$$DSE = (C - II)(CR) = 1,000,000(1.0227) = 1,022,700,$$

which only differs from the DSE for case A above by 3,100 people (or 0.3%). The coverage correction factor is 1,022,700 divided by 1 million (C) = 1.0227. The net undercount rate is $(DSE - C)/DSE$ = 2.22 percent, which is essentially the same net undercount rate as 1.92 percent.

C. Finally, suppose that all of the IIs are, instead, able to be included in the A.C.E., but that one-half of them (10,000) are erroneous enumerations and the rest are matches (8,200) and other correct enumerations (1,800). Then the P-sample match rate is (8,200 + 916,000)/1,000,000 = 92.42. The E-sample correct enumeration rate is [(10,000 + (0.953)(980,000)] /1,000,000 = 94.394. In this case, the P-sample match rate increases by a smaller amount than in case B above; the E-sample correct enumeration rate *decreases*. Now the correction ratio is 1.0214 and the DSE is:

$$DSE = (C - II)(CR) = 1,000,000(1.0214) = 1,021,400,$$

which only differs from the DSE for case A by 1,800 people (or less than 0.2%). The coverage correction factor is 1,021,400 divided by 1 million (C) = 1.0214. The net undercount rate is $(DSE - C)/DSE$ = 2.10 percent.

These examples illustrate the negligible effect that the IIs have on the value of the DSE. At the same time, they illustrate how the larger number of IIs in 2000 clouds the interpretation of the A.C.E. results in comparison with the 1990 PES. The correction ratio is considerably higher than the coverage correction factor for A.C.E. Also, estimates of duplicates and other kinds of erroneous enumerations are lower than they would otherwise be because so many more census records are excluded from A.C.E. processing.

PEOPLE REQUIRING IMPUTATION

Situations Requiring Imputation

The Census Bureau distinguishes five situations in which imputation of person records is required (see Appendix A for the methods used for each situation):

(1) Individual imputed person(s) in an enumerated household. An example in 2000 would be a household of seven members that had characteristics reported for six members, and the telephone follow-up failed to obtain information for the seventh person listed on the household roster. Individual persons requiring imputation comprised 0.9 percent of the total household population in 2000, 2.33 million people (Schindler, 2001), compared with 0.2 percent of the total population in 1990, 373,000 people (including some imputations for persons in group quarters; Love and Dalzell, 2001).

(2) Person imputations in a household for which the number of residents was known (perhaps from a neighbor or landlord), but no characteristics were available for them. Whole households that required imputation included 0.8 percent of the household population in 2000, 2.27 million people, and 0.6 percent in 1990, 1.55 million people.

(3), (4), and (5) Persons imputed in a household or at an address for which there was no information on household size (category 3), or sometimes no information on occupancy status (category 4), or sometimes not even information on status as a housing unit (category 5). Together, these three categories comprised 0.4 percent of the household population counted in 2000, 1.17 million people, compared with only 0.02 percent of the household population counted in 1990, 54,000 people.

Information is available on each of the three categories, (3), (4), and (5), separately for 2000 (but not for 1990). Category (3) includes persons imputed in a household that was known with reasonable certainty to be occupied but the household size was not known. Members of such households were 0.2 percent of the household population (496,000 people). Category (4) includes persons imputed in a housing unit that was known to exist but for which its status as occupied or vacant was not certain. Members of households with occupied status, size, and person characteristics imputed were 0.1 percent of the household population in 2000 (260,000 people). Finally, category (5) includes people imputed at an address for which nothing was certain—not its existence as a housing unit, its occupancy status, its size, or household composition. Members of households in this category were 0.2 percent of the household population (415,000 people).

Distribution of Imputations Among Population Groups

Race/Ethnicity Domain and Housing Tenure

Table 8-3 shows the distribution of people requiring imputation in 2000 among race/ethnicity and housing tenure groups by type of imputation required. It also shows the total percentage of people requiring imputation for each group; note that the overall percentages are low.

Several patterns stand out. First, the proportion of imputations that involved filling in a data record for one (or possibly more) individuals missing in an enumerated household (type 1) is higher for owners (43%) than renters (37%), and this pattern holds for all race/ethnicity groups except American Indians and Alaska Natives. In contrast, the proportion of imputations that involved supplying data records for all people in a household for which the number of people, but not their characteristics, was known (type 2) is higher for renters (45%) than owners (34%), and this pattern holds uniformly for all race/ethnicity groups.

These differences could make sense in light of knowledge of different response propensities and other characteristics for owners and renters. Owners have higher mail return rates than renters, and average household size also tends to be larger for owner-occupied housing than renter-occupied housing.[4] Consequently, it is at least plausible to assume that proportionately more owners than renters sent in questionnaires indicating a larger household size than the number of people for whom they reported characteristics. If telephone follow-up did not locate these households, then one or more of their members would require imputation. Conversely, one could conjecture that enumerators would more often have a hard time gleaning any information for a rented housing unit beyond the household size (and the fact it was rented) than would be true for owned units. Hence, more renter-occupied units would require imputation of all their members.

Another striking pattern in Table 8-3 is that American Indians and Alaska Natives on reservations have the highest proportions of imputations for status as a housing unit (type 5). This finding suggests that there may have been difficulties in developing the address list for reservations. American Indians and Alaska Natives on reservations also have the highest total proportion of people requiring imputation of any race/ethnicity group (5%).

---

[4]Mail return rates in 2000 were about 77 percent for owners and 57 percent for renters (from tabulations by panel staff of U.S. Census Bureau, E-Sample Person Dual-System Estimation Output File, February 16, 2001; weighted using TESFINWT); see U.S. General Demographic Characteristics Quick Table for average household size by tenure at http://factfinder.census.gov/home/en/c2ss.html.

TABLE 8-3 Distribution of People Requiring Imputation by Type of Imputation, by Race/Ethnicity Domain and Housing Tenure, 2000

Domain and Tenure Group	Percent of People Requiring Imputation by Type[a]					Percent of Total Household Population Requiring Imputation
	Person (1)	Household (2)	Size (3)	Occupancy (4)	Housing Unit (5)	
American Indian/Alaska Native on Reservation						
Owner	41.4	9.2	12.1	1.9	35.7	5.1
Renter	42.9	10.1	14.5	1.2	31.2	4.7
American Indian/Alaska Native off Reservation						
Owner	38.6	34.7	9.3	4.5	12.9	2.4
Renter	40.5	40.5	7.8	3.7	7.5	3.0
Hispanic Origin						
Owner	61.5	22.8	7.0	2.2	6.5	3.7
Renter	54.3	32.0	7.2	2.3	4.2	4.0
Black (Non-Hispanic)						
Owner	43.2	39.3	9.4	3.4	4.7	2.8
Renter	34.1	49.1	10.4	3.2	3.3	4.0
Native Hawaiian and Pacific Islander						
Owner	60.6	25.7	6.5	1.5	5.6	3.7
Renter	49.3	36.3	7.6	1.7	5.1	3.8
Asian (Non-Hispanic)						
Owner	62.1	25.6	5.2	2.4	4.8	2.5
Renter	39.9	45.5	8.0	2.9	3.7	3.4
White and Other Races (Non-Hispanic)						
Owner	35.3	38.1	8.8	7.0	10.9	1.2
Renter	27.1	51.9	9.1	5.1	6.8	2.4
Total	40.3	39.3	8.6	4.5	7.2	2.1
Owner	43.2	34.3	8.4	5.2	8.9	1.7
Renter	37.0	45.3	8.9	3.7	5.1	3.1

[a] See text for definitions of imputation types.

SOURCE: Tabulations by panel staff from U.S. Census Bureau, Census Imputations by Post-Stratum File, July 30, 2001 (see Schindler, 2001).

Age/Sex Categories

For age/sex categories (data not shown in Table 8-3), the most striking finding is that children under 18 have not only the highest total proportion of people requiring imputation of any age group (3.1%), but also the highest share of imputations that occurred in otherwise enumerated households (60% were type 1 imputations). No other age/sex group has as high a share of person imputations; the next highest proportions of type 1 imputations are for men aged 18–29 (37.9%) and women aged 18–29 (35%). This finding is consistent with an assumption that imputation of individuals in large households that did not report (or lacked enough room to report) characteristics for all their members most often involved children.

It is true that type 1 imputations could occur not only in households with more than six members, but also in smaller households that did not report characteristics for all of their members. It is at least plausible to assume, however, that the decision to reduce the size of the questionnaire by limiting the number of persons for whom characteristics could be reported from seven in 1990 to six in 2000 was a primary cause of the large increase in type 1 imputations in 2000 compared with 1990 and the predominance of type 1 imputations among children.

Indirect evidence for this assumption comes from analysis by panel staff of matched P-sample and E-sample cases in the 2000 A.C.E. by household composition. The analysis finds that the percentage of E-sample households for which the P-sample found one or more people in the household who were missed, or possibly missed, in the census rises almost from about 3 percent of single-person and two-person households to about 17 percent of households with nine or more members. In the middle of the E-sample household size distribution, the percentages of households with one or more P-sample omissions are, respectively, 5.8 percent, 11.5 percent, 9.0 percent, and 12.1 percent for five-person, six-person, seven-person and eight-person households. This pattern, in which the percentage for six-person households does not fit the sequence, suggests that the telephone follow-up to fill in the characteristics of all persons in households with more than six persons did not work completely. Alternatively, some households with more than six members may have chosen to report only six to forestall follow-up.

Distribution of Imputations by State

Figure 8-3 shows for each state the percentage of its population in 2000 that represented people requiring imputation. The percentage varied from 1 percent in Iowa and Nebraska to 3.74 percent in the District of Columbia. States with the highest proportions of people requiring imputation included a group in the Southwest: Arizona, California, Nevada, New Mexico, and Texas, plus

Delaware, the District of Columbia, Hawaii, New York, and Wyoming. States with the lowest proportions of people requiring imputation included a group of Midwest states: Iowa, Kansas, Minnesota, Missouri, Nebraska, and North Dakota, plus Kentucky, Ohio, and West Virginia.

Figures 8-4 through 8-6 show the state variation in the three major types of imputation situations: category (1), partial household imputation, with some but not all members of the household fully enumerated (Figure 8-4); category (2), whole household imputation, with household size reported but not the characteristics of the members (Figure 8-5); and categories (3)–(5), housing status imputation, with household size and possibly occupancy status and housing unit status imputed first (Figure 8-6). Generally, they show similar patterns to those in Figure 8-3.[5]

Thus, several Southwest states, Alaska, Hawaii, and New York had higher-than-average proportions of people requiring partial household imputation (Figure 8-4), with California having the highest rate. This result is consonant with the finding that many California census tracts had marked increases in mail return rates in 2000 versus 1990 (see Appendix B), and so could have had relatively high proportions of mailed-back returns that did not (or could not) provide characteristics for all household members.

There is a wider range among states of proportions of people requiring whole household imputation than of people requiring only partial household imputation. Delaware, Maryland, and New York had the highest rates of people requiring whole household imputation, and Maine, Nebraska, North and South Dakota, and West Virginia had the lowest rates (Figure 8-5). Proportions of people requiring housing status imputation are the lowest and the most evenly distributed across states (Figure 8-6). Relatively high rates of housing status imputations for New Mexico and Wyoming may be associated with larger numbers of American Indians living on reservations. Data are not yet available with which to analyze distributions of people requiring imputation for smaller geographic areas.

---

[5]The same four groupings are used in Figures 8-4 through 8-6: from 1 to 2 standard deviations below the mean to greater than 2 standard deviations above the mean. The distribution from which the groupings derive includes 153 state percentages—those for partial household imputations, whole household imputations, and housing status imputations for each state and the District of Columbia.

144

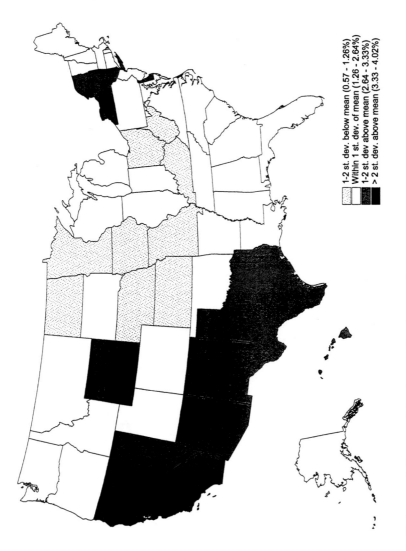

1-2 st. dev. below mean (0.57 - 1.26%)
Within 1 st. dev. of mean (1.26 - 2.64%)
1-2 st. dev above mean (2.64 - 3.33%)
> 2 st. dev. above mean (3.33 - 4.02%)

FIGURE 8-3 State population requiring imputation (percent).

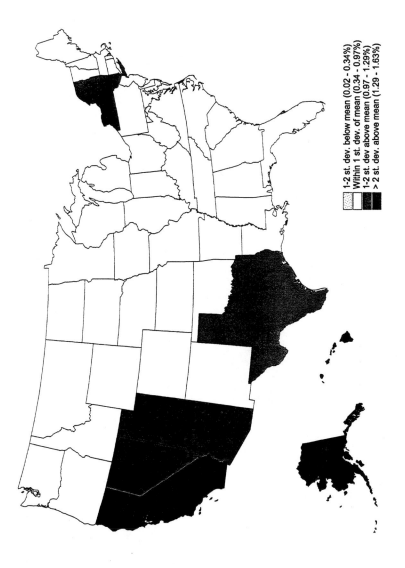

FIGURE 8-4 State population requiring partial household imputation (percent).

NOTE: Groupings by standard deviations are computed with respect to all three imputation types illustrated in Figures 8-4, 8-5, and 8-6. Accordingly, each of the four gradations may not appear in each individual figure.

146

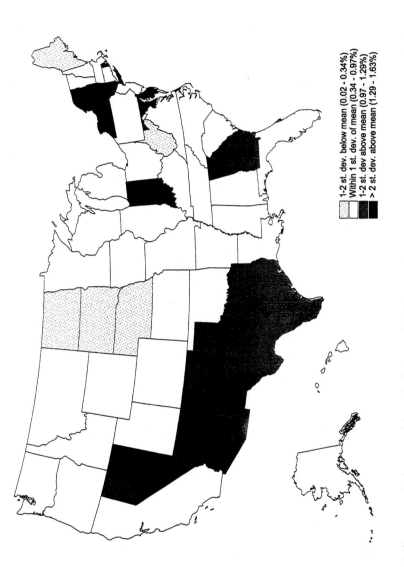

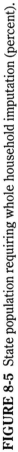

1-2 st. dev. below mean (0.02 - 0.34%)
Within 1 st. dev. of mean (0.34 - 0.97%)
1-2 st. dev above mean (0.97 - 1.29%)
> 2 st. dev. above mean (1.29 - 1.63%)

FIGURE 8-5 State population requiring whole household imputation (percent).

NOTE: Groupings by standard deviations are computed with respect to all three imputation types illustrated in Figures 8-4, 8-5, and 8-6. Accordingly, each of the four gradations may not appear in each individual figure.

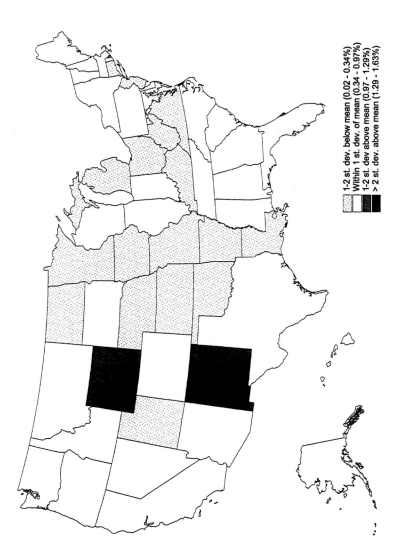

1-2 st. dev. below mean (0.02 - 0.34%)
Within 1 st. dev. of mean (0.34 - 0.97%)
1-2 st. dev above mean (0.97 - 1.29%)
> 2 st. dev. above mean (1.29 - 1.63%)

FIGURE 8-6 State population requiring imputation of housing status (percent).

NOTE: Groupings by standard deviations are computed with respect to all three imputation types illustrated in Figures 8-4, 8-5, and 8-6. Accordingly, each of the four gradations may not appear in each individual figure.

LATE ADDITIONS

Of 6 million people whose census records were removed from processing in summer 2000 because they were thought to duplicate enumerations for other households, 2.4 million were reinstated in the census but too late for A.C.E. processing. As noted above, there was little variation in the distribution of people reinstated in the census by race/ethnicity group, housing tenure, or age/sex categories. In this section we look at their distribution by geographic area. We also consider the possibility that people reinstated in the census still contain a high proportion of duplicates and what the A.C.E. can explain about duplicates in the census.

Geographic Variation

Figure 8-7 shows for each state the percentage of its census count that represented people reinstated in the census at the conclusion of the summer 2000 program that identified duplicates in the Master Address File (MAF). The percentage of people reinstated in the census varied relatively little among states—from 0.1 percent in the District of Columbia and 0.4 percent in Delaware to 1.7 percent in New York and Vermont, compared with a national average of 0.9 percent. States with the largest proportions of people reinstated in the census included Arkansas, Hawaii, Maine, Mississippi, Montana, New Mexico, New York, Vermont, West Virginia, and Wyoming. States with the lowest proportions of late additions included California, Delaware, District of Columbia, Florida, Indiana, Michigan, Ohio, Oregon, Washington, and Wisconsin.

There is probably more variation in percentages of people reinstated in the census at smaller levels of geographic aggregation than at the state level. The Census Bureau indicated that the decision to reinstate people who were originally identified as duplicates was most often made in rural areas with nonstandard addressing styles and in apartment buildings in cities, for which individual apartment addresses were not clear (Miskura, 2000b). In other words, when there was cause for doubt about a duplication because the addresses could not clearly be compared, the person record was often reinstated.

Percentages of people reinstated in the census for certain A.C.E. poststrata categorized by region show several patterns (Farber, 2001b:Table 3-1). The highest percentages of people reinstated in the census (2–4%) are most often found in strata for either rural areas or large cities, specifically in strata for:

- mailout/mailback areas with low mail return rates in the largest cities of the Northeast for non-Hispanic white owners, black owners, and Hispanic owners;

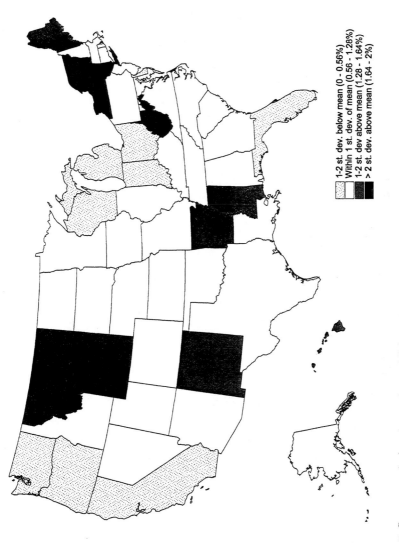

FIGURE 8-7 State population due to late additions (percent).

- non-mailout/mailback (i.e., update/leave and list/enumerate) areas in all regions of the country for non-Hispanic white renters; and

- non-mailout/mailback areas with low mail return rates (update/leave areas) in all regions of the country for non-Hispanic white owners and in the South and West for Hispanic renters.

Of course, no census can be conducted completely uniformly for all geographic areas. However, the concern is that sizable geographic variation in the completeness of the census count could affect uses of the census that are based on population shares. Moreover, adjustment of the census counts in the presence of substantial local variations could be problematic: a disproportionately well-counted area would receive an adjustment that is likely too great and the reverse would be true for a disproportionately less well-counted area.

Further research is needed on geographic variations in the completeness of the census due not only to people reinstated in the census, but also to people requiring imputation. Such research needs to be at a finer geographic level than states and needs to trace variations to their sources in the MAF.

Duplication

An often-voiced worry about the 2000 census was that changes in the method used to construct the MAF and additional opportunities for enumeration would lead to an increase in erroneous enumerations, particularly duplicates. Construction of the MAF encouraged acceptance of addresses from multiple sources. Enumeration opportunities included mail, telephone, Internet, the "Be Counted" forms that were widely distributed just prior to Census Day, and various follow-up operations.

In fact, duplicates from additional opportunities for enumeration in 2000 appeared relatively low (see Appendix A). However, extensive unduplication operations had to be undertaken for the MAF, including the special unduplication effort in summer 2000.

It is likely that the Bureau's efforts to remove duplications from the MAF were not completely successful. In particular, the people reinstated in the census at the conclusion of the special unduplication operation may have contained a larger-than-average proportion of duplicates and other erroneous enumerations. Also, some of the people requiring imputation, particularly those at addresses for which the housing unit status had to be imputed first, may have been duplicates or other types of erroneous enumerations.

The reason for concern about duplications is that they may not simply offset people with the same characteristics who were omitted from the census. Research from previous censuses (see Ericksen et al., 1991; see also Appendix B) suggests that not only omissions, but also duplicate and other erroneous enumerations are more likely to occur among historically less well-counted groups. However, the relationship is not as strong for duplicates as it is for omissions, so that duplication can increase, not reduce, differences in net undercount rates between less well-counted and better-counted groups.

Because net undercount rates in 2000 declined proportionally more from 1990 rates for historically less well-counted groups than for others, it does not appear that duplication had a serious effect on differential coverage of population groups in 2000. In fact, it may have helped reduce differential coverage. However, duplication could well have varied across geographic areas.

Measurement of Duplication in the A.C.E.

The A.C.E. estimated duplicates in the E-sample universe, and it found many fewer than the number estimated by the 1990 PES. In addition, the estimated number of duplicates in both the A.C.E. and the PES, but particularly the A.C.E., seems too low in relation to the total number of erroneous enumerations of all types (see Table 7-10 in Chapter 7). These results are not entirely unexpected for at least three reasons.

First, neither the A.C.E. nor the PES is well designed to measure duplicates as distinct from other kinds of erroneous enumerations. They will not, for example, identify enumerations of snowbirds at both their winter and their summer residences as duplicates because the search area is limited to a block cluster or a ring of surrounding blocks (the A.C.E. used a targeted extended search—see Chapter 6). For the same reason, they will not identify enumerations for children of divorced or separated parents who spend time with each parent or enumerations for college students who were counted at home and at college as duplicates.[6]

Second, the A.C.E., as distinct from the PES, likely underestimated duplicate enumerations because it was not designed to measure duplicates (or omissions) that occurred within the group quarters population (the PES included group quarters residents not in institutions). Third, the A.C.E. could not measure the extent to which people not part of the E-sample universe (those requiring imputation or reinstated in the census too late for A.C.E. processing) contained duplicates, and there were many more such cases in 2000 than in 1990. Also, if the special operation to unduplicate addresses in the MAF had not permanently deleted 3.6 million people of the 6 million originally set aside for examination, then the A.C.E. would have measured more duplicate enumerations. For all these reasons, the A.C.E. estimates of duplicate census enumerations should be viewed as a lower bound.

---

[6]It can be demonstrated that the A.C.E. estimate of erroneous enumerations in the aggregate will likely include duplicate enumerations for snowbirds and others with multiple residences, even though the A.C.E. cannot identify them as duplicates as such. With regard to group quarters residents, the A.C.E. was supposed to exclude them (in contrast to the PES). One of the concerns currently under investigation at the Census Bureau is that the A.C.E. may not have properly identified erroneous enumerations in E-sample households for college students and other residents of group quarters who were reported at, say, their parental home.

CONCLUSIONS

We have devoted considerable attention to people requiring imputation and people whose census records were reinstated too late for A.C.E. processing, even though the numbers involved are small relative to the total population. We have done so because of the small size of the estimated net undercount, which means that relatively small changes in the enumeration of population groups can affect their net undercount rates. We conclude that the exclusion from the A.C.E. of people requiring imputation and people reinstated in the census did not likely affect the DSE to any appreciable degree (as explained in Hogan, 2001b; see also Box 8-1). We find that the larger numbers of imputed and reinstated people lead mathematically to a reduction in the overall net undercount rate; specifically, the larger numbers of people requiring imputation contributed to reducing net undercount rates for historically less well-counted groups. However, the larger numbers of imputed and reinstated people also made the results from the A.C.E. less easy to interpret and less useful as a guide to gross errors in the census. It is not yet known whether the imputed and reinstated people resulted in more variation in population coverage across geographic areas.

While there will always be people who require imputation to complete their census records and other people who are enumerated too late for inclusion in coverage evaluation, it seems clearly desirable to reduce their numbers from 2000 levels. Direct information from respondents—collected in time to support normal census and coverage evaluation procedures—is always preferable to imputed and reinstated responses. For planning the 2010 census, considerable research is needed on the sources of addresses for which people were imputed or reinstated in 2000; features of census operations that may have increased the number of people requiring imputation; and methods and their associated costs and benefits for reducing the number of people requiring imputation and minimizing the number of late or reinstated enumerations. For purposes of evaluating the 2000 census data, research is also needed on the exact nature and quality of the imputation and reinstatement procedures used in the 2000 census.

People Requiring Imputation

It is important to keep in mind that many cases of whole person imputations are based on definite knowledge that one or more individuals should be counted at an address. Indeed, the largest group of people requiring imputation in 2000 were individual members of an enumerated household, not the entire household (type 1). These cases were genuine household enumerations for which the computer was used to supply characteristics of the missing members on the basis of knowing a great deal about the household. Further analysis is needed of type 1 imputations, which contributed to reducing the net undercount of children in 2000: Were most such imputations among households with more than six members? On mailed-back returns rather than enumerator-obtained returns? On returns that lacked a telephone number, which is a reason that the coverage edit and telephone follow-up operation could have missed them? Did the imputations produce a reasonable distribution of households by size?

Most important, can it be established that the reduced size of the questionnaire in 2000 encouraged mail returns from large households that might otherwise have failed to respond or have been poorly enumerated in follow-up? If so, then there is an argument for continuing to use a shorter questionnaire in 2010, even though more people may require type 1 imputations as a consequence. In that regard, a thorough evaluation is needed of the performance of the coverage edit and telephone follow-up operation, which was intended to complete the census records for partially enumerated households. If many of the households in the telephone follow-up workload did not provide telephone numbers or could not be reached despite repeated calls, then there is an argument for considering the benefits and costs of field follow-up of partially enumerated households as a supplement to telephone follow-up in 2010.

Looking at the numbers of people requiring imputation in a household for which occupancy status and size were known, but not characteristics (type 2), they are similar to 1990. There apparently will always be some households that are reported to be occupied and for which a household size can be obtained but not other characteristics. We believe it makes sense to include people for these households in the census by using information for other households in the immediate neighborhood rather than drop the addresses. Imputations for these kinds of households were proportionately greater among renter households than owner households in 2000, which helps explain the narrowing of the difference in net undercount rates between owners and renters from the 1990 levels.

Looking at categories (3)–(5), it is difficult to explain the much larger number of people in 2000 than in 1990 (1.17 million and 54,000) who required imputation when characteristics of the housing unit had to be imputed first.[7] It

---

[7]There were similarly large numbers of housing status imputations in 1970 (the number in 1980 was between the 1990 and 2000 numbers). However, the 1970 case was different in that most of the housing status imputations involved sample-based imputation of occupancy status to housing units that were originally classified as vacant in nonresponse follow-up. A small sample of such vacant units were rechecked in the field when it appeared that vacancy rates were too high; the sample results were used for imputation.

is possible that some of these cases—perhaps a large proportion—were erroneous or duplicates (type 2 situations could also include duplicates). Research is needed on the geographic distribution of housing status imputations, the sources of addresses for them in the MAF, and the extent to which features of the 2000 nonresponse and coverage improvement follow-up operations (e.g., instructions to enumerators) may have contributed to the larger number of such cases. Research is also needed on the quality of the housing status imputation process, which was refined somewhat from the 1990 procedure (see Appendix A). Although it may result that the housing status imputations in the 2000 census appear reasonable, it is clearly desirable to minimize the number of census enumerations for which so little is known. Hence, research on the sources of these enumerations is important to carry out for planning the 2010 census.

Late Additions

Research is needed on the sources and geographic distribution of the MAF addresses that necessitated the special unduplication operation in summer 2000. This operation was unprecedented. Not only did it pose a risk for census data processing, but it also meant that the A.C.E. was less informative about erroneous enumerations than if the records that were reinstated at the conclusion of the special operation had been available to include in the A.C.E. It seems desirable to preclude the necessity for any such late-occurring address clean-up operation in future censuses, which means that the Census Bureau's plans for reengineering the MAF development process for the 2010 census are critically important (see Chapter 4).

Research is also needed on the quality of the reinstated records in 2000. Field work may be needed to estimate the extent of duplication among the reinstated records (and among some types of imputations). In addition, research is needed on the extent of duplication of people with more than one residence. A possible way to study the issue would be to use the American Community Survey to ask about multiple residences at the time of the census and then to check the census records to determine how such cases were enumerated.

Appendix A

Census Operations

This appendix describes the operations of the 2000 census, noting differences from 1990 census procedures. It covers five topics:

- the Master Address File (MAF) (including local review and internal checks for duplicate addresses);

- questionnaire delivery and mail return (including redesign of mailings and materials and multiple response modes);

- field follow-up (including nonresponse follow-up, NRFU, and coverage improvement follow-up, CIFU);

- outreach efforts; and

- data processing (including data capture, coverage edit and telephone follow-up, unduplication of households and people, editing and imputation, and other processing).

MASTER ADDRESS FILE

The 2000 census was conducted primarily by mailing or delivering questionnaires to addresses on a computerized mailing list—the MAF—and asking residents to fill out the questionnaires and mail them back.[1] The Census Bureau first used mailout/mailback techniques with an address list in the 1970 census,[2] but the procedures to develop the 2000 MAF differed in several important respects from those used in past censuses (see LUCA Working Group, 2001; Owens, 2000). The major difference from 1990 was that the 2000 MAF was constructed using more sources.

---

[1]The Census Bureau refers to the version of the MAF that was used in the census as the Decennial Master Address File or DMAF. It is an extract of the full MAF, which includes business as well as residential addresses. Use of the term "MAF" in this report refers to the DMAF.

[2]Unaddressed short-form questionnaires were delivered by the U.S. Postal Service in the 1960 census to 80 percent of households, but residents were to hold the questionnaires for enumerators to pick up. At every fourth household, enumerators left a long-form questionnaire, which respondents were to fill out and mail back (National Research Council, 1995:189).

Initial Development

The Census Bureau used somewhat different procedures to develop the MAF for areas believed to have predominantly city-style mailing addresses (house number and street) than for areas believed to have predominantly rural route and post office box mailing addresses (see Box A-1). City-style areas were those inside the "blue line," and non-city-style areas were those outside the "blue line."[3] For areas inside the blue line, the Bureau expected to have U.S. Postal Service carriers deliver questionnaires to most addresses on the list; for areas outside the blue line, the Bureau expected to use its own field workers to deliver questionnaires.

For remote rural areas, which have less than 1 percent of the population, Census Bureau enumerators developed the address list concurrently with enumerating households in person. For special places in which people live in non-residential settings, such as college dormitories, prisons, nursing homes and other group quarters, the Bureau used a variety of sources to develop an address list. About 2.8 percent of the population was enumerated in group quarters in 2000 (tabulations of Census Bureau data); the comparable 1990 figure is 2.7 percent (U.S. Census Bureau, 1996:68).

Inside the "Blue Line"

As the starting point for the MAF for city-style areas inside the blue line, the Census Bureau took the 1990 census address list for these areas and updated it from the Delivery Sequence File (DSF) of the Postal Service. The DSF contains a listing of addresses to which mail is delivered, ordered by carrier routes. It is updated regularly. Legislation passed in 1994 allows the Postal Service to share the DSF with the Bureau.

Although not part of its original plan, the Bureau determined that a complete field check of the city-style list should be conducted, which was done in a block canvass operation for all mailout/mailback areas conducted in January-May 1999. The Bureau also provided an opportunity for local review in 1998–1999 (see "Local Review," below). Approximately 101 million addresses were included in the MAF for areas inside the blue line at the time when questionnaires were labeled and prepared for mailing in July 1999. The Postal Service conducted an intensive check of the DSF in early 2000, and updates were made to the MAF based on that check prior to questionnaire delivery.

Outside the "Blue Line"

To develop the MAF for non-city-style areas, the Bureau first conducted a block canvass operation, called address listing, in July 1998-February 1999.

---

[3]The blue line was a late-1997 Census Bureau demarcation.

BOX A-1
Basic Steps to Develop the Master Address File Prior to Census Day, 2000 and 1990

2000 CENSUS MASTER ADDRESS FILE

City-Style Areas (mailout/mailback areas inside the "blue line")

1. Start with the 1990 Census Address Control File.
2. Refresh the 1990 list with periodic updates of the U.S. Postal Service Delivery Sequence File.
3. Conduct complete block canvass in the field in January-May 1999 (not in original plans).
4. Provide opportunity for counties, minor civil divisions, places, and tribal governments to review the MAF for their areas in the Local Update of Census Addresses Program, called LUCA98. LUCA98 spanned February 1998-March 2000; it included:
   (a) local review of initial MAF and census maps;
   (b) Census Bureau verification of address changes provided by localities (reconciliation);
   (c) local review of feedback/final determination materials from the Bureau; and
   (d) review of local appeals by Census Address List Appeals Office in the Office of Management and Budget.
5. Provide opportunity for localities to review the address list for dormitories, nursing homes, and other special places in December 1999-April 2000 (Special Places LUCA).
6. Incorporate updates from Postal Service's final intensive check of Delivery Sequence File prior to questionnaire delivery.
7. Provide opportunity for localities to supply addresses for newly constructed housing units in January-March 2000 to be enumerated in summer 2000 (New Construction LUCA).

Non-City-Style Areas (update/leave areas outside the "blue line")

1. Conduct an address list creation operation in July 1998-February 1999.
2. Provide opportunity for localities to review the list in the LUCA99 Program. LUCA99 spanned July 1998-March 2000. It was similar to LUCA98 except that localities were asked to challenge housing unit counts for blocks in their initial review. They had to challenge and provide evidence for specific addresses in the appeals phase.
3. Provide opportunity for localities to review the address list for special places.
4. Instruct Census Bureau enumerators to update the MAF when they drop off questionnaires in February-March 2000.

1990 ADDRESS CONTROL FILE

City-Style Areas

1. Purchase lists from two vendors; supplement with field listing operation (prelist).
2. Recheck the vendor-supplied lists in 1989.
3. Provide the opportunity for localities to review housing unit counts by block in summer 1989.
4. Have the Postal Service conduct several checks in 1988–1990.

Non-City-Style Areas

1. Conduct a prelisting operation in fall 1989.
2. Instruct Census Bureau enumerators to update the list when they drop off questionnaires.

The 1990 list was not used. There was also a LUCA Program conducted in 1999. Approximately 21 million addresses were included on the MAF for areas outside the blue line at the time when questionnaires were labeled and prepared for delivery. Census enumerators further updated the MAF in these areas when they delivered questionnaires in February-March 2000.

Local Review

The same legislation that made it possible for the Postal Service to share the DSF with the Census Bureau also permitted the Bureau to invite local governments—counties, places, and minor civil divisions, over 39,000 jurisdictions in all—to review the MAF for their areas and provide additions, deletions, and corrections to the Bureau (LUCA Working Group, 2001).[4] The Local Update of Census Addresses (LUCA) Program was conducted separately in areas inside the blue line (LUCA98) and areas outside the blue line (LUCA99). There was also a Special Places LUCA Program.

LUCA required participating local governments to sign a pledge to treat the address list as confidential. The program involved several steps of local review, field verification by the Bureau, and appeal to the U.S. Office of Management and Budget when localities disagreed with the Bureau's decision to reject local changes to the MAF. Due to time constraints, some planned LUCA operations were combined and rescheduled (LUCA Working Group, 2001:Fig.1-1). In response to local concerns, a New Construction LUCA Program was added to give localities inside the blue line an opportunity during January-March 2000 to identify newly constructed housing units. Addresses identified in the program were not mailed questionnaires; instead, they were visited by enumerators during the coverage improvement follow-up operation in summer 2000.

Of the total 39,051 jurisdictions that were eligible for either or both LUCA98 or LUCA99, it is estimated that 25 percent participated fully in one or both programs by informing the Census Bureau of needed changes to the address list for their area (LUCA Working Group, 2001:Ch.2). Participation varied by such characteristics as geographic region of the country, population size of jurisdiction, type of government, and city-style or non-city-style area (see Chapter 4). Not yet known is what proportion of the MAF in city-style areas and non-city-style areas represented valid addresses that LUCA contributed (rather than repeating information from another operation, such as an update from the DSF).

Further Development of MAF

MAF was a dynamic file during the operation of the census. Not only were addresses added from each stage of census field operations, they were deleted

---

[4]Local review procedures were used in the 1980 and 1990 censuses, but localities were not permitted to examine the list of individual addresses for their areas.

in an effort to minimize duplicate and erroneous entries. In total, the Census Bureau estimates that about 4 million addresses were added to the MAF during census field operations—2.3 million addresses during questionnaire delivery in update/leave, update/enumerate, and list/enumerate areas (see "Questionnaire Delivery and Mail Return," below) and 1.7 million addresses during follow-up. About 10.4 million addresses were removed as duplicative of other addresses or nonexistent. About 5 million of these addresses were removed on the basis of two internal consistency checks, one of which was planned and the other of which was designed and implemented while the census data were being processed; the remaining addresses were deleted on the basis of field operations (see "Field Follow-up," below). Whether the combination of internal checks and field checks reduced duplicate and erroneous addresses to a minimum or went too far or not far enough is a matter for evaluation. The final number of addresses on the MAF of occupied and vacant housing units counted in 2000 was 115.9 million (Farber, 2001a:Tables 1, 2).

Internal Checks for Duplicates

The Census Bureau anticipated that multiple sources to develop the MAF could result in duplication of addresses by carrying out a planned internal consistency check in April in order to reduce the nonresponse follow-up workload. Subsequently, the Bureau responded promptly to evidence that the MAF still contained duplicates by designing and implementing a second internal consistency check in summer 2000.

Reducing the NRFU Workload

In April 2000 the Census Bureau conducted an internal consistency check of the MAF prior to the beginning of nonresponse follow-up in order to remove from the NRFU workload as many addresses as possible that could clearly be identified as duplicative or nonexistent (Miskura, 2000a). At the conclusion of this operation, 3.6 million addresses were dropped or merged with another MAF address.

One source of potential duplicates and errors came about because LUCA, which was essentially a new, untested program, did not run as smoothly as intended (LUCA Working Group, 2001). Because of delays in providing materials to local governments to review, the Census Bureau agreed to include every address provided by a LUCA participant on the MAF that was used to label questionnaires in July 1999, even when there had not been time to verify the address in the field. LUCA-supplied addresses that the Bureau believed likely did not exist, based on field checks after July, were flagged. Processing specifications were developed to delete many of these addresses and other addresses of doubtful existence when no questionnaire was returned for them.

In all, 2.5 million addresses that the Bureau had reason to believe did not exist were deleted from the MAF prior to nonresponse follow-up.

Also as part of this review, the Bureau attempted to identify duplicate addresses originating from LUCA or other sources. About 1.1 million addresses were merged with another address on the MAF when the addresses appeared to be exact duplicates. Follow-up was conducted either only for the one (merged) address or not at all if a questionnaire had been received for that address.[5]

Unduplication and Late Additions

Another important set of MAF internal checks, not previously planned, was put into place in summer 2000. From evaluations of MAF housing unit counts during January-June 2000 against estimates prepared from other sources, such as building permits, the Census Bureau determined that there were likely still a sizable number of duplicate addresses on the MAF (West and Robinson, 2001). Field verification carried out in June 2000 in a small number of localities substantiated this conclusion (Nash, 2000).

Consequently, the Bureau mounted a special operation to identify duplicate addresses and associated duplicate census returns to remove them from the MAF and the census. Software was written for this operation to match addresses and person records to identify potential duplicates. The flagged records were deleted from the census file of valid, completed returns and further examined. After examination, it was decided that a portion of the potential duplicates were likely valid returns for addresses not already in the census, and they were restored to the census file (late additions). At the conclusion of the operation, 1.4 million housing units and 3.6 million people were permanently deleted from the census file, from a total of 2.4 million housing units and 6.0 million people that had been initially flagged as potential duplicates (Miskura, 2000b).

Comparison: Address List Development in 1990

The procedures used to develop the 1990 Address Control File (ACF) differed in important respects from those used to develop the 2000 MAF (see National Research Council, 1995:App.B). Overall, the Census Bureau used fewer sources in developing the 1990 ACF than it used for the 2000 MAF; also, the 1990 local review operation was considerably less extensive than the 2000 LUCA Program (see Box A-1, above).

For 1990 in areas with city-style addresses, the Census Bureau made no use of the 1980 census address list or the Postal Service DSF. Instead, the

---

[5]If questionnaires were received for two addresses that were deemed to be exact duplicates, the data on the two questionnaires were merged.

starting point for the Address Control File was two files of lists purchased from vendors, supplemented by a field listing operation carried out by census field staff in summer 1988 (precanvass). The Postal Service performed several reviews of the list in 1988–1990; Bureau staff also checked the part of the ACF that derived from the commercial lists in 1989. Governmental jurisdictions in the city-style areas were given an opportunity for review in summer 1989; however, they could not review specific addresses but only counts of addresses at the block level. About 16 percent of eligible local governments responded, adding about 400,000 housing units to the ACF (U.S. Census Bureau, 1993:6-44). By comparison, twice as many eligible governments—36 percent—participated in the LUCA98 Program in city-style areas.

In areas with non-city-style addresses, the development of the 1990 address list was similar to 2000, in that census field staff conducted a prelisting operation in fall 1989. Census enumerators also checked the list in March 1990 when they delivered questionnaires in the areas in which the update/leave technique (new for the 1990 census) was used. However, there was no pre-census local review program for the ACF in these areas.

QUESTIONNAIRE DELIVERY AND MAIL RETURN

The 2000 census, like the 1980 and 1990 censuses, was conducted primarily by delivering questionnaires to households and asking them to mail back a completed form. Procedures differed somewhat depending on such factors as type of addresses in an area and accessibility; in all, there were nine types of enumeration areas. Box A-2 provides brief descriptions of the nine types in 2000.

The two largest types of enumeration areas were: (1) mailout/mailback, covering almost 82 percent of the population, in which Postal Service carriers delivered questionnaires and (2) update/leave/mailback (usually termed update/leave), covering almost 17 percent of the population, in which Census Bureau field staff delivered questionnaires and updated the MAF at the same time. These two types, together with small numbers of addresses in areas (6), (7), and (9), comprised the mailback universe, covering about 99 percent of the household population (calculated from Baumgardner et al., 2001). The remaining 1 percent of the household population was enumerated in person (see areas (3), (4), (5), and (8) in Box A-2). Separate enumeration procedures were used for such special populations as homeless people, residents of group quarters, and transients (see Citro, 2000c).

Approaches to boost mail response were to redesign the questionnaire and mailing package, adapt enumeration procedures to special situations (the reason for having nine types of enumeration areas), and allow multiple modes for response. Advertising and outreach efforts were also expanded from 1990 (see "Outreach Efforts," below).

BOX A-2
Types of Enumeration Areas (TEAs)

① **Mailout/mailback** In areas with predominantly city-style addresses (inside the blue line), U.S. Postal Service carriers delivered an address-labeled advance letter to every housing unit on the MAF the week of March 6. In mid-March the carriers delivered address-labeled questionnaires, followed 2 weeks later by a reminder postcard. Households were to fill out the questionnaire and mail it back.

② **Update/leave** In areas outside the blue line in which there were many rural route and post office box addresses that could not be tied to a specific location, census enumerators dropped off address-labeled questionnaires to housing units in their assignment areas. At the same time, they checked the address list and updated it to include new units not on the list, noting for each its location on a map (map spot), so that follow-up enumerators could find units that did not mail back a questionnaire. The update/leave effort began in late February in some areas and continued through March.

③ **List/enumerate** In remote, sparsely populated, and hard-to-visit areas, census enumerators combined address listing and enumeration. There was no MAF for these areas created in advance. The enumerators searched for housing units, listed each unit in an address register (also its map spot), and enumerated the household at the same time. This operation was conducted in March-May 2000.

④ **Remote Alaska** The enumeration procedure in remote areas of Alaska was similar to list/enumerate. It was conducted earlier (in February) before ice breakup and snow melt.

⑤ **Rural update/enumerate** It was determined in some instances that blocks originally planned to be enumerated by update/leave would be better handled by a procedure in which address list updating and enumeration were conducted concurrently. "Rural" refers to the source of the address list—the prelist and LUCA99 operations conducted outside the blue line.

⑥ **Military** Mailout/mailback procedures were used for all residential blocks on military bases (excluding group quarters). Such blocks in type 2 enumeration areas (but not those in type 1 enumeration areas) were assigned an enumeration area code of 6 because there was no need to update the address list or provide map spots.

⑦ **"Urban" update/leave** It was determined that some blocks originally planned to have questionnaire delivery by the Postal Service would be better handled by having census enumerators follow an update/leave procedure. Such blocks contained older apartment buildings that lacked clear apartment unit designators, or they had many residents, despite having city-style addresses, who elected to receive mail at post office boxes. "Urban" refers to the source of the address list—the 1990 list updated by the DSF, the LUCA98 Program, and the Postal Service check in early 2000. No map-spotting was needed for these addresses.

⑧ **"Urban" update/enumerate** Some American Indian reservations contained blocks in more than one TEA. In these instances, all blocks in the reservation were enumerated using update/enumerate methods (see TEA 5). However, those blocks for which the mailing list was developed using "urban" procedures and for which no map-spotting was required were assigned a TEA code of 8 and not 5.

⑨ **Mailout/mailback conversion to update/leave** Some blocks originally in TEA 1 areas contained a significant number of non-city-style addresses. They were identified and converted to "rural" address listing procedures before the urban block canvassing operation was carried out in 1999; they were reviewed as a special component of the LUCA99 Program.

NOTE: For details, see U.S. Census Bureau (1999).

The mail response rate in 2000 (66%) was similar to the rate in 1990 (65%); it was also considerably higher than the rate that was budgeted (61%), which reduced the burden of field follow-up. The mail *return* rate in 2000 (72%) was slightly lower than the rate in 1990 (74%). This rate is a more refined measure of public cooperation than the mail response rate, which includes vacant and nonresidential addresses in the denominator in addition to occupied housing units (see Box 3-1 in Chapter 3).

Redesign of Mailings and Materials to Boost Response

To encourage mail response, a new questionnaire format was adopted for 2000. Based on extensive research (see National Research Council, 1995:Ch.6), a design was chosen that appeared as attractive and easy to fill out as possible. The use of new processing technology greatly facilitated the redesign (see "Data Processing," below). The mailing package was also redesigned to distinguish the questionnaire from junk mail and to motivate response (e.g., the envelope noted that responses were required by law).

One design change for the questionnaire was to ask households to list all members but to limit the space for characteristics to six members—instead of seven, as in 1990—in order to reduce bulk and make the questionnaire less intimidating. It was planned to follow up households with more than six members by telephone (see "Data Processing," below).

In the mailout/mailback area, multiple mailings were used to increase response. The first mailing was an advance letter (a new approach for 2000). The purpose of the letter was to alert residents to watch for the questionnaire, to provide a means for them to request a questionnaire in a language other than English, and to inform them of employment opportunities in census local offices. The second and third mailings were the questionnaire and a reminder postcard.

In both mailout/mailback and update/leave areas, the Bureau originally planned to deliver a second questionnaire to households not returning a form. Early testing showed that the use of a second questionnaire could increase mail response rates by as much as 10 percent (National Research Council, 1995:120). However, the Bureau determined that vendors could not process the list of nonresponding households quickly enough to be able to mail out a replacement questionnaire on the schedule required. Mailing a second questionnaire to all households, as was done in the 1998 dress rehearsal, was deemed too expensive and likely to lead to negative publicity and confusion.

The advance letter operation did not proceed as smoothly as hoped. A programming error resulted in an extra digit being inserted in every address, although the Postal Service caught the mistake and was able to deliver the letters as planned. In addition, the final version of the letter was not fully tested when it was decided after the 1998 dress rehearsal to add to the letter a way to request a foreign-language questionnaire. There was considerable public confusion about what to do with the enclosed return envelope if one did not need a special questionnaire. However, there were no apparent untoward effects of these problems on the public's cooperation with the census, and the publicity may have been helpful in alerting people to the need to respond.

Multiple Response Modes

Another innovation for 2000 to encourage response was to allow multiple response modes. Households that received a short-form questionnaire could fill out a short form on the Internet or by telephone. To answer questions and also permit telephone response, the Bureau contracted with a commercial phone center to operate a toll-free telephone questionnaire assistance system. This system provided assistance in English, Spanish, and several other languages. Individuals could also pick up "Be Counted" forms, which were made available in six languages at various local sites throughout the country just prior to Census Day.

Because multiple response modes might not only boost return rates but also result in more duplicate responses that could not be weeded out in later processing, the Census Bureau did not promote the "Be Counted" Program vigorously. Also, it did not widely publicize the Internet response option because of concerns about being able to handle a large response and maintain security. As it turned out, of 76 million questionnaires that were returned by households, 99 percent arrived by mail and only 1 percent by other modes: 66,000 were Internet returns; 605,000 were "Be Counted" forms; and 200,000 were forms completed by telephone. Not all "Be Counted" and telephone forms were included in the census: they were not counted if they did not have a valid address or if they duplicated another return.

Comparison: 1990 Questionnaire Delivery and Return

Questionnaire delivery procedures in the 1990 census differed in some respects from those used in 2000 (National Research Council, 1995:App.B). In 1990 about 84 percent of total housing units were in mailout/mailback areas; 11 percent—less than in 2000—were in update/leave areas (update/leave was a new procedure in 1990); and 5 percent—more than in 2000—were in list/enumerate areas. The list/enumerate procedure in 1990 differed somewhat from that used in 2000: Postal Service carriers delivered unaddressed short-form questionnaires to housing units in 1990 and census enumerators then came by to pick up completed questionnaires or obtain the answers, list the housing units in an address register, and at a predesignated subset of units, collect responses to the sample (long-form) questions. In 2000 Census Bureau field staff took questionnaires with them as they listed housing units and enumerated residents at the same time.

The 1990 census mailout procedures had not included an advance letter; however, a reminder postcard was delivered to all addresses in both mailout/mailback and update/leave areas. Responding by the Internet (which did not exist) was not an option. The questionnaire and mailing package were designed not to facilitate response as much as to permit data processing with the technology used in the 1960–1980 censuses (see "Data Processing," below).

Overall, the mailing strategies used in the 1990 census did not appear to help mail response. The mail response rate declined from 75 percent in 1980 to 65 percent in 1990; the mail return rate declined from 81 percent in 1980 to 74 percent in 1990.

FIELD FOLLOW-UP

Because not all households will mail back a form and because many addresses to which questionnaires are delivered will turn out to be vacant or nonresidential, the 2000 census, like previous censuses, included a large field follow-up operation (see Thompson, 2000). Over 500 local census offices (LCOs) were set up across the country, which reported to 12 regional census centers. The LCOs were responsible for hiring the temporary enumerators and crew leaders who would be needed to conduct follow-up operations. In update/leave areas, enumerators were hired to deliver questionnaires prior to Census Day and to return to follow up nonresponding households. LCOs also carried out operations to enumerate special groups, such as group quarters residents, transients, and the homeless.

In anticipation of possible difficulties in hiring and also the possibility that the mail response rate would decline from 1990, LCOs were authorized to recruit aggressively in advance of Census Day, to hire more enumerators than they thought would be needed, and to pay above-minimum wages (which differed according to prevailing area wages). Most offices were successful in meeting their hiring goals before the first follow-up operations began in mid-April 2000.

Follow-up operations were carried out in two separate stages, discussed below. The first stage, conducted in April-June, was the nonresponse follow-up, designed to obtain a questionnaire from every nonresponding unit in the mailback universe (or to determine that an address was vacant or nonresidential). The second stage, conducted in June-August, was coverage improvement follow-up (CIFU), which included specific operations designed to check and supplement NRFU. Several operations included in CIFU for 1990 were dropped for 2000.

Nonresponse Follow-Up

Preparation for NRFU began in early April 2000. Lists of addresses for inclusion in the NRFU workload were provided to the LCOs the week of April 11; a week later, notification was sent of late mail returns, which the LCOs deleted manually from their follow-up lists. The final workload totaled 41.7 million addresses. This total included addresses in the MAF for which a completed questionnaire was not checked in prior to April 18 and new addresses from DSF updates. It also included addresses marked for deletion in the update/leave operation and addresses for which postal carriers returned the questionnaires as not deliverable and no attempt was made to redeliver them by census staff. The purpose of NRFU for these addresses was to doublecheck their status and, if they were in fact occupied, to obtain an enumeration.[6]

In most LCOs, NRFU enumerators went into the field beginning April 27. Their first objective was to visit each household in person to try to obtain an interview, even if the residents said they had already mailed back a form.[7] If unsuccessful, the enumerators were to try up to five additional times to obtain an interview, unless the residents were known to be out of town for an extended period or the housing unit was verified to be vacant or nonexistent by a proxy respondent (someone not a member of the household, such as a neighbor or landlord). Three of the follow-up attempts could be made by telephone if the enumerator could obtain a phone number. In the case of refusals, field observations indicated that some offices adhered to the six-visit rule, sometimes using different enumerators, while others allowed the use of proxy respondents without making all six visits. If no interview was obtained after the specified number of visits, then enumerators were instructed to obtain information from a proxy respondent, noting the name and address on the interview form. When an office had obtained information for 95 percent of its workload, the best enumerators were given the remaining cases to make one last attempt to obtain information from the household or a proxy, even if fewer than six visits had been made to the household. Some offices required that at least three visits be made to a household before allowing a last attempt.

Conducted concurrently with the NRFU enumeration was a quality assurance program, in which selected cases were reinterviewed to identify fabrication ("curbstoning"). A random sample of the workload of each enumerator was reinterviewed; also, cases were selected purposively for reinterview by identifying enumerators whose work did not match that of other enumerators in the area. About 6 percent of the workload was reinterviewed in all, and

---

[6]NRFU enumerators could also enumerate housing units they identified that were not on the address list; however, field observation suggested that LCOs and enumerators did not consider checking the completeness of the address list to be part of the enumerator's job.

[7]Enumerators were instructed to be very diligent in this regard and to assure households that duplicate responses would be handled in the census processing.

preliminary analysis found discrepant results in a relatively small proportion of the reinterview batches (3.0%).[8]

NRFU operations were completed in most LCOs by June 26, so that the entire operation took only 8 weeks, shortening the original schedule by 1 week. At the conclusion of NRFU, enumerators had classified 62.3 percent of the 41.7 million addresses in their workload as occupied, 23.4 percent as vacant, 14.3 percent as "delete" (e.g., because the unit was demolished or nonresidential), and a handful (0.01%) as "not resolved" (Baumgardner et al., 2001:Table 4).

Coverage Improvement Follow-Up

The coverage improvement follow-up effort that followed NRFU included several operations that involved about 8.7 million housing units. The largest portion of the workload comprised 6.5 million housing units that had been classified as vacant or delete in NRFU. These units, which CIFU rechecked to determine if they might have been occupied on Census Day, were only 41 percent of total addresses identified as vacant or delete in NRFU. If such an address had not already been marked vacant or delete in another operation, it was revisited, but not otherwise. Examples of vacant or deleted units *not* included in CIFU were those classified as vacant or delete by an update/leave enumerator and a NRFU enumerator and those marked as undeliverable by a postal carrier and classified as vacant by a NRFU enumerator.[9]

There were four other components of the CIFU workload to visit or reinterview: (1) 717,000 addresses that were added to the MAF in update/leave, but from which no questionnaire was mailed back; (2) 372,000 addresses that were added to the MAF from the New Construction LUCA Program (in city-style areas); (3) 539,000 addresses for which forms were essentially blank because NRFU enumerators could not determine even the number of household residents (and a small number of forms that were lost in the process of data capture); and (4) 570,000 addresses that were visited for some other reason. The fourth category included addresses that were added to the MAF from late updates from the Postal Service DSF and the LUCA appeals process. It also included verification of addresses on "Be Counted" forms and those filled out by telephone questionnaire assistance staff.

Addresses initially classified by CIFU itself as vacant or delete that had not been visited in any previous operation (e.g., an address added from the New Construction Program) were reinterviewed for quality control purposes. The

---

[8]The quality control reinterview process was delayed in some LCOs in 2000; also, some reinterview forms were lost or not filled out correctly so that analysis of the reinterview results must be interpreted with caution (Baumgardner et al., 2001:17).

[9]The Census Bureau used a "two strikes and you're out" rule for assigning a final status of vacant or delete: if two separate operations classified an address as vacant or delete, then it was not checked again in CIFU.

entire workload for one district office, in Hialeah, Florida, was reinterviewed because of problems that came to light in that office, and selected housing units were reinterviewed in seven other offices for which problems were identified. The operations in 15 local offices were questioned by the House Subcommittee on the Census, but the Census Bureau determined, on review, that only two of these offices warranted some reenumeration. (These two offices are included in the total of seven in which partial reenumeration occurred.)

Overall, CIFU determined that 27 percent of the 8.7 million housing units visited were occupied, 43 percent were vacant, and 30 percent should be deleted. (Almost no units had an unresolved status at the end of CIFU; Baumgardner et al., 2001:Table 5.) CIFU enumerators were most likely to find occupied units among the addresses added in update/leave; they classified 45 percent of these addresses as occupied. Other categories had lower percentages of units classified as occupied: 35 percent for lost or blank returns, 27 percent for new construction addresses (53% of these addresses were not yet completed and so were deleted); and 24 percent for addresses classified as vacant or delete in NRFU that were rechecked in CIFU. The percentage of NRFU vacant and delete addresses that CIFU reclassified as occupied, however, was 2 to 3 times the percentage of vacant and delete units found to be occupied in previous censuses for which a vacancy recheck was carried out (see "1990 Coverage Improvement," below). The reason may be that, as noted at the beginning of the section, CIFU rechecked less than half of the addresses that were classified as vacant or delete by NRFU.

Comparison: 1990 Field Follow-Up and Coverage Improvement

NRFU procedures in 1990 were similar in broad outline to the procedures used in 2000 (see U.S. Census Bureau, 1993:Ch.6). The NRFU enumerators were instructed to visit each household in person. If an enumerator could not obtain an interview but was able to obtain a telephone number, then he or she was to make up to five additional attempts to interview the household—three telephone attempts and two more personal visits at different times of the day. If the enumerator did not have a telephone number, he or she was to make two additional personal visits. When all of these attempts failed to result in an interview or if the case was a refusal or the respondent was away for an extended period of time, the enumerator was instructed to talk to someone outside the household to obtain "last resort" information. Such information was defined as three of the four characteristics of relationship to head of household, sex, race, and marital status for each household member and a description of the housing unit. When 95 percent of the caseload had been completed, the remaining cases were given to the best enumerators who were to make one last visit to try to gather "closeout" data, defined as at least two characteristics for each household member.

Concurrently with NRFU enumeration, a reinterview program was carried out to detect falsification, similar to the program in 2000. The 1990 quality control program reinterviewed 4.8 percent of the NRFU workload of 34 million housing units and estimated a very low rate of falsification overall (0.09%; see U.S. Census Bureau, 1994:30-34).

In contrast to 2000, the 1990 NRFU operations fell considerably behind schedule, largely because of the Census Bureau's failure to forecast the extent of the decline in the mail response rate from 1980 to 1990—the Bureau projected a 70 percent response rate (down from 75% in 1980), but the actual rate at the time NRFU began was 63 percent (the rate subsequently rose to 65%). The Bureau had to obtain additional appropriations and scramble to hire sufficient workers for NRFU and other follow-up activities; it raised pay rates in 140 of the 449 district offices (equivalent to LCOs) and took other steps to increase productivity. The NRFU operation was planned to take 6 weeks from when it began in late April; however, only 72 percent of the workload was completed by that time (by June 6). Another 18 percent of the workload was completed in 2 more weeks, but it took another 6 weeks—until early August—to complete the remaining 10 percent of the workload (U.S. General Accounting Office, 1992:46).

A subsequent stage of follow-up in 1990 included several coverage improvement procedures (U.S. Census Bureau, 1993:6-37 to 6-38;6-53 to 6-56). An operation called field follow-up, carried out in June-August, rechecked most units classified as vacant or delete in NRFU. Units that were not rechecked included those in areas with high proportions of seasonal housing or boarded-up buildings, plus units classified as delete by two precensus address update operations and a NRFU enumerator (a more stringent criterion than that used in 2000). By August 1, 5.3 percent of deleted units and 7.1 percent of vacant units that were rechecked in field follow-up were converted to occupied. (The corresponding percentages in 1980 were 7.5% deleted units and 10% of vacant units converted to occupied.) These figures are considerably below the rate of conversion from vacant or delete to occupied in the 2000 CIFU (24%).

In addition to the recheck of vacant and delete units, the 1990 field follow-up operation revisited failed-edit mail returns. These cases were mail returns that lacked sufficient information to be processed and for which telephone follow-up was not successful (see "Data Processing," below). For cost reasons, only a 10 percent sample of failed-edit short forms requiring field follow-up were included in the workload; in contrast, all long forms requiring field follow-up were included. The 1990 field follow-up also revisited a number of mailback cases for which there was no record of data capture.

Another 1990 coverage improvement operation was the "Were You Counted Campaign," in which people who thought they had been missed were encouraged by media announcements in June-July 1990 to send in a special form. Those forms with addresses that could be assigned to census geography and with complete content were put through an operation to determine if they duplicated other forms. There was no field verification of the address, except in the Detroit district office, from which an unusually large number of forms were received.

Another special operation was the recanvass, carried out in July-November 1990, in which selected blocks, including those in high growth areas and those identified by postcensus local review, were relisted. The households were then reenumerated, provided the enumerator determined that the unit existed as of April 1. In all, the Bureau recanvassed more than 650,000 blocks containing about 20 million housing units (20% of all units).

Blocks identified for recanvassing by localities came about because in 1990 (though not 2000), local jurisdictions nationwide were invited to review preliminary census counts of housing units by block for their areas (U.S. Census Bureau, 1993:6-45 to 6-46). The counts were provided in August 1990, and localities had 15 days to challenge them. Responses were received from about 25 percent of all jurisdictions, including all of the 51 largest cities. All challenged blocks in which the discrepancy between the census count and that provided by the locality exceeded a specified amount were added to the recanvass operation, for which additional funding had to be obtained.

As part of the coverage improvement effort in 1990, in 24 local offices, all households for which the questionnaires reported only one household member were reenumerated. This procedure was implemented in response to allegations in late summer 1990 that enumerators in some offices during the closeout phase of NRFU had recorded households as one-person households without actually obtaining an interview (i.e., they were curbstoning). In addition, seven local offices in New Jersey were identified in which it appeared that fabrication may have occurred; households in these offices were reinterviewed when the questionnaires indicated household size but recorded no characteristics of household members.

Finally, a special program was implemented to improve the coverage of people who were on parole or probation (U.S. Census Bureau, 1993:6-55). The first step was to contact each state to ask its parole or probation officers to distribute census forms to their assignees to be filled out and mailed back. This operation had a very low response rate, so census enumerators were sent to correction departments in designated counties to obtain information for parolees and probationers from administrative records. No attempt was made to contact parolees or probationers unless their addresses could not be verified. The operation was not completed until late November-early December 1990. The forms obtained were processed through an unduplication operation (see "Data Processing," below); however, subsequent analysis determined that many of the parolee/probationer forms that were accepted in the census count represented duplicate enumerations (Ericksen, 1991:43-46).

Summary: 1990 and 2000

The description of 2000 and 1990 follow-up procedures makes it clear that they were large-scale, complex operations, similar in broad outline but sufficiently different in detail to make it difficult to compare results across years. It is difficult, for example, to compare results from the 2000 CIFU recheck of vacant and delete units with the 1990 field follow-up vacancy check because of differences in how the workload was defined. Also, it is not clear exactly how such terms as "proxy" (2000), "last resort" (1990), "closeout," and "non-data-defined" were similar or dissimilar, again complicating the task of comparative evaluation.

One can, however, conclude that the Census Bureau was more successful in 2000 than in 1990 in controlling field follow-up operations and keeping them on schedule. Coverage improvement operations were more focused, and programs that appeared problematic in 1990 (e.g., the parolee and probationers check) were not repeated in 2000.

OUTREACH EFFORTS

To supplement field operations and special programs to improve population coverage and cooperation with the census, the Census Bureau engaged in large-scale advertising and outreach efforts for 2000. For the first time, the Census Bureau budget included funds ($167 million) for a paid advertising campaign (recommended by a National Research Council panel in 1978).[10]

The 2000 advertising campaign was extensive, involving a major contractor, Young and Rubicam, which contracted with four other agencies to prepare ads targeted to particular population groups and communities. The advertising ran from October 1999 through May 2000 and included a phase to alert people to the importance of the upcoming census, a phase to encourage filling out the form, and a phase to encourage people who had not returned a form to cooperate with the follow-up enumerator. Ads were placed on television (including one during the 2000 Super Bowl), radio, newspapers, and other media, using multiple languages. Based on market research, the ads stressed the benefits to people and their communities from the census, such as better targeting of government funds to needy areas for schools, day care, and other services.

In addition to the ad campaign, the Census Bureau hired partnership and outreach specialists in local census offices, who worked with community and public interest groups to develop special initiatives to encourage participation in the census. The Bureau signed partnership agreements with over 30,000 organizations, including federal agencies, state and local governments, business firms, nonprofit groups, and others. The Bureau did not fund these groups,

---

[10]In previous censuses, the Advertising Council arranged for advertising firms to develop ads and air them on a pro bono, public service basis (Anderson, 2000).

but it provided materials and staff time to help them encourage a complete count. A special program was developed to put materials on the census in local schools to inform school children about the benefits of the census and motivate them to encourage their adult relatives to participate.

The Census Bureau director and other staff made numerous public appearances throughout the census period to stress the importance of a complete count and respond to questions and concerns. The director also put into place a program to use the Internet to challenge communities to raise their mail response rates. The 1990 response rates were posted for local areas on the Bureau's web site beginning in mid-March, and 2000 response rates were regularly updated on the site through mid-April. Communities were challenged to exceed their 1990 rates by 5 percent. Although few communities achieved this goal, the overall response rate did not continue its decline from previous censuses.

The 1990 census had also included advertising and outreach efforts; however, their extent was less than in 2000. The advertising was prepared by a firm selected by the Advertising Council, which conducted its work on a pro bono basis. Ads were placed as public service announcements, which meant that many ads ran in undesirable times (e.g., middle of the night). The partnership program was not as extensive as in 2000.

In both censuses, perhaps more so in 2000, advertising and outreach efforts varied in intensity across the country. Some localities were more active than others in coordinating and supplementing outreach and media contacts. Whether this variability narrowed or widened the difference in net undercount rates among major population groups depends on the extent to which outreach efforts were more (or less) effective in hard-to-count areas in comparison with other areas.

DATA PROCESSING

Data processing for the 2000 census was a continuing, high-volume series of operations that began with the capture of raw responses and ended with the production of voluminous data products for the user community, which will be made available in 2001–2003.[11] Important innovations were adopted for 2000. For the first time, the Census Bureau contracted with outside vendors for major components of data processing. Also for the first time, data capture was carried out with optical mark and optical character recognition technology. A telecommunications network linked Census Bureau headquarters in Suitland, Maryland; 12 permanent regional offices; the Bureau's permanent computer center in Bowie, Maryland; 12 regional census centers and the Puerto Rico

---

[11]Data processing also included a series of computer systems for management of operations, including payroll, personnel, and management information systems.

Area Office; the Bureau's permanent National Processing Center in Jefferson-ville, Indiana; 3 contracted data capture centers in Phoenix, Arizona, Pomona, California, and Baltimore County, Maryland; 520 local census offices; and con-tracted telephone centers for questionnaire assistance (U.S. Census Bureau, 1999:XI-1).

Five operations in 2000 are described in this section: data capture, cover-age edit and telephone follow-up, unduplication, editing and imputation, and other data processing. Data processing operations for 1990 are also summa-rized.

Data Capture

The first step in data processing was to check in the questionnaires and capture the data on them in computerized form. The return address on mail-back questionnaires directed them to one of four data capture centers—the Bureau's National Processing Center and three run by contractors. Each ques-tionnaire had a bar code that was scanned to record its receipt. The question-naires were then imaged electronically, check-box data items were read by optical mark recognition (OMR), and write-in character-based data items were read by optical character recognition (OCR). Clerks keyed data from images in cases when the OMR/OCR technology could not make sense of the data. Images of the long-form items were set aside temporarily to permit the fastest possible processing of short-form data.

Coverage Edit and Telephone Follow-up

The data on the questionnaires were reviewed by computer to identify those returns that failed coverage edit specifications. These failed-edit cases were reinterviewed by telephone, using contractor-provided clerical telephone staff. The workload for the coverage edit and telephone follow-up operation totaled about 2.3 million cases. It included returns that reported more house-hold members in question one ("How many people were living or staying in this house, apartment, or mobile home on April 1, 2000?") than the number of members for which individual information (e.g., age, race, sex) was provided; mailed-back returns in which question one was left blank and individual infor-mation was provided for exactly six people (the limit of the space provided); mailed-back returns that reported household counts of seven people or more; and returns of four or more people that contained nonrelatives of the household head.

The purpose of the edit and telephone follow-up was to reduce undercount-ing of people in large households and nonfamily households. There was no field follow-up for failed-edit households for which telephone follow-up was unsuccessful. Because of computer problems, the start of the coverage edit and telephone follow-up operation was delayed. Originally planned to be conducted in April-June 2000, it was carried out in May through mid-August.

Unduplication of Households and People

Two major, computer-based unduplication operations were carried out subsequent to field follow-up. One of those operations, the use of the primary selection algorithm (PSA) to unduplicate multiple returns for the same address, was planned from the outset and is described below. The other operation, the use of special software and procedures to reduce duplication of addresses in the MAF, was planned and implemented in summer 2000 to respond to evidence of duplicate addresses not eliminated by previous processing (described in "Master Address File," above). The PSA and MAF unduplication operations were linked: final determination of which returns to delete from the census because they duplicated a return from another MAF address was not made until after the PSA had processed multiple returns for the same address.

The purpose of the PSA was to identify unique households and people to include in the census when more than one questionnaire was returned with the same census address identification number. Such duplication could occur in a number of ways: when a respondent mailed back a census form after the cutoff date for determining the NRFU workload and the enumerator then obtained a second form from the household (or perhaps identified the household as vacant); when someone was enumerated in a group quarters but provided another "usual" address to which his or her information was assigned; or when a respondent filled out a "Be Counted" form, thinking that he or she had been missed, but another member of the household also mailed back a questionnaire for the household (which might or might not contain information for the individual).

For each housing unit, returns with one or more persons in common were combined to form a single PSA household. All vacant returns for a housing unit were also combined to form a PSA household. In some cases more than one PSA household might exist for a unit. For each PSA household, the algorithm selected which return best represented the Census Day household ("basic" return) and which people from the other returns were part of that household.[12]

In all, 9 percent of census housing units had two returns and 0.4 percent had three or more returns. In most instances, the operation of the PSA discarded duplicate household returns or extra vacant returns. Less often, the PSA found additional people to assign to a basic return or identified more than one household at an address (see Baumgardner et al., 2001:22-27).

---

[12]The Census Bureau does not make public the criteria for the PSA.

Editing and Imputation

Editing and imputation were carried out for all data-captured questionnaires. This operation included whole person and whole household imputation, called substitution, when there was minimal or no information for the person or household; editing content items for consistency and to fill in a missing item on the basis of a related item (e.g., to calculate age when only date of birth was provided); and imputation of specific content items, called allocation, when values were missing for one or more items.

All editing and imputation were computer based; there was no clerical editing of the questionnaires as in past censuses. When it was not possible to perform an edit that used other information for the same person or household, imputation was performed with hot deck methods that made use of information for other people and households in the immediate neighborhood. First used in processing the 1960 census, the Census Bureau's computerized hot deck procedures have been refined to search for the best match for a person or household missing one or more related data items on the basis of a large number of known characteristics. The best match search is geographically restricted to take advantage of common characteristics among small-area populations (see Box A-3; see also Citro, 2000b).

Household and Person Imputation

There were 5.8 million people imputed or substituted in the 2000 census, amounting to 2.1 percent of the census household population count (Schindler, 2001). Substituted people broke down into three main groups:

1. 1.172 million people (0.4% of the household population) were substituted because there was no information about the number of people living at that address or their characteristics. For units reported as occupied but for which household size was not known, the imputation process first categorized them as units at single-unit or multi-unit addresses. Then, household size was imputed from an occupied unit at a single-unit or multi-unit address with a reported population count from an enumerator-completed form. (In a refinement from 1990, mail returns that were not subject to field follow-up activities were excluded from the donor pool.) A similar process was followed for units for which occupancy status was not clear (the donor pool consisted of occupied and vacant units from enumerator-completed forms), and for units for which it was not even clear that they existed (the donor pool consisted of occupied, vacant, and deleted units from enumerator-completed forms). A potential donor record could be used as a donor only once and, in general, was selected from the same census tract as the unit requiring imputation. After imputing household size (and, if necessary, first imputing occupancy status and status as a housing unit), the computer duplicated another occupied

---

BOX A-3
Imputation Methods and Uses

It is standard practice to process censuses and surveys to review the input data, employ editing techniques to reconcile inconsistent or anomalous answers for a person or household, and employ imputation techniques to provide values for missing responses by making use of information reported for other items, persons, or households. In surveys, reweighting is often used to adjust for cases in which there is no information for a respondent.

Why Perform Editing and Imputation?

The reason to supply values for missing data and perform other edits is that the resulting data set is more useful for its intended uses, particularly when the data have multiple purposes and serve different users. The alternative of deleting records that have any missing values is to reduce the data that are available for analysis. Moreover, such a reduced data set may exhibit biases that a well-designed imputation system will moderate, or at least not make worse.

Editing

An example of a simple edit is when age or relationship is changed according to a specified rule when they are inconsistent (e.g., a child of the household head is reported as older than the head). Another example is when an item that was not supposed to be answered is changed from a reported value to a "not applicable" code (e.g., when hours worked last week is reported on the long form for someone who is unemployed).

Clerks reviewed census responses and noted errors as early as the 1830 census. By the end of the 19th century, clerical editing procedures had become quite elaborate. Computers were first used for machine editing in the 1960 census, although some clerical editing and follow-up was still conducted in censuses through 1990. Editing of data content was completely computerized in 2000.

Imputation

The first use of imputation to supply values for missing data took place in the 1940 census when a method was devised to impute age for people who did not report their age. The 1960 census employed computers for imputation, using **cold decks** and **hot decks**.

The hot deck method was developed and refined so that by the 1980 census, the computer could search for the best match for a person or household missing one or more related data items on the basis of a large number of known characteristics instead of the one or two characteristics used in the past.

Sometimes imputation supplies values for all characteristics for some or all persons in a household by replicating (substituting) the record of a neighboring person or household. More often, imputation fills in the values for one or a few characteristics that are missing.

Cold and Hot Decks

Cold decks were originally sets of punched cards that contained numeric values to represent known distributions of answers to questions in a previous census or survey. (The term *deck* continued to be used even after the distributions were provided to computers in other media.) A cold deck might, for example, contain a random sequence of values for marital status such that a certain percentage of men would have the value for "married" assigned to them. The values in the cold deck would be assigned sequentially to men not reporting their marital status.

Hot decks, in contrast, are distributions of values that are constantly altered as questionnaires are processed and data for the latest person or housing unit are substituted for the values already in the hot deck matrix. Imputation for a missing entry is made from the latest value stored in the matrix that fits other known characteristics of the person or housing unit.

Hot decks have the advantages that they use data from the current, not past, census for imputation, that they preserve more of the variability in responses that occurs in the population, and that they take advantage of common characteristics among households in the same small geographic area.

housing unit record of the same size in the nearby area to provide characteristics for people in the household (see Griffin, 2001).

2. 2.269 million people (0.8% of the household population) were substituted because the number of persons was known for their household but no other information was available. For these households, the computer duplicated another housing unit record in the nearby area of the same household size.

3. 2.333 million people (0.9% of the household population) were substituted because no information was provided for them, although other members of their households had data reported. This situation could occur, for example, when a large household listed more than six people and the telephone follow-up was not successful in reaching the household to obtain information for the additional members. For these people, the computer duplicated a person from a nearby housing unit with the same characteristics as the unit with person(s) requiring substitution.[13]

Content Editing and Imputation

For short-form content items, editing and imputation rates for missing values were low: 1.1 percent for sex, 4.3 percent for age, 3.2 percent for race, 3.8 percent for Hispanic origin, 1.6 percent for household relationship, and 4.2 percent for housing tenure.[14] These rates are for people who were missing one or more but not every short-form item (i.e., they exclude substituted people). In many instances, it was possible to fill in an answer from other information for the person or household, so that rates of hot deck imputation for short-form items were lower: 0.2 percent for sex, 2.9 percent for age, 3.2 percent for race, 3.4 percent for Hispanic origin, 1.3 percent for household relationship, and 3.6 percent for housing tenure. Information about editing and imputation rates for long-form content items is not yet available.

Other Data Processing

A number of other data processing steps were carried out, or are still in process, to generate data files and publications from the 2000 census records. Such steps for the short-form records include tabulating the data on various dimensions and modifying the data appropriately on files that are to be released

[13]Terminology has not been consistent across censuses for the process of imputation. "Substitution" most often refers to cases when an entire household is imputed. When individual people are imputed into a household with other respondents, they are often referred to as "totally allocated persons," as distinct from allocations for one or a few missing items.

[14]Item edit and imputation rates are from tabulations by panel staff from U.S. Census Bureau, E-Sample Person Dual-System Estimation Output File, February 16, 2001 (weighted using TESFINWT). The rate for age excludes cases in which it was possible to estimate age from date of birth and vice versa. See also Chapter 6.

to the public in order to protect the confidentiality of individual responses. For the long-form records, there are the added steps of coding such variables as occupation and industry and weighting the records to short-form control totals on several dimensions.

Comparison: 1990 Data Processing

The 1990 census data processing system was more decentralized than in 2000 and made more use of clerical editing (see National Research Council, 1995:App.B). There were 7 processing offices and 559 district offices. Mailback questionnaires in district offices in hard-to-enumerate areas in central cities went directly to a processing office for check-in and data capture. Mailback questionnaires in other district offices and all enumerator-obtained returns went first to the district office for check-in and editing.

Mailback questionnaires sent to processing offices were checked in by scanning bar codes. The data were then captured by using the Census Bureau's Film Optical Sensing Device for Input to Computers (FOSDIC), first developed for the 1960 census (Salvo, 2000). The computerized records were put through edit checks to identify households that had not provided complete data or would otherwise need telephone or personal visit follow-up (see "Field Follow-Up," above). Once any further data had been received from the field, computerized editing, allocation, and imputation routines were used to fill in remaining missing or inconsistent data

Mailback questionnaires sent to district offices were checked in by scanning bar codes and then reviewed by clerks to identify cases that required follow-up. After completion of follow-up, the questionnaires were sent to the processing offices for data capture and computerized editing and imputation.

Another step in data processing included the search/match operation, in which forms received from various activities were checked against completed questionnaires for the same address to determine which people should be added to the household roster and which were duplicates. This operation was carried out for "Were You Counted" forms, parolee/probationer forms, and for people who sent in a questionnaire from one location with an indication that their usual home was elsewhere. Such people might have two homes, such as people who spend the winter in a southern state and the summer in a northern state. There was no way on the 2000 form to indicate usual home elsewhere.

At the conclusion of data processing in 1990, about 1.9 million people had their information imputed (substituted) from data for another person. Substituted people accounted for 0.8 percent of the household population in 1990, compared with 2.1 percent in 2000. Obtaining comparable rates of imputations of characteristics for people with partial data is difficult. It appears that rates of editing and imputation for short-form items were similar in 1990 and 2000— somewhat lower for some items and somewhat higher for other items.

Appendix B

Mail Returns

Research has shown that a census mail return filled out by a household member tends to be more complete in coverage and content than an enumerator-obtained return (see National Research Council, 1995:122, App.L).[1] For this reason we decided at the outset of our assessment to examine the population coverage on mail returns in comparison with enumerator returns and to analyze similarities and differences in mail return rate patterns between 1990 and 2000.

In 2000, "mail" returns included returns filed over the Internet and telephone and "Be Counted" returns that had valid addresses and did not duplicate another return. The denominator for mail return rates in both 2000 and 1990 was restricted to occupied housing units in the mailback universe. The mail return rate is therefore a better measure of public cooperation than the mail response rate, which includes vacant and nonresidential units in the denominator as well (see Box 3-1 in Chapter 3).

We note that higher coverage error rates for enumerator returns do not reflect on them so much as on the difficulties of the task. With relatively little training or experience for the job, enumerators work under difficult conditions to try to obtain responses within a short period of time from households that, for whatever reason, declined or neglected to fill out and mail back their forms as requested. In that light, attempts to push mail return rates to very high levels, say, 85 or 90 percent or more, could reduce their overall quality because people who responded by mail only after extraordinary effort would likely do a poorer job of filling out their forms than other respondents. However, at the levels of mail return seen in recent censuses, the positive effect on data quality from maintaining or somewhat raising those rates appears to hold, and, hence, it is useful to understand the factors that facilitate response. Moreover, every return from a household by the mail or other medium is one less return that requires expensive follow-up in the field.

---

[1]Indeed, a primary impetus for the adoption of mailout/mailback procedures for census-taking came from the results of experiments in the 1950 and 1960 censuses, which found much higher rates of enumerator error in responses to all but the simplest questions, compared with self-enumeration (Bailar, 2000; Goldfield and Pemberton, 2000).

In the remainder of this chapter we summarize research from 1990 documenting the superiority of population coverage on mail returns and present largely confirmatory results from 2000. We then analyze changes in mail return rate rates for census tracts between 1990 and 2000 by a variety of characteristics. We knew that the overall reduction in net undercount in 2000 could not likely be due to mail returns, given that the total mail return rate was somewhat lower in 2000 than in 1990.[2] However, we thought it possible that changes in mail return rates for particular types of areas, such as those with many renters or minority residents, might help explain the reductions in net undercount rates that the Accuracy and Coverage Evaluation (A.C.E.) Program measured for usually hard-to-count groups.

QUALITY IN 1990

Research from the 1990 census, based on a match of P-sample and E-sample records in the 1990 Post-Enumeration Survey (PES), found that mail returns were substantially more likely than returns obtained by enumerators to cover all people in the household. Only 1.8 percent of mail returns had within-household misses, defined as cases in which a mail return in the E-sample matched a P-sample housing unit but the P-sample case included one or more people who were not present in the E-sample unit. In contrast, 11.6 percent of returns obtained by enumerators had within-household misses (Siegel, 1993; see also Keeley, 1993). These rates did not vary by type of form: within-household misses were 1.9 percent and 1.8 percent for short-form and long-form mail returns and 11.7 percent and 11.3 percent for short-form and long-form enumerator-filled returns.

In an analysis of the 1990 PES for 1,392 post-strata, Ericksen et al. (1991: Table 1) found that both the gross omission rate and the gross erroneous enumeration rate were inversely related to the "mailback rate" (equivalent to the mail response rate) for PES cases grouped by mailback rate category.[3] The relationship was stronger for omissions than for erroneous enumerations— the omission rate was 3 percent in the highest mailback rate category and 19 percent in the lowest mailback rate category, compared with 4 percent and 10 percent, respectively, for the erroneous enumeration rate. Consequently, the net undercount rate also varied inversely with the mailback rate.

---

[2]The somewhat lower mail return rate in 2000 than in 1990 is not explained by the larger mailback universe in 2000 (99% of the population and 95% in 1990). We calculated mail return rates for tracts in the 2000 mailback universe, which included people previously enumerated in person and for tracts in both the 2000 and the 1990 universes; the latter rate was only 0.2 percentage point higher than the former. There were larger effects for individual states: for example, in Alaska, the 2000 mail return rate for tracts in both the 1990 and the 2000 mailback universes was 65 percent, compared with 61 percent for all tracts in the 2000 universe.

[3]Ericksen et al. (1991) defined 10 mailback rate categories: one for under 55 percent, eight intervals of 5 percentage points from 55–59.9 percent to 80–84.9 percent, and one for 85 percent and over.

QUALITY IN 2000

Using data from the A.C.E. P-sample and E-sample, we carried out several analyses of the relationship between mail returns and population coverage for 2000. The analyses are not as comparable as we would have liked to the 1990 analyses summarized above: not only are there differences between the PES and the A.C.E., but also it is difficult a decade later to determine exactly how the 1990 analyses were performed. Nonetheless, the work is sufficiently similar that we are confident that the findings, which largely confirm the 1990 results, are valid. All results presented below are weighted, using the TES-FINWT variable[4] in the P-Sample or E-Sample Person Dual-System Estimation Output File, as appropriate.

Within-Household Omissions and Erroneous Enumerations by Type of Return

We linked P-sample and E-sample records in the same housing units to provide a basis for calculating rates of within-household omissions for 2000 that could be compared to the 1990 rates from Siegel (1993). We also developed other classifications of linked P-sample and E-sample households.

Table B-1 shows our results: E-sample mail returns received before the cutoff for determining the nonresponse follow-up workload included proportionally fewer cases with one or more omissions or possible omissions (2.8%) than did E-sample returns that were obtained by enumerators in nonresponse follow-up (7%). The difference was in the same direction as in 1990, but it was not as pronounced. Perhaps more striking, enumerator-obtained returns in 2000 included a much higher proportion with one or more erroneous or unresolved enumerations (15.5%) than did mail returns (5.3%) (comparable data are not available for 1990). Such enumerations included duplicates, geocoding errors, people lacking enough reported data for matching, and other erroneous and unresolved enumerations.

By housing tenure, both owner-occupied households and renter households showed the same patterns: mail returns included proportionally fewer cases of within-household omissions or cases with one or more erroneous or unresolved enumerations than enumerator returns. Consistently, renter households had higher proportions of these kinds of households than owner households (comparable data are not available for 1990).

---

[4]TESFINWT is the final person-level weight assigned to P-sample and E-sample records by the Census Bureau. It is based on each individual's estimated probability of being included in the sample as well as their inclusion in the targeted extended search operation (see Chapter 7).

TABLE B-1 Composition of 2000 Census Households, as Measured in the A.C.E. E-Sample, by Enumeration Status, Mail and Enumerator Returns, and Housing Tenure (weighted)

Type of Census (E-Sample) Household	Total		Owner		Renter	
	Mail Return (%)	Enumerator Return (%)	Mail Return (%)	Enumerator Return (%)	Mail Return (%)	Enumerator Return (%)
No Valid Omissions from P-Sample	97.1	93.0	97.5	93.8	96.3	92.3
All Members Match with P-Sample	81.5	62.9	84.6	69.4	73.0	56.1
All Matches or Correct (nonmatched) Enumerations	10.3	14.6	8.7	12.7	14.7	16.6
At Least One Correct and One Erroneous or Unresolved Enumeration	2.1	4.2	1.9	3.6	2.8	4.9
All Erroneous or Unresolved Enumerations	3.2	11.3	2.3	8.1	5.8	14.7
One or More Omissions or Possible (Unresolved) Omissions	2.8	7.0	2.5	6.2	3.7	7.6
One or More Omissions	2.3	5.7	2.2	5.3	2.9	6.0
One or More Possible Omissions	0.5	1.3	0.3	0.9	0.8	1.6

NOTE: Households in all categories may contain P-sample cases classified as unresolved or removed.

SOURCE: Tabulations by panel staff of U.S. Census Bureau, P-Sample and E-Sample Person Dual-System Estimation Output Files, February 16, 2001. Data files matched by household and weighted using the median value of TESFINWT within households.

Omissions and Erroneous Enumerations by Mail Return Rate Deciles

In an analysis similar to Ericksen et al. (1991), Table B-2 classifies P-sample cases and E-sample cases in the 2000 mailback universe into 10 mail return rate categories, with each category defined to include 10 percent of the total. (The decile cutoffs are very similar between the two samples.) The mail return rate associated with each case is the rate for the census tract in which the P-sample or E-sample person resided. Within each P-sample decile, the omission rate is calculated as the ratio of valid P-sample cases that did not match an E-sample person to the total of nonmatches plus matches. Within each E-sample decile, the erroneous enumeration rate is calculated as the ratio of erroneous enumerations (duplicates, fictitious persons, etc.) to the total of erroneous enumerations plus correct enumerations.

The omission rate ranges from 3.8 percent in the highest mail return rate decile to 14.8 percent in the lowest decile. The erroneous enumeration rate ranges from 2.5 percent in the highest return rate decile to 7.2 percent in the lowest return rate decile. The differences are in the same direction as those estimated for 1990, although they are not as pronounced.[5]

The rate of unresolved cases in the P-sample and E-sample (cases whose match status or enumeration status could not be resolved even after field follow-up) also shows a relationship to mail return rate deciles (see Table B-2). The unresolved rate (unresolved cases as a percentage of unresolved plus matches and nonmatches for the P-sample, and as a percentage of unresolved plus correct and erroneous enumerations for the E-sample) ranges from 1.2 percent in the highest P-sample mail return rate decile to 3.6 percent in the lowest decile and from 1.3 percent in the lowest E-sample mail return rate decile to 4.5 percent in the highest decile. These results indicate that it was easier to determine match or enumeration status in areas with higher mail return rates.

Erroneous Enumerations by Domain and Tenure

In an analysis of 2000 data—for which we have not seen comparable findings for 1990—we examined erroneous enumeration rates for E-sample people (including unresolved cases) by whether their household mailed back a return or was enumerated in the field. This analysis finds considerable overall differences and for domain (race/ethnicity) and tenure groups. The analysis differs from that reported above for mail return rate deciles for 1990 and 2000 in that it uses the mail return status of the individual household to classify E-sample people and not the return rate of either the post-stratum (as in 1990) or the census tract (as in 2000).

---

[5]We cannot determine the comparability of the 1990 and 2000 analysis due to missing details on how mail return, omission, and erroneous enumeration rates were calculated in 1990. Hence, the comparison between the 1990 and 2000 results should be limited to order of magnitude and direction.

TABLE B-2 Rates of P-Sample Omissions, E-Sample Erroneous Enumerations, and P-Sample and E-Sample Unresolved Cases in the 2000 A.C.E., by Mail Return Rate Decile of Census Tract (weighted)

Census Tract Decile (Return Rate Range)[a]	P-Sample Rates (%)		E-Sample Rates (%)	
	Omissions[b]	Unresolved Cases[c]	Erroneous Enumerations[d]	Unresolved Cases[e]
10th (82.8–100.0)	3.8	1.2	2.5	1.3
9th (79.7–82.7)	4.8	1.7	2.7	1.7
8th (77.3–79.6)	5.2	1.9	3.2	1.9
7th (74.9–77.2)	5.8	2.0	3.6	1.9
6th (72.6–74.8)	6.8	2.2	3.9	2.1
5th (69.9–72.5)	7.6	2.3	4.6	2.8
4th (66.8–69.8)	8.3	2.4	4.6	2.6
3rd (63.2–66.7)	9.4	2.5	5.0	3.5
2nd (57.7–63.1)	11.6	3.0	5.7	4.3
1st (19.9–57.6)	14.8	3.6	7.2	4.5

[a] The return rate ranges shown are for the P-sample; the ranges for the E-sample are almost identical.
[b] The omission rate is omissions divided by the sum of omissions plus matches (excluding unresolved cases, cases removed from the P-sample as not appropriately in the sample of Census Day household residents, and inmovers who were not sent through the matching process—see Chapter 6).
[c] The unresolved rate for the P-sample is unresolved cases divided by the sum of omissions, matches, and unresolved cases.
[d] The erroneous enumeration rate is erroneous enumerations divided by the sum of erroneous enumerations, matches, and other correct enumerations.
[e] The unresolved rate for the E-sample is unresolved cases divided by the sum of unresolved cases, erroneous enumerations, matches, and other correct enumerations.

SOURCE: Tabulations by panel staff of U.S. Census Bureau, P-Sample and E-Sample Dual-System Estimation Output Files, February 16, 2001; weighted using TESFINWT.

As shown in Table B-3, the rate of erroneous and unresolved enumerations for people on mail returns is 4.3 percent, compared with 12.6 percent for people on returns obtained by a nonresponse follow-up enumerator. For most race/ethnicity groups, people on mail returns have lower erroneous and unresolved enumeration rates than do people on enumerator-obtained returns, and owners have lower rates than renters. There are two exceptions: American Indian and Alaska Native owners living off reservations and Hawaiian and other Pacific Islander owners, for whom the rates of erroneous and unresolved enumerations are similar between mail and enumerator-obtained returns; and American Indian and Alaska Native renters living on reservations, for whom the rates of erroneous and unresolved enumerations are higher for mail returns than for enumerator-obtained returns.

For the update/leave cases, the patterns are similar to mailout/mailback cases: the rate of erroneous and unresolved enumerations for people on mail returns in update/leave areas is 3.1 percent, compared with 9.2 percent for people on enumerator-obtained returns, with rates for owners lower than those

TABLE B-3 Rates of E-Sample Erroneous Enumerations and Unresolved Cases, in Mailout/Mailback and Update/Leave Types of Enumeration Area (TEA), by Mail or Enumerator Return, Race/Ethnicity Domain, and Housing Tenure, 2000 A.C.E. (weighted)

Race/Ethnicity Domain and Tenure Category	Percent Erroneous and Unresolved Cases of Total E-Sample Enumerations			
	Mailout/Mailback TEA		Update/Leave TEA	
	Mail Return	Enumerator Return	Mail Return	Enumerator Return
American Indian and Alaska Native on Reservation				
Owner	0.0	6.5	13.5	9.0
Renter	5.1	1.9	10.2	3.9
American Indian and Alaska Native off Reservation				
Owner	7.2	7.7	2.2	8.7
Renter	9.1	12.8	5.5	11.3
Hispanic				
Owner	3.4	8.2	4.0	7.3
Renter	7.0	15.2	7.1	15.1
Black				
Owner	4.6	11.7	3.7	7.3
Renter	8.4	16.8	5.6	10.6
Native Hawaiian and Pacific Islander				
Owner	6.6	6.9	7.4	6.7
Renter	5.3	13.8	10.8	13.5
Asian				
Owner	4.0	8.8	3.5	8.5
Renter	8.4	17.5	8.4	23.2
White and Other Non-Hispanic				
Owner	3.0	8.5	2.6	8.0
Renter	7.2	16.6	5.2	12.9
Total	4.3	12.6	3.1	9.2

SOURCE: Tabulations by panel staff of U.S. Census Bureau, E-Sample Person Dual-System Estimation Output File, February 16, 2001; weighted using TESFINWT.

for renters (see Table B-3). The exceptions are American Indians and Alaska Natives living on reservations, for whom people on mail returns have higher (not lower) rates of erroneous enumerations than do people on enumerator-obtained returns, and for whom owners have higher rates than renters.

There were very few list/enumerate cases, but they have high rates of erroneous and unresolved enumerations—18.3 percent (data not shown). In contrast, the rates are relatively low for rural update/enumeration (5.2%) and urban update/enumeration (2.9%). For all other enumerator-obtained returns (e.g., those obtained from new construction), the rates of erroneous and unresolved enumerations are relatively high—14.3 percent.

1990–2000 DIFFERENCES IN MAIL RETURN RATES

In this section, we examine the differences in mail return rates by census tract, to determine whether part of the reduction in net undercount for historically hard-to-count groups estimated in the 2000 census may be attributable to a higher rate of higher-quality mail returns than enumerator returns. We were also interested in the structure of return rates in the 2000 census relative to the 1990 experience: Do returns in the two censuses appear to behave similarly, and do they bear the same relationships to such factors as the demographic and socioeconomic composition of a particular tract?

The data used in this analysis are drawn from two sources. The first—detailing the 2000 mail return rates by tract—is a summary file of return rates by collection tracts provided by the Census Bureau; this file was used to determine cutoffs of "high" versus "low" return rates for different racial/ethnic domains in constructing A.C.E. post-strata.[6] The second source provides 1990 return rates for tracts and links them to a set of characteristics; this source is the Bureau's "1990 Data for Census 2000 Planning" dataset (hereafter, the planning database). This database contains tract-level data from the 1990 census on a variety of demographic and housing-stock characteristics, as well as the estimated 1990 undercount for the tract. Among the variables included in the planning database is a hard-to-count score—based on percentile ranks in 11 of the demographic variables—that was used by the Bureau to identify "areas with concentrations of attributes that make enumeration difficult." This hard-to-count score can range from 0 to 132, with higher values indicating more difficult-to-count areas.

Since our primary interest is in comparing the 1990 and 2000 return rates, we restricted our attention to those tracts for which both rates are available: that is, we excluded those cases that did not have a mailout/mailback or update/leave component in both censuses. We also tried to avoid some of the noise created by small "sliver" tracts with little to no population; hence, we omitted those tracts for which either the 1990 or the 2000 mail return rates were exactly equal to zero. Our analysis set consisted of 55,688 tracts; our effective sample size when we performed regression analyses using the planning database characteristics is reduced slightly from that total due to missing values in the database.

This analysis should be considered tentative because the range of variables available for explanatory purposes is limited by geographic differences: the return rate summary files are given in 2000 census collection geography, which has somewhat different boundaries and very different numbering mechanisms from the geography used to tabulate data files for public release (e.g., the 2000

---

[6]These preliminary return rates from the A.C.E. should not be confused with the official census return rates, yet to be released.

census redistricting data files). It may be of interest to use demographic information from the 2000 census as explanatory variables rather than just the 1990 figures—for instance, one might be interested in looking at mail return rates in areas that underwent major changes in their racial or age composition over the 1990s. Such analyses await the release of full information from the census, including the long form, and should be part of the Census Bureau's program of evaluations.

Comparison

In general, a tract's mail return rate in the 2000 census tended to be close to its 1990 mail return rate; this conclusion is made clear in Figure B-1, which plots the mail return rates by tract for both censuses. The points are fairly tightly clustered near the 45-degree line; the correlation between the two variables is 0.79, and a simple linear regression fit to the data registers a slope of 0.78. The agreement between 1990 and 2000 rates is far from perfect, however; there is a fringe of points with near-perfect rates in one of the two censuses (mainly less-populated tracts). More significantly, the scatterplot suggests a slight bulge below the 45-degree line in the central cloud of points; this suggests a considerable number of tracts for which high 1990 mail return rates dropped off in 2000.

The boxplots along the margins of the scatterplot indicate the marginal distributions of the return rates in the two censuses.[7] The boxplots suggest that the tract-level return rates in 2000 tend to be slightly lower than in 1990; the median among the 2000 return rates is 72.2; the 1990 median is 76.5. However, the two distributions share essentially the same variability as measured by interquartile range: for 2000 the first and third quartiles are 64.5 and 78.7, respectively; for 1990 the quartiles are 68.5 and 82.9, respectively.

In general, then, 2000 mail return rates closely resembled 1990 mail return rates by tract, with some tendency for high-return tracts from 1990 to register a lower return rate in 2000. This conclusion is consistent with previous Census Bureau research on the structure of mail response rates, which are a slightly different construct than the mail return rates we examine here (Word, 1997).

Correlates of Rates and Change in Return Rate

Previous research on mail return rates for the census indicated fairly stable relationships between small-area demographic characteristics and response rates. For instance, high return rates have been found to be positively correlated with higher income and educational attainment, while impoverished

---

[7]Each box is bounded by the first and third quartiles (25th and 75th percentiles) of the distribution; the center line is the median value. The "whisker" lines extend from the end of the box to the most extreme data points within 1.5 times the interquartile range. Points outside the whiskers are outliers for the distribution.

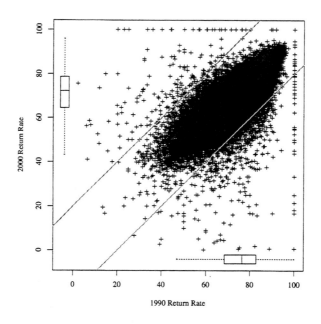

FIGURE B-1 Plot of 2000 and 1990 mail return rates.

NOTES: Each point represents one of 55,688 tracts for which both rates are available and for which neither the 1990 nor the 2000 mail return rate equals zero. Boxplots along the margins of the plot summarize the univariate (marginal) distribution of the two rates; see text for details. Two diagonal lines (intercepts ±20 and slope 1) demarcate those tracts whose mail return rates experienced changes of 20 percentage points or more between 1990 and 2000.

areas and areas with high concentrations of residents with limited English proficiency usually have lower return rates (Word, 1997; Salvo and Lobo, 1997).

Table B-4 displays the results of stepwise regression analysis, using the 1990 census characteristics from the planning database as predictors of three separate dependent variables: the change in mail return rate from 1990 to 2000, the raw 2000 return rate, and the raw 1990 return rate. Terms in the model had to achieve significance at the 0.05 level in order to enter or remain in the model. Achieving statistical significance in a dataset of over 50,000 records is not as telling as practical significance, though. To gauge the impact of each predictor, we multiplied the estimated coefficient by the interquartile range (third quartile minus first quartile); this value is tabulated as the "impact" and may be interpreted as the change in the response variable induced by a change from low to high values of the predictor, controlling for the effects of the other variables in the model.

It is apparent that none of the predictor variables available in the planning

TABLE B-4 Summary of Tract-Level Regression Models Using the Planning Database as the Source of Predictor Variables

Variable	Change in Return Rate, 1990–2000 ($R^2 = 0.19$)		2000 Return Rate ($R^2 = 0.69$)		1990 Return Rate ($R^2 = 0.75$)	
	Coef	Impact[a]	Coef	Impact[a]	Coef	Impact[a]
Census-Related Variables						
1990 PES % Net Undercount	−0.13	−0.28	−0.90	−1.90	−0.77	−1.62
Hard-to-Count Score	−0.03	−1.31	−0.12	−5.14	−0.09	−3.85
Demographic Composition						
Log(1990 Population + 1)	0.51	0.33	1.34	0.87	0.83	0.54
% American Indian/Alaska Native			−0.21	−0.08	−0.19	−0.08
% Asian/Pacific Islander	−0.05	−0.11	−0.06	−0.13	−0.01	−0.02
% Black	0.03	0.37	−0.08	−0.96	−0.11	−1.33
% Hispanic	−0.01	−0.08	0.03	0.15	0.04	0.22
% Population Over Age 65	−0.04	−0.30	0.24	1.94	0.28	2.25
% Population Under Age 18	0.06	0.42			−0.05	−0.41
% Linguistically Isolated Households			0.05	0.14	0.06	0.16
% Recent Movers	0.10	1.16	0.04	0.44	−0.06	−0.71
% People in Group Quarters	0.03	0.05	−0.01	−0.02	−0.04	−0.07
% Non-Husband/Wife Families	0.02	0.48	−0.02	−0.45	−0.04	−0.92
% Occupied Units with No Phone	−0.07	−0.53	−0.15	−1.13	−0.08	−0.61
Housing Stock						
% Units in 10+ Unit Structures	0.04	0.62	0.08	1.20	0.04	0.57
% Units in 2+ Unit Structures	−0.02	−0.54	−0.11	−3.30	−0.09	−2.72
% Crowded Units	0.20	0.88	0.02	0.07	−0.19	−0.82
% Housing Units Vacant	−0.02	−0.16	−0.11	−0.74	−0.09	−0.57
% Renter-Occupied Units			−0.01	−0.27	−0.01	−0.34
% Trailers/Mobile Homes			−0.04	−0.38	−0.04	−0.41
Economic and Educational Conditions						
% People Unemployed	0.11	0.56	0.05	0.24	−0.06	−0.32
% People Not High School Graduates	−0.04	−0.98	−0.11	−2.45	−0.07	−1.46
% Households on Public Assistance	0.08	0.58	0.17	1.29	0.09	0.71
% People Below Poverty	−0.06	−0.88	0.03	0.38	0.09	1.26
Geographic Division Indicators						
East North Central		−3.18		1.33		4.52
East South Central		−3.42		−0.93		2.51
Mid-Atlantic		−2.40		−2.07		0.33
Mountain		−1.42		−0.45		0.98
New England		1.49		−1.77		−3.28
South Atlantic		−2.08				2.12
West North Central		−3.57		1.14		4.72
West South Central		−4.17		−0.66		3.51

NOTES: Separate models were fit using each of three response variables indicated in the column headings. The operative sample size was 54,278, which includes tracts for which both rates are non-zero and none of the predictor variables includes missing values. Models were fit using stepwise regression, requiring significance at the 0.05 level to enter or remain in the model. In the set of geographic region indicators, the Pacific division is the omitted dummy variable.

[a] Number equals the estimated coefficient multiplied by the interquartile range (third quartile minus first quartile) and may be interpreted as the change in the response variable induced by a change from low to high values of the predictor, controlling for the effects of other variables in the model.

SOURCE: Analysis by panel staff of U.S. Census Bureau, Return Rate Summary File (U.S.), February 26, 2001, and 1990 Planning Database.

database is very informative in explaining the change in return rate from 1990 to 2000. The strongest correlations between any of them and the change in return rate are ±0.16 (positive for the percentage of persons living in crowded units, negative for the percentage of persons aged 65 and older), and the R^2 of the stepwise regression model searching over this set of variables is only 0.19. None of the planning database predictors in the model for change in return rate has a noticeable effect. However, it is interesting to note that the largest practical effects are those created through the dummy variables for census geographic division. The size of the coefficients suggests that the Pacific division (the omitted dummy variable) and New England both tended to have tracts that increased their return rates, while other areas—notably the West Central divisions—showed marked declines (see below).

The other two models illustrated in Table B-4 are those using the 2000 and 1990 return rates, respectively, as the dependent variable; the fitted models that result are strikingly similar in both the sign and the magnitude of the coefficients. Some discrepancies between the two models arise—signs differ on the coefficient associated with percentage of recent movers, and the geographic effects are consistent with markedly higher rates in the central regions of the country in 1990 than in 2000. Except for local geographic differences, 1990 and 2000 mail return rates may effectively be estimated by the same regression equation, in which the 1990 hard-to-count score, percentage net undercount, percentage people in multi-unit structures, and percentage people who were not high school graduates have large negative effects and 1990 percentage population over age 65 has a strong positive effect.

Geographic Variation

While none of the characteristics that are readily accessible are strongly related to the change in mail return rate between 1990 and 2000, the geographic region indicators we included in the model do show some of the largest effects. Further analysis of the change in return rates suggests interesting geographic patterning—more subtle than can be captured by simple regional dummies—for reasons that are not immediately obvious.

In this section of the analysis, we further restrict our focus to the 965 tracts in our dataset for which the 2000 mail return was either 20 percentage points higher or lower than in 1990. The 20 percent cutoff is arbitrary in the sense that it is not motivated by any theoretical concern; visually, though, the 20 percent cutoff does appear to shear off much of the bulge below the 45-degree line that is depicted in Figure B-1. Of these tracts thus considered, 780 had a 2000 mail return rate at least 20 percent lower than in 1990 levels, and 185 had a 20 percent higher rate than in 1990. Points representing these 965 tracts are shown on a national-level map in Figure B-2. For finer detail, Figure B-3 shows the Northeast corridor from Washington to New York.

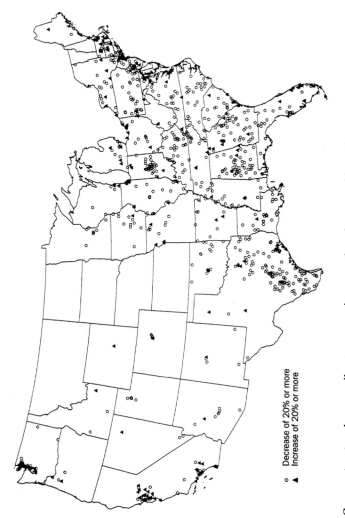

Decrease of 20% or more
Increase of 20% or more

FIGURE B-2 Census tracts whose mail return rate increased or decreased by at least 20 percent between 1990 and 2000.

NOTES: Census tracts are indicated by a randomly-selected point inside the tract's boundary. Not shown on the map are two sharp-decline tracts in Anchorage, Alaska, and two sharp-decline tracts and two sharp-increase tracts in Honolulu, Hawaii.

o   Decrease of 20% or more

▲   Increase of 20% or more

FIGURE B-3 Census tracts in the Washington-New York corridor whose mail return rate increased or decreased by at least 20 percent between 1990 and 2000.

The maps reveal a surprising level of structure and suggest how localized clustering of similar return rates can be. There is a strong concordance between 1990 and 2000 rates in the Plains and Mountain states. In contrast, the large majority of the tracts experiencing 20 percent or more dips in return rate lie in the eastern United States, beginning in central Texas. Large clusters of lower return rates are evident in various parts of the map, perhaps most strikingly in central Indiana and in Brooklyn, New York (Figure B-3), and abound throughout Kentucky, Tennessee, and the Carolinas. At the other extreme, as suggested by our regression models, the tracts that experienced higher mail return rates are concentrated in the Pacific division (particularly around Los Angeles and the extended Bay Area) and also in New England. Within the nation's largest cities (save, perhaps, Los Angeles), similar return rates are concentrated in portions of the city; a zoom-in on Chicago highlights a cluster of tracts with lower return rates on the west and south sides of the city (data not shown), while the striking cluster of tracts with lower rates in Brooklyn contrasts markedly with other portions of New York City (see Figure B-3).

These geographic effects are consistent with the broad geographic dummies (by division) incorporated in our regression models. Furthermore, these extreme-value tracts have higher hard-to-count scores (with half of the values lying between the first quartile 22 and third quartile 58, with median 39) than do tracts whose change in return rates was less than 20 percent (first quartile 9 and third quartile 51, with median 27). But the effects do not suggest any other obvious explanatory factors. There does not, for instance, appear to be an urban/suburban/rural divide at work, nor do areas of either growth or decline in return rate appear to correspond with areas experiencing greater population growth over the 1990s and for which new construction might be a major part of the address list. Again, our analysis here is limited by the available data; we look forward to the Census Bureau's evaluations of factors influencing mail return rates.

CONCLUSION

We did not find that changes in mail return rates explain the reductions in net undercount rates shown in the A.C.E. In fact, our analysis found very similar mail return patterns between the 1990 and 2000 censuses. The patterns in each census were explained by much the same variables, and the available demographic and socioeconomic characteristics for tracts did not explain changes between 1990 and 2000. However, census tracts experiencing unusually large increases or decreases in mail return rates did show a tendency to cluster geographically. Further investigation of these clusters and of local operations and outreach activities in these areas would be useful to identify possible problems and successes to consider for 2010 census planning.

Appendix C

A.C.E. Operations

This appendix describes the operations of the 2000 Accuracy and Coverage Evaluation (A.C.E.) Program.[1] Differences from the analogous 1990 Post-Enumeration Survey (PES) are summarized in Chapter 6, which also describes the dual-systems estimation (DSE) method used to develop population estimates for post-strata from the A.C.E. results. This appendix covers six topics:

- sampling, address listing, and housing unit match;

- P-sample interviewing;

- initial matching and targeted extended search;

- field follow-up and final matching;

- weighting and imputation; and

- post-strata estimation.

SAMPLING, ADDRESS LISTING, AND HOUSING UNIT MATCH

The 2000 A.C.E. process began in spring 1999 with the selection of a sample of block clusters for which an independent listing of addresses was carried out in fall 1999. The selection process was designed to balance such factors as the desired precision of the DSE estimates, not only for the total population, but also for minority groups, and the cost of field operations for address listing and subsequent interviewing. In addition, the A.C.E. selection process had to work within the constraints of the design originally developed for integrated coverage measurement (ICM).

---

[1]See Childers and Fenstermaker (2000) and Childers (2000) for detailed documentation of A.C.E. procedures.

First-Stage Sampling and Address Listing of Block Clusters

Over 3.7 million block clusters were formed that covered the entire United States, except remote Alaska.[2] Each cluster included one census collection block or a group of geographically contiguous blocks, in which the block(s) were expected to be enumerated using the same procedure (e.g., mailout/mailback) and to contain, on average, about 30 housing units on the basis of housing unit counts from an early version of the 2000 Master Address File (MAF). The average cluster size was 1.9 blocks.

Next, clusters were grouped into four sampling strata: small (0–2 housing units), medium (3–79 housing units), large (80 or more housing units), and American Indian reservations (in states with sufficient numbers of American Indians living on reservations). Systematic samples of block clusters were selected from each stratum using equal probabilities, yielding about 29,000 block clusters containing about 2 million housing units, which were then visited by Census Bureau field staff to develop address lists.

The sample at this stage was considerably larger than that needed for the A.C.E. The reason was that the Census Bureau had originally planned to field a P-sample of 750,000 housing units for use in ICM, and there was not time to develop a separate design for the planned A.C.E. size of about 300,000 housing units. So the ICM block cluster sample design was implemented first and then block clusters were subsampled for A.C.E., making use of updated information from the address listing about housing unit counts.[3]

Sample Reduction for Medium and Large Block Clusters

After completion of the address listing and an update of the MAF, the number of medium and large block clusters was reduced, using differential sampling rates within each state. Specifically, medium and large clusters classified as minority on the basis of 1990 data were oversampled to improve the precision of the DSE estimates for minority groups. Also, clusters with large differences in housing unit counts from the P-sample address list and the January 2000 version of the MAF were oversampled in order to minimize their effect on the variance of the DSE estimates.

Sample Reduction for Small Block Clusters

The next step was to stratify small block clusters by size, based on the current version of the MAF, and sample them systematically with equal probability

---

[2]A.C.E. operations were also conducted in Puerto Rico; the Puerto Rico A.C.E. is not discussed here.

[3]Our panel reviewed this decision and found it satisfactory because the development of direct dual-systems estimates for states was not necessary in the A.C.E. as it would have been under the ICM design (National Research Council, 1999a).

at a rate of 1 in 10. However, all small block clusters that were determined to have 10 or more housing units and all small block clusters on American Indian reservations, in other American Indian areas, or in list/enumerate areas were retained. After completion of the cluster subsampling operations, the A.C.E. sample totaled about 11,000 block clusters.

Initial Housing Unit Match

The addresses on the P-sample address listing were matched with the MAF addresses in the sampled block clusters. The purpose of this match was to permit automated subsampling of housing units in large blocks for both the P-sample and the E-sample and to identify nonmatched P-sample and E-sample housing units for field follow-up to confirm their existence. Possible duplicate housing units in the P-sample or E-sample were also followed up in the field. When there were large discrepancies between the housing units on the two samples, indicative of possible geocoding errors, the block clusters were relisted for the P-sample.

Last Step in Sampling: Reduce Housing Units in Large Block Clusters

After completion of housing unit matching and follow-up, the final step in developing the P-sample was to subsample segments of housing units on the P-sample address list in large block clusters in order to reduce the interviewing workload. The resulting P-sample contained about 301,000 housing units. Subsequently, segments of housing units in the census were similarly subsampled from large block clusters in order to reduce the E-sample follow-up workload. For cost reasons, the subsampling was done to maximize overlapping of the P-sample and E-sample. Table C-1 shows the distribution of the P-sample by sampling stratum, number of block clusters, number of housing units, and number of people.

P-SAMPLE INTERVIEWING

The goal of the A.C.E. interviewing of P-sample households was to determine who lived at each sampled address on Census Day, April 1. This procedure required that information be obtained not only about nonmovers between Census Day and the A.C.E. interview day, but also about people who had lived at the address but were no longer living there (outmovers). In addition, the P-sample interviewing ascertained the characteristics of people who were now living at the address but had not lived there on Census Day (inmovers).

The reason for including both inmovers and outmovers was to implement a procedure called PES-C, in which the P-sample match rates for movers would be estimated from the data obtained for outmovers, but these rates would then

TABLE C-1 Distribution of the 2000 A.C.E. P-Sample Block Clusters, Households, and People, by Sampling Stratum (unweighted)

Sampling Stratum	Block Clusters		Households		People		Average Households per Block Cluster
	Number	Percent	Number	Percent	Number	Percent	
Small Block Clusters (0–2 housing units)	446	4.4	3,080	1.2	7,233	1.1	6.9
Medium Block Clusters (3–79 housing units)	5,776	57.6	146,265	56.7	386,556	57.8	25.3
Large Block Clusters (80 or more housing units)	3,466	34.6	102,286	39.6	253,730	38.0	29.5
Large and Medium Block Clusters on American Indian Reservations	341	3.4	6,449	2.5	21,018	3.1	18.9
Total	10,029	100.1	258,080	100.0	668,537	100.0	25.7

NOTES: Block clusters are those in the sample after all stages of sampling that contained one or more P-sample cases; households are those that contain at least one valid nonmover or inmover; people are valid nonmovers and inmovers. Outmovers are not included, nor are people that were removed from the sample.

SOURCE: Tabulations by panel staff of U.S. Census Bureau, P-Sample Person Dual-System Estimation Output File, February 16, 2001.

be applied to the weighted number of inmovers. The assumption was that fewer inmovers would be missed in the interviewing than outmovers, so that the number of inmovers would be a better estimate of the number of movers. PES-C differed from the procedure used in the 1990 PES (see Chapter 6).

It was important to conduct the P-sample interviewing as soon as possible after Census Day, so as to minimize errors by respondents in reporting the composition of the household on April 1 and to be able to complete the interviewing in a timely manner. However, independence of the P-sample and E-sample could be compromised if A.C.E. interviewers were in the field at the same time as census nonresponse follow-up interviewers. An innovative solution for 2000 was to conduct the first wave of interviewing by telephone, using a computerized questionnaire. Units that were eligible for telephone interviewing included occupied households for which a census questionnaire (either a mail or an enumerator-obtained return) had been captured that included a telephone number, had a city-style address, and was either a single-family home or in a large multi-unit structure. Units in small multi-unit structures or with no house number or street name on the address were not eligible for telephone interviewing. Telephone interviewing began on April 23, 2000, and continued through June 11. Fully 29 percent of the P-sample household interviews were obtained by telephone, a higher percentage than expected.

Interviewing began in the field the week of June 18, using laptop computers. Interviewers were to ascertain who lived at the address currently and who had lived there on Census Day, April 1. The computerized interview—an innovation for 2000—was intended to reduce interviewer variance and to speed up data capture and processing by having interviewers send their completed interviews each evening over secure telephone lines to the Bureau's main computer center, in Bowie, MD.

For the first three weeks, interviewers were instructed to speak only with a household resident; after then, they could obtain a proxy interview from a nonhousehold member, such as a neighbor or landlord. (Most outmover interviews were by proxy.) During the last two weeks of interviewing, the best interviewers were sent to the remaining nonrespondents to try to obtain an interview with a household member or proxy. Of all P-sample interviewing, 99 percent was completed by August 6; the remaining 1 percent of interviews were obtained by September 10 (Farber, 2001b:Table 4.1).

INITIAL MATCHING AND TARGETED EXTENDED SEARCH

After the P-sample interviews were completed, census records for households in the E-sample block clusters were drawn from the census unedited file; census enumerations in group quarters (e.g., college dormitories, nursing homes) were not part of the E-sample. Also excluded from the E-sample were people with insufficient information (*IIs*), as they could not be matched, and late additions to the census whose records were not available in time for matching. People with insufficient data lacked reported information for at least two characteristics (among name, age, sex, race, ethnicity, and household relationship); computer imputation routines were used to complete their census records. Census terms for these people are "non-data-defined" and "whole person imputation;" we refer to them in this report as "people requiring imputation." In 2000, there were 5.8 million people requiring imputation, as well as 2.4 million late additions due to the special operation to reduce duplication in the MAF in summer 2000 (see Chapter 8).

For the P-sample, nonmovers and outmovers were retained in the sample for matching, as were people whose residence status was not determined. Inmovers or people clearly identified from the interview as not belonging in the sample (e.g., because they resided in a group quarters on Census Day) were not matched.

E-Sample and P-Sample Matching Within Block Cluster

Matching was initially performed by a computer algorithm, which searched within each block cluster and identified clear matches, possible matches, nonmatches, and P-sample or E-sample people lacking enough reported data for matching and follow-up. (For the A.C.E., in addition to meeting the census definition of data defined, each person had to have a complete name and at least two other characteristics). Clerical staff next reviewed possible matches and nonmatches, converting some to matches and classifying others as lacking enough reported data, erroneous (e.g., duplicates within the P-sample or E-sample, fictitious people in the E-sample), or (when the case was unclear or unusual) as requiring higher-level review.[4] The work of the clerical staff was greatly facilitated by the use of a computerized system for searching and coding (see Childers et al., 2001).

On the P-sample side, the clerks searched for matches within a block cluster not only with E-sample people, but also with non-E-sample census people. Such people may have been in group quarters or in enumerated housing units in the cluster that were excluded when large block clusters were subsampled.

Targeted Extended Search

In selected block clusters, the clerks performed a targeted extended search (TES) for certain kinds of P-sample and E-sample households (see Navarro and Olson, 2001). The search looked for P-sample matches to census enumerations in the ring of blocks adjacent to the block cluster; it also looked for E-sample

---

[4]Duplicates in the E-sample were classified as erroneous enumerations; duplicate individuals in a P-sample household with other members were removed from the final P-sample; wholehousehold duplications in the P-sample were treated as household noninterviews.

correct enumerations in the adjacent ring of blocks. The clerks searched only for those cases that were whole household nonmatches in certain types of housing units. The purpose was to reduce the variance of the DSE estimates due to geocoding errors (when a housing unit is coded incorrectly to the wrong census block). Given geocoding errors, it is likely that additional P-sample matches and E-sample correct enumerations will be found when the search area is extended to the blocks surrounding the A.C.E.-defined block cluster.

Three kinds of clusters were included in TES with certainty: clusters for which the P-sample address list was relisted; 5 percent of clusters with the most census geocoding errors and P-sample address nonmatches; and 5 percent of clusters with the most weighted census geocoding errors and P-sample address nonmatches. Clusters were also selected at random from among those clusters with P-sample housing unit nonmatches and census housing units identified as geocoding errors. About 20 percent of block clusters were included in the TES sample. Prior to matching, field work was conducted in the TES clusters to identify census housing units in the surrounding ring of blocks.

Only some cases in TES block clusters were included in the extended clerical search. These cases were P-sample nonmatched households for which there was no match to an E-sample housing unit address and E-sample cases identified as geocoding errors. When an E-sample geocoding error case was found in an adjacent block, there was a further search to determine if it duplicated another housing unit or was a correct enumeration.

Following the clerical matching and targeted extended search, a small, highly experienced staff of technicians reviewed difficult cases and other cases for quality assurance. Then a yet smaller analyst staff reviewed the cases the technicians could not resolve.

FIELD FOLLOW-UP AND FINAL MATCHING

Matching and correct enumeration rates would be biased if there were not a further step of follow-up in the field to check certain types of cases. On the E-sample side, almost all cases that were assigned a nonmatch or unresolved code by the computer and clerical matchers were followed up, as were people at addresses that were added to the MAF subsequent to the housing unit match. The purpose of the follow-up was to determine if these cases were correct (nonmatching) enumerations or erroneous.

On the P-sample side, about half of the cases that were assigned a nonmatch code and most cases that were assigned an unresolved code were followed up in the field. The purpose was to determine if they were residents on Census Day and if they were a genuine nonmatch. Specifically, P-sample nonmatches were followed up when they occurred in: a partially matched household; a whole household that did not match a census address and the interview was conducted with a proxy respondent; a whole household that matched an address with no census person records and the interview was conducted with a proxy; or a whole household that did not match the people in the E-sample for that household. In addition, P-sample whole household nonmatches were followed up when: an analyst recommended follow-up; when the cluster had a high rate of P-sample person nonmatches (greater than 45%); when the original interviewer had changed the address for the household; and when the cluster was not included in the initial housing unit match (e.g., list/enumerate clusters, relisted clusters).

The field follow-up interviews were conducted with a paper questionnaire, and interviewers were instructed to try even harder than in the original interview to speak with a household member. After field follow-up, each P-sample and E-sample case was assigned a final match and residence status code by clerks and, in some cases, technicians or analysts.

WEIGHTING AND IMPUTATION

The last steps prior to estimation were to:[5]

- weight the P-sample and E-sample cases to reflect their probabilities of selection;

- adjust the P-sample weights for household noninterviews;

- impute missing characteristics for P-sample persons that were needed to define post-strata (e.g., age, sex, race); and

- impute residence and/or match status to unresolved P-sample cases; impute enumeration status to unresolved E-sample cases.

Weighting is necessary to account for different probabilities of selection at various stages of sampling. Applying a weight adjustment to account for household noninterviews is standard survey procedure, as is imputation for individual characteristics. The assumption is that weighting and imputation procedures for missing data reduce the variance of the estimates, compared with estimates that do not include cases with missing data, and that such procedures may also reduce bias, or at least not increase it.

For the P-sample weighting, an initial weight was constructed for housing units that took account of the probabilities of selection at each phase of sampling. Then a weighting adjustment was performed to account for household noninterviews. Two weight adjustments were performed, one for occupied households as of the interview day and the other for occupied households as of

---

[5]Cantwell et al. (2001) provide details of the noninterview adjustment and imputation procedures used.

Census Day. The adjusted interview day weight was used for inmovers; the adjusted Census Day weight, with a further adjustment for the targeted extended search sampling, was used for nonmovers and outmovers. E-sample weighting was similar but did not require a household noninterview adjustment.[6]

Item imputation was performed separately for each missing characteristic on a P-sample record. The census editing and imputation process provided imputations for missing characteristics on the E-sample records (see Appendix A). Finally, probabilities of being a Census Day resident and of matching the census were assigned to P-sample people with unresolved status, and probabilities of being a correct enumeration were assigned to E-sample people with unresolved enumeration status (see Chapter 6).

POST-STRATA ESTIMATION

Estimation of the DSE for post-strata and the variance associated with the estimates was the final step in the A.C.E. process. The post-strata were specified in advance on the basis of research with 1990 census data (see Griffin and Haines, 2000), and each E-sample and P-sample record was assigned to a post-stratum as applicable. Post-strata that had fewer than 100 cases of nonmovers and outmovers were combined with other post-strata for estimation. In all, the originally defined 448 post-strata, consisting of 64 groups defined by race/ethnicity, housing tenure, and other characteristics cross-classified by 7 age/sex groups (see Figure 6-2 in Chapter 6), were reduced to 416, by combining age/sex groups as needed within one of the other post-strata.

Weighted estimates were prepared for each of the 416 post-strata for the following:

- P-sample total nonmover cases (NON), total outmover cases (OUT), and total inmover cases (IN) (including multiplication of the weights for nonmovers and outmovers by residence status probability, which was 1 for known Census Day residents and 0 for confirmed nonresidents);

- P-sample matched nonmover cases (MNON) and matched outmover cases (MOUT) (including multiplication of the weights by match status probability, which was 1 for known matches and 0 for known nonmatches);

- E-sample total cases (E); and

- E-sample correct enumeration cases (CE) (including multiplication of the weights by correct enumeration status probability).

Also tabulated for each post-stratum was the census count (C) and the count of IIs (people with insufficient information, including people requiring

---

[6]The weights were trimmed for one outlier block cluster.

imputation and late additions). The DSE for each post-stratum was calculated as the census count minus IIs, times the correct enumeration rate (CE/E), times the inverse of the match rate, or

$$(C - II)\left(\frac{CE}{E}\right)\left(\frac{P}{M}\right).$$

The match rate (M/P) was calculated for most post-strata by applying the out-mover match rate (MOUT/OUT) to the weighted number of inmovers (IN) to obtain an estimate of matched inmovers (MIN), and then solving for

$$\frac{M}{P} = \frac{\text{MIN} + \text{MNON}}{\text{IN} + \text{NON}}.$$

However, for post-strata with fewer than 10 outmovers (63 of the 416), the match rate was calculated as

$$\frac{M}{P} = \frac{\text{MOUT} + \text{MNON}}{\text{OUT} + \text{NON}}.$$

Procedures were implemented to estimate the variance in the DSE estimates for post-strata. Direct variance estimates were developed for the collapsed post-strata DSEs that took account of the error due to sampling variability from the initial listing sample, the A.C.E. reduction and small block subsampling, and the targeted extended search sampling. The variance estimates also took account of the variability from imputation of correct enumeration, match, and residence probabilities for unresolved cases. Not included in the variance estimation were the effects of nonsampling errors, other than the error introduced by the imputation models. In particular, there was no allowance for synthetic or model error; the variance calculations assume that the probabilities of being included in the census are uniform across all areas in a post-stratum (see Starsinic et al., 2001).

Glossary

Accuracy and Coverage Evaluation (A.C.E.) Program. A *coverage evaluation* program conducted by the Census Bureau following the 2000 census; it produces estimates of *undercount* and *overcount* in the census and forms the basis for statistical adjustment of census counts through *dual-systems estimation*. In the A.C.E., a sample survey is conducted in a sample of *census blocks* after the *nonresponse follow-up* phase of the census is complete. The resulting sample of individuals found by the survey in the selected blocks—called the *P-sample*—is matched to the set of census enumerations from the sample blocks (the *E-sample*).

Address Control File (ACF). The 1990 census analogue to the *Master Address File* used in 2000. The ACF was the residential address list used to label questionnaires, control the mail response check-in operation, and determine the *nonresponse follow-up* workload.

Address List Improvement Act of 1994 (P.L. 103-430). The law that enabled two innovations in the construction of the *Master Address File* for the 2000 census: the *Local Update of Census Addresses* Program (allowing local governments to receive and review the address list) and address list updates from the U.S. Postal Service's *Delivery Sequence File*.

Administrative records. Records that are collected as part of the operation of federal, state, and local programs, typically fund allocation and tax programs, such as Internal Revenue Service and Food Stamp Program records.

American Community Survey. A new continuous survey program currently being developed by the Census Bureau to collect the detailed socioeconomic and other data currently included on the census long form, based on monthly surveys of respondents and released annually. It is hoped that implementation of the American Community Survey will allow the Bureau to switch to a short-form-only census in 2010. The planned sample size is about three million households per year.

205

Balancing error. Type of error cited by the *Executive Steering Committee for A.C.E. Policy* in its recommendation not to adjust census counts for congressional redistricting. Balancing error occurs when cases in the *P-sample* and *E-sample* are not treated identically (e.g., when the search area used to identify P-sample matches and E-sample correct enumerations is defined differently).

"Be Counted." A program introduced in the 2000 census that made census questionnaires available in public places, so that residents who believed that they had been missed in the regular census enumeration could file a questionnaire.

Blue line. Descriptive term used to differentiate basic types of addresses. Areas of residences with mainly city-style addresses (number and street) are said to be inside the blue line, and areas of residences with mainly non-city-style addresses (such as rural route and post office boxes) are said to be outside the blue line. The term derives from the color used on initial sets of maps generated prior to the *Local Update of Census Addresses* (LUCA) Program; the 1998 implementation of LUCA targeted addresses inside the blue line and the 1999 implementation targeted those outside. *Mailout/mailback* enumeration was used inside the blue line and *update/leave* enumeration was used outside the blue line.

Block cluster. Group of one or more *census blocks* expected to contain about 30 housing units, defined for use in the *Accuracy and Coverage Evaluation Program.*

Casing check. A program in which postal workers determine addresses for which they did not receive a questionnaire and notify the Census Bureau.

Census block. The smallest entity for which the Census Bureau collects and tabulates decennial census information; bounded on all sides by visible and nonvisible features shown on Census Bureau maps. Occasionally, especially in rural areas, drainage ditches or power lines may be used to define blocks. Because most blocks have small population and housing unit counts, only 100 percent data, or *short-form* data, are tabulated for them.

Census Day. The target date of a decennial census. Census Day is the date for which census respondents are supposed to describe their household population, and for which the results of a decennial census are supposed to be an accurate representation of the nation's population. Since 1930, Census Day has been April 1 of years ending in zero.

Census tract. A census-defined geographic area of roughly 2,500 households. Census tracts are aggregations of *census blocks* (roughly 150 blocks, dependent on the population of the area). Tracts are intended to be relatively stable entities over time, though their definitions do shift with each census.

Census 2000 Supplementary Survey. Pilot program for the *American Community Survey*; a survey to collect data items from the census long form that was conducted in monthly samples totaling 700,000 households in 2000.

Closeout. The last stage of *nonresponse follow-up* when enumerators are instructed to make a last attempt to obtain at least minimal information, from a *proxy* if necessary. *Imputation* is used to fill in any missing information.

Coefficient of variation. An assessment of the variability of an estimate as a percentage of the size of the quantity being measured.

Computer-aided personal interview (CAPI). The use of a computer to assist an interviewer in carrying out an interview. Advantages include avoiding errors in skip patterns, providing immediate edit checks, and expediting electronic data capture.

Computer-assisted interviewing (CAI). A group of methods for using computers to assist with data collection. CAI surveys can be either interviewer-administered (conducted in person using a laptop computer or by telephone using a shared computer) or self-administered (conducted by surveys disseminated to respondents by telephone, by the Internet, or on a computer disk).

Correlation bias. A (technical) bias in *dual-systems estimation* by which the estimated counts would be, on the average, either too low or too high, caused by heterogeneity in enumeration probabilities for both the census and the *postenumeration survey*. The heterogeneities of the probabilities for these two attempted enumerations are typically positively related, which causes the estimated counts to be on the average too low.

Coverage correction factor (CCF). A term related to *dual-systems estimation*. The CCF is defined as the dual-systems estimate for a *post-stratum* divided by the census count (including whole person imputations and late additions); hence, it is the multiplier that can be applied to the population count for a post-stratum in a particular area to generate an adjusted count.

Coverage evaluation. Statistical studies conducted to evaluate the level and sources of coverage error in censuses and surveys.

Coverage improvement follow-up (CIFU). The second-stage follow-up operation used in the 2000 census (performed between June and August, 2000), verifying findings from the initial *nonresponse follow-up*.

Coverage improvement programs. Often (but not always) nationally applied methods and programs that attempt to collect information from individuals and households that might be missed using *mailout/mailback* or *nonresponse follow-up*. Before the 2000 census cycle this term referred to such programs as the parolee and probationer program (used in 1990), in which lists of these individuals were checked to see whether they were enumerated, and the non-household sources program, in which several *administrative record* lists were matched to census records to try to identify people missed in the census for purposes of field follow-up (used in 1980). For the 2000 census, coverage improvement refers more to efforts to complete the address list, use of *multiple response modes*, and *service-based enumeration*.

Curbstoning. The practice by which a census enumerator fabricates a questionnaire for a residence without actually visiting it.

Current Population Survey (CPS). Monthly sample survey of the U.S. population that provides employment and unemployment figures as well as current data about other social and economic characteristics of the population. The CPS is collected for the Bureau of Labor Statistics by the Census Bureau. The sample size for the CPS is about 50,000 households per month.

Data capture. The process by which survey responses are transferred from written questionnaires to an electronic format for tabulation. In the 2000 census, data capture was done by *optical scanning*; from 1890 to 1950, punch cards were used for data capture, and the *FOSDIC* process was used from 1960 to 1990.

Delivery Sequence File (DSF). The master list of deliverable mail addresses maintained by the U.S. Postal Service, organized by carrier route. The Delivery Sequence File was first used as a source of updates to the *Master Address File* for the 2000 census, following enactment of the *Address List Improvement Act of 1994*.

Demographic analysis. A method that uses various *administrative records* (especially birth and death records, information on immigration and emigration, and Medicare records) and information from previous censuses to estimate the total number of people in various demographic groups resident in the United States on a specific date, and therefore their census undercoverage.

Dress rehearsal. The largest census test, typically 2 years before the decennial census, in which the methods and procedures of the upcoming decennial census are given their final test to identify any operational problems.

Dual-systems estimation. An estimation methodology that uses two independent attempts to collect information from households to estimate the total population, including the number of people missed by both attempts.

E-sample. The set of census enumerations for a sample of census blocks; part of the *Accuracy and Coverage Evaluation*.

Enumerator. A census field operations employee who collects information from respondents through interviews.

Erroneous enumeration. The inclusion of someone in the census in error. Such inclusions may be people born after *Census Day* or deceased before Census Day, people in the United States temporarily, and people in the wrong location. They also include people counted more than once, i.e., duplicates.

Error. The difference between an estimate and the true value.

Executive Steering Committee for A.C.E. Policy (ESCAP). The committee of senior Census Bureau staff charged with analyzing information from the 2000 census and *Accuracy and Coverage Evaluation* in order to decide whether census counts should be adjusted for net *undercount*. The ESCAP reports to the director of the Census Bureau, who in turn submits a formal recommendation to the U.S. Secretary of Commerce.

Follow-up. A secondary census or survey operation, predominately in data collection, carried out to successfully complete an initial operation. It is most often a telephone or personal visit interview to obtain missing data or clarify original responses.

FOSDIC (Film Optical Sensing Device for Input to Computers). From 1960 to 1990, census questionnaires were microfilmed. The answers were read from the microfilmed questionnaires using FOSDIC and converted to electronic codes on computer tape.

Gross error. The sum of erroneous enumerations and omissions in the census. See also *Erroneous enumeration*; *Omission*; *Overcount*; *Undercount*.

Group quarters. A place where people live that is not a housing unit. There are two types of group quarters: institutional (for example, nursing homes, mental hospitals, and correctional institutions) and noninstitutional (for example, college dormitories, ships, hotels, group homes, and shelters).

Hot-deck imputation. The technique used by the Census Bureau to impute missing responses on census questionnaires. Imputations are made based on a continually updated distribution of responses from other, filled-in questionnaires that match characteristics that are known from an incomplete questionnaire.

Household. All the persons who occupy a *housing unit*.

Housing unit. A house, an apartment, etc., that is occupied (or, if vacant, is intended for occupancy) as separate living quarters, which are those in which the occupants live and eat separately from any other persons in the building. See also *household*.

***II*s.** Census respondents whose records contain insufficient information for matching, such as would be necessary to obtain adjusted counts through *dual-systems estimation*. For the 2000 census in particular, the set of *II*s contained both persons with substantially incomplete questionnaires and people who were reinstated in the census count at a late stage of processing but excluded from the *Accuracy and Coverage Evaluation*.

Imputation. A method for filling in missing information. Sequential *hot-deck imputation* fills in information from a previously processed respondent (and therefore geographically close) with other similar characteristics.

Integrated coverage measurement (ICM). The use of a *postenumeration survey* and some type of estimation method, e.g., *dual-systems estimation*, to produce adjusted census counts in time for apportionment and therefore all uses of census data. ICM was a key part of initial Census Bureau plans for the 2000 census, but was abandoned after the Supreme Court's 1999 decision ruling out the use of sampling in generating apportionment counts.

Last resort. Term used in the 1990 census to describe the collection of data from neighbors, apartment managers, post office employees, etc., when a response from a resident could not be obtained.

List/enumerate. A method of enumeration in which enumerators canvass a geographic area, list each residential address, and collect a questionnaire from or enumerate a household.

List/leave. A method of enumeration in which the enumerators list each residential address and at the same time deliver the census form for return by mail.

Local review. Census Bureau program in the 1980 and 1990 censuses in which local officials were given the opportunity to review housing unit counts in census blocks.

Local Update of Census Addresses (LUCA). A Census Bureau program in which local officials were given the opportunity to review individual addresses on the *Master Address File* and make corrections, additions, and deletions to that list, and to make corrections to census maps to match any changes that may be needed. The LUCA98 Program covered only local governments in *mailout/mailback* enumeration areas; LUCA99 covered governments in *update/leave* enumeration areas.

Long form. The census questionnaire that is delivered to a (roughly) one-sixth sample of *households*, which includes the short-form questions and additional questions about income, commuting patterns, etc. See also *short form*.

Mail Response Rate. Measure of respondent cooperation in the census, defined as the number of households returning a questionnaire by mail divided by the total number of questionnaires sent out in mailback areas. See also *mail return rate*.

Mail Return Rate. Measure of respondent cooperation in the census, defined as the number of households returning a questionnaire by mail divided by the total number of occupied households that were sent questionnaires in mailback areas (excluding vacant households and nonresidential units). The mail return rate is considered a more refined measure of cooperation than the earlier-available mail response rate.

Mailout/mailback. A method of census enumeration used primarily in urban areas in which questionnaires are mailed to each address and the residents are asked to mail back the completed questionnaires.

Master Address File (MAF). The list of addresses on which the 2000 census enumeration was based. It is derived from the 1990 census address list or a prelisting by census field staff, and is updated using a variety of sources, including information from the U.S. Postal Service and local officials. See also *Topologically Integrated Geographic Encoding and Referencing (TIGER) System*.

Master Trace Sample. A sample of census records (possibly by selecting all records in a sample of decennial census blocks) for which all information relevant to census data collection is retained to assist in analyzing and comparing methodologies suggested for use in the subsequent census.

Matching. The process through which it is determined how many persons are included in both the *postenumeration survey* and the census (in PES blocks) and how many persons are only included in one or the other attempted enumeration.

Multiple response modes. Generally speaking, methods for being enumerated, not including *mailout/mailback* and enumeration as part of usual *nonresponse follow-up*. In 2000 these methods included obtaining and returning questionnaires available in public places (*"Be Counted"* forms), the use of the telephone and the Internet to obtain or provide census information, and the enumeration of persons at places that offer services to the homeless.

Nonresponse. The failure to obtain all or part of the information requested on a questionnaire.

Nonresponse follow-up (NRFU). The field operation whereby census enumerators attempt to obtain completed questionnaires from interviewing members of households for which no questionnaire was returned in the mail. For the 2000 census, NRFU was performed between April and June, 2000. NRFU was conducted on a 100 percent basis in accordance with the Supreme Court's decision on sampling for apportionment; the Census Bureau's initial plans for the 2000 census called for sampling in this follow-up phase, which was then sampling for nonresponse follow-up (SNRFU).

Omission. A person missed in the census. See also *Erroneous enumeration*; *Overcount*; *Undercount*.

Overcount. The total number of people counted more than once or otherwise enumerated erroneously in the census. See also *Erroneous enumeration*; *Omission*; *Undercount*.

P-sample. Sample survey of respondents in a sample of *block clusters* conducted after (and independent of) the census enumeration; part of the *Accuracy and Coverage Evaluation*.

P.L. 94-171. The public law that requires the Census Bureau to provide the decennial census data required for congressional redistricting to the states by April of the year following the year of the census enumeration.

Post-Enumeration Survey (PES). The 1990 census analogue of the *Accuracy and Coverage Evaluation* in 2000.

Post-stratification. Separating a data set collected through use of sampling into strata on the basis of information gathered during data collection, and then treating each stratum separately in estimation.

Post-stratum. A collection (of individuals in the census context) that share some characteristics (e.g., race, age, sex, region, owner/renter) obtained during data collection and that are separately treated in estimation.

Primary selection algorithm (PSA). Algorithm developed by the Census Bureau to consolidate multiple responses from the same household into a single return; given concerns about opening a loophole for duplicates, the details of the PSA have not been made public.

Service-based enumeration. Enumeration of typically homeless people at food kitchens and shelters.

Short form. The census questionnaire that is mailed to about five-sixths of all *households*. The short form concentrates on basic demographic information. See also *long form*.

Special place. A place where people live or stay that is different from the usual private house, apartment, or mobile home and that requires different decennial census procedures. Examples are hospitals, prisons, hotels, motels, orphanages, nursing homes, dormitories, marinas, military installations, and large rooming or boarding houses. See also *group quarters*.

Synthetic error. Type of error cited by the *Executive Steering Committee for A.C.E. Policy* in its recommendation not to adjust census counts for congressional redistricting. The population post-strata used to assign coverage correction (adjustment) factors are supposed to be homogeneous in that members of a post-stratum are supposed to be equally likely to be counted in the census and the A.C.E.; synthetic error is produced in adjusted counts when this homogeneity assumption is not satisfied.

Title 13. The section of the U.S. Code under which the Census Bureau operates. It also protects the confidentiality of census information and establishes penalties for disclosing this information.

Topologically Integrated Geographic Encoding and Referencing (TIGER) System. The framework for identifying the exact geographic location of residential addresses (as well as other physical features).

Under(over)coverage; under(over)count. A nonspecific term representing either the rate or number of individuals missed (erroneously included) in the decennial census. More specifically, gross undercoverage and gross undercount are the rate or number of those missed for a demographic group or geographic area (similarly for gross overcoverage and gross overcount); net undercoverage and net undercount are the difference between the rate or number of those missed for a demographic group or geographic area and the rate or number of those erroneously included; differential (net) undercoverage and differential (net) undercount are the difference between the rate or number of net undercoverage between two demographic groups or between two geographic areas.

Unduplication. The process by which individuals reported on more than one census questionnaire are identified and counted once at only one geographic location.

Update/leave (also known as **update/leave/mailback**). A method of census enumeration used in areas lacking city-style addresses in which the census questionnaire is delivered to an address by a census enumerator. The *Master Address File* is corrected at the time of delivery (if necessary). Residents at the address are asked to fill out the questionnaire and mail it back.

References

Adams, Tamara, and Elizabeth A. Krejsa
    2001 ESCAP II: Results of the Person Followup and Evaluation Followup Forms Review. Executive Steering Committee for A.C.E. Policy II, Report 24. U.S. Census Bureau, Washington, D.C. (October 12).

Adams, Tamara, and Xijan Liu
    2001 ESCAP II: Evaluation of Lack of Balance and Geographic Errors Affecting Person Estimates. Executive Steering Committee for A.C.E. Policy II, Report 2. U.S. Census Bureau, Washington, D.C. (October 11).

Anderson, Margo J.
    1988 *The American Census: A Social History.* New Haven, Conn.: Yale University Press.
    2000 Advertising and the census. Pp. 13-14 in *Encyclopedia of the U.S. Census*, Margo J. Anderson, editor-in-chief. Washington, D.C.: CQ Press.

Anderson, Margo J., and Stephen E. Fienberg
    2001a Counting and Estimation: Methodology for Improving the Quality of Censuses— The U.S. 2000 Census Adjustment Decision. Paper presented at the International Conference on Quality in Official Statistics, Stockholm. Department of History, University of Wisconsin-Milwaukee, and Department of Statistics and Center for Automated Learning and Discovery, Carnegie Mellon University, Pittsburgh. (August).
    2001b *Who Counts? Census-Taking in Contemporary America.* Revised Paperback Edition. New York: Russell Sage Foundation.

Bailar, Barbara A.
    2000 Census testing. Pp. 62-66 in *Encyclopedia of the U.S. Census*, Margo J. Anderson, editor-in-chief. Washington, D.C.: CQ Press.

Bateman, David V.
    1991 Post Enumeration Survey Evaluation Project P11: Balancing Error Evaluation. 1990 Coverage Studies and Evaluation Memorandum Series M-2. U.S. Census Bureau, Washington, D.C.

Baumgardner, Stephanie K., Darlene A. Moul, Robin A. Pennington, Rebecca I. Piegari, Herbert F. Stackhouse, Kevin J. Zajac, Nick S. Alberti, Jennifer W. Reichert, and James B. Treat
    2001 Quality of 2000 Census Processes. DSSD Census 2000 Procedures and Operations Memorandum Series B-3. U.S. Census Bureau, Washington, D.C. (February 28).

Bean, Susanne L.
    2001 ESCAP II: Accuracy and Coverage Evaluation Matching Error. Executive Steering Committee for A.C.E. Policy II, Report 7. U.S. Census Bureau, Washington, D.C. (October 12).

Brown, Lawrence D., M.L. Eaton, David A. Freedman, S.P. Klein, Richard A. Olshen, Kenneth W. Wachter, Martin T. Wells, and Donald Ylvisaker
    1999 Statistical controversies in Census 2000. *Jurimetrics* 39:347-375.

215

Cantwell, Patrick J., David McGrath, Nganha Nguyen, and Mary Frances Zelenak
    2001 Accuracy and Coverage Evaluation: Missing Data Results. DSSD Census 2000 Procedures and Operations Memorandum Series B-7. U.S. Census Bureau, Washington, D.C. (February 28).
Childers, Danny R.
    2000 Accuracy and Coverage Evaluation: The Design Document. DSSD Census 2000 Procedures and Operations Memorandum Series, Chapter S-DT-01. U.S. Census Bureau, Washington, D.C. (February 2000, revised January 26, 2001).
Childers, Danny R., and Deborah A. Fenstermaker
    2000 Accuracy and Coverage Evaluation: Overview of Design. DSSD Census 2000 Procedures and Operations Memorandum Series, Chapter S-DT-2. U.S. Census Bureau, Washington, D.C. (January).
Childers, Danny R., Rosemary L. Byrne, Tamara S. Adams, and Roxanne Feldpausch
    2001 Accuracy and Coverage Evaluation: Person Matching and Follow-up Results. DSSD Census 2000 Procedures and Operations Memorandum Series B-6. U.S. Census Bureau, Washington, D.C. (February 28).
Citro, Constance F.
    2000a Advisory committees. Pp. 14-18 in *Encyclopedia of the U.S. Census*, Margo J. Anderson, editor-in-chief. Washington, D.C.: CQ Press.
    2000b Editing and imputation. Pp. 195-197 in *Encyclopedia of the U.S. Census*, Margo J. Anderson, editor-in-chief. Washington, D.C.: CQ Press.
    2000c Enumeration: Special populations. Pp. 201-206 in *Encyclopedia of the U.S. Census*, Margo J. Anderson, editor-in-chief. Washington, D.C.: CQ Press.
Davis, Peter P.
    2001 Accuracy and Coverage Evaluation: Dual System Estimation Results. DSSD Census 2000 Procedures and Operations Memorandum Series B-9. U.S. Census Bureau, Washington, D.C. (February 28).
Dillman, Don, Jon R. Clark, and Michael D. Sinclair
    1993 The 1992 simplified questionnaire test: Effects of questionnaire length, respondent-friendly design, and request for Social Security numbers on completion rates. Pp. 8-17 in *Proceedings of the 1993 Bureau of the Census Annual Research Conference*. Washington, D.C.: U.S. Department of Commerce.
Ericksen, Eugene P., Leobardo F. Estrada, John W. Tukey, and Kirk M. Wolter
    1991 *Report on the 1990 Decennial Census and the Post-Enumeration Survey*. Washington, D.C.: U.S. Department of Commerce.
Executive Steering Committee for A.C.E. Policy
    2001a Report: Recommendation Concerning the Methodology to be Used in Producing Tabulations of Population Reported to States and Localities Pursuant to 13 U.S.C. 141(c). U.S. Census Bureau, Washington, D.C. (March 1).
    2001b Analysis Plan for Further ESCAP Deliberations Regarding the Adjustment of Census 2000 Data for Future Uses. U.S. Census Bureau, Washington, D.C. (July 26).
    2001c Report of the Executive Steering Committee for Accuracy and Coverage Evaluation Policy on Adjustment for Non-Redistricting Uses. U.S. Census Bureau, Washington, D.C. (October 17).
Farber, James
    2001a Accuracy and Coverage Evaluation: Consistency of Post-Stratification Variables. DSSD Census 2000 Procedures and Operations Memorandum Series B-10. U.S. Census Bureau, Washington, D.C. (February 28).
    2001b Quality Indicators of Census 2000 and the Accuracy and Coverage Evaluation. DSSD Census 2000 Procedures and Operations Memorandum Series B-2. U.S. Census Bureau, Washington, D.C. (February 28).

Fay, Robert E.
  2001 Evidence of Additional Erroneous Enumerations from the Person Duplication Study.
        Executive Steering Committee for A.C.E. Policy II, Report 9. U.S. Census Bureau,
        Washington, D.C. (Preliminary version, October 26).
Feldpausch, Roxanne
  2001 Census Person Duplication and the Corresponding A.C.E. Enumeration Status. Ex-
        ecutive Steering Committee for A.C.E. Policy II, Report 6. U.S. Census Bureau,
        Washington, D.C. (October 13).
Fienberg, Stephen E.
  2000 Capture-recapture methods. Pp. 49-55 in *Encyclopedia of the U.S. Census*, Margo J.
        Anderson, editor-in-chief. Washington, D.C.: CQ Press.
Freedman, David A.
  1991 Adjusting the 1990 census. *Science* 252:1233-1236.
Freedman, David A., and W. Navidi
  1992 Should we have adjusted the U.S. census of 1980? (with discussion). *Survey
        Methodology* 18:3-74.
Goldfield, Edwin D., and David M. Pemberton
  2000 1960 census. Pp. 148-153 in *Encyclopedia of the U.S. Census*, Margo J. Anderson,
        editor-in-chief. Washington, D.C.: CQ Press.
Griffin, Richard
  2001 Census 2000: Missing Housing Unit Status and Population Data. DSSD Census
        2000 Procedures and Operations Memorandum Series B-17. U.S. Census Bureau,
        Washington, D.C. (February 28).
Griffin, Richard, and Dawn Haines
  2000 Accuracy and Coverage Evaluation Survey: Post-Stratification for Dual System Es-
        timation. DSSD Census 2000 Procedures and Operations Memorandum Series Q-
        21. U.S. Census Bureau, Washington, D.C. (January).
Haines, Dawn
  2000 Accuracy and Coverage Evaluation Survey: Final Post-Stratification Plan for Dual-
        System Estimation. DSSD Census 2000 Procedures and Operations Memorandum
        Series Q-24. U.S. Census Bureau, Washington, D.C. (April).
Hogan, Howard
  1992 The 1990 Post-Enumeration Survey: an overview. *American Statistician* 46:261-
        269.
  1993 The 1990 Post-Enumeration Survey: operations and results. *Journal of the Ameri-
        can Statistical Association* 88:1047-1060.
  2000a Accuracy and Coverage Evaluation. Pp. 3-5 in *Encyclopedia of the U.S. Census*,
        Margo J. Anderson, editor-in-chief. Washington, D.C.: CQ Press.
  2000b Accuracy and Coverage Evaluation: Theory and Application. Paper prepared for the
        Second Workshop of the Panel to Review the 2000 Census. U.S. Census Bureau,
        Washington, D.C. (February 2).
  2001a Accuracy and Coverage Evaluation: Data and Analysis to Inform the ESCAP Re-
        port. DSSD Census 2000 Procedures and Operations Memorandum Series B-1.
        U.S. Census Bureau, Washington, D.C. (March 1).
  2001b Accuracy and Coverage Evaluation Survey: Effect of Excluding "Late Census Adds."
        DSSD Census 2000 Procedures and Operations Memorandum Series Q-43. U.S.
        Census Bureau, Washington, D.C. (March 22).
Keathley, Don, Anne Kearney, and William Bell
  2001 ESCAP II: Analysis of Missing Data Alternatives for the Accuracy and Coverage
        Evaluation. Executive Steering Committee for A.C.E. Policy II, Report 12. U.S.
        Census Bureau, Washington, D.C. (October 11).
Keeley, Charles
  1993 Could the Census Bureau Reduce the Undercount by Not Using a "Long Form?"
        U.S. Census Bureau, Washington, D.C.

Killion, Ruth Ann
    1997 Group Quarters and the Integrated Coverage Measurement Survey. Memorandum
          for Census 2000 Committee on Statistical Policy. U.S. Census Bureau, Washington,
          D.C. (August 7).
Krejsa, Elizabeth A., and David A. Raglin
    2001 ESCAP II: Evaluation Results for Changes in A.C.E. Enumeration Status. Exec-
          utive Steering Committee for A.C.E. Policy II, Report 3. U.S. Census Bureau,
          Washington, D.C. (October 15).
Love, Susan, and Don Dalzell
    2001 Comparison of Record Substitution and 100% Data Allocation. Memorandum for
          the Record. U.S. Census Bureau, Washington, D.C. (March 27).
LUCA Working Group [Joseph Salvo (chair), Shoreh Elhami, Abby Hughes, Terry Jackson, Tim
Koss, Harry Wolfe, Patricia Becker (consultant)]
    2001 Assessment of the 2000 Census LUCA Program. Report prepared for the Panel
          to Review the 2000 Census, Committee on National Statistics, National Research
          Council, Washington, D.C. (April, revised September).
Marks, Eli S.
    1978 The role of dual system estimation in census evaluation. Chapter 20 in *Develop-
          ments in Dual Systems Estimation of Population Size and Growth*, Karol J. Krotki,
          ed. Edmonton: University of Alberta Press.
McMillen, David B.
    1998 The census under attack. *CHANCE* 11(2)(spring):50-55.
Miskura, Susan M.
    2000a Addressses in the Master Address File (MAF) Excluded from the April 7, 2000
          MAF Extract. Census 2000 Informational Memorandum No. 67. U.S. Bureau of
          the Census, Washington, D.C. (August 15).
    2000b Results of Reinstatement Rules for the Housing Unit Duplication Operations. Cen-
          sus 2000 Informational Memorandum No. 82. U.S. Census Bureau, Washington,
          D.C. (November 21).
Miskura, Susan M., Robert W. Marx, Charlene A. Leggieri, Charles H. Alexander, Jr., and A. Ed-
ward Pike III
    2001 2010 Census Planning: Opportunities to Meet the Challenges. Paper prepared
          for the Joint Statistical Meetings, Atlanta. U.S. Census Bureau, Washington, D.C.
          (August).
Mule, Thomas
    2001 ESCAP II: Person Duplication in Census 2000. Executive Steering Committee for
          A.C.E. Policy II, Report 20. U.S. Census Bureau, Washington, D.C. (October 11).
Mulry, Mary, and Bruce D. Spencer
    2001 Overview of Total Error Modeling and Loss Function Analysis. Prepared for U.S.
          Census Bureau. Abt Associates, Inc., Washington, D.C. (February 28).
Nash, Fay F.
    2000 Overview of the Duplicate Housing Unit Operations. U.S. Census Bureau, Wash-
          ington, D.C. (November 7).
    2001 ESCAP II: Analysis of Census Imputations. Executive Steering Committee for
          A.C.E. Policy II, Report 21. U.S. Census Bureau, Washington, D.C. (September
          24).
National Research Council
    1978 *Counting the People in 1980: An Appraisal of Census Plans*. Panel on Decennial Cen-
          sus Plans, Committee on National Statistics. Washington, D.C.: National Academy
          Press.
    1985 *The Bicentennial Census: New Directions for Methodology in 1990*. Panel on Decen-
          nial Census Methodology, Constance F. Citro and Michael L. Cohen, eds., Commit-
          tee on National Statistics. Washington, D.C.: National Academy Press.

1994 *Counting People in an Information Age*. Panel to Evaluate Alternative Census Methodologies, Norman Bradburn and Duane Steffey, eds., Committee on National Statistics. Washington, D.C.: National Academy Press.

1995 *Modernizing the U.S. Census*. Panel on Census Requirements in the Year 2000 and Beyond, Barry Edmonston and Charles Schultze, eds., Committee on National Statistics. Washington, D.C.: National Academy Press.

1999a Letter from Janet L. Norwood to Kenneth Prewitt, Director, U.S. Census Bureau. Panel to Review the 2000 Census, Committee on National Statistics, Washington, D.C. (May).

1999b *Measuring a Changing Nation: Modern Methods for the 2000 Census*. Panel on Alternative Census Methodologies, Michael L. Cohen, Andrew A. White, and Keith F. Rust, eds., Committee on National Statistics. Washington, D.C.: National Academy Press.

2000a *Designing the 2010 Census. First Interim Report*. Panel on Research on Future Census Methods, Michael L. Cohen and Benjamin F. King, eds., Committee on National Statistics. Washington, D.C.: National Academy Press.

2000b Letter from Janet L. Norwood to Kenneth Prewitt, Director, U.S. Census Bureau. Panel to Review the 2000 Census, Committee on National Statistics, Washington, D.C. (November).

2000c *Small-Area Income and Poverty Estimates—Priorities for 2000 and Beyond*. Panel on Estimates of Poverty for Small Geographic Areas, Constance F. Citro and Graham Kalton, eds., Committee on National Statistics. Washington, D.C.: National Academy Press.

2001a *Proceedings, First Workshop of Panel to Review the 2000 Census* (October 6, 1999). Committee on National Statistics. Washington, D.C.: National Academy Press.

2001b *Proceedings, Second Workshop of Panel to Review the 2000 Census* (February 2-3, 2000). Committee on National Statistics. Washington, D.C.: National Academy Press.

2001c *Proceedings, Third Workshop of Panel to Review the 2000 Census* (October 2, 2000). Committee on National Statistics. Washington, D.C.: National Academy Press.

Navarro, Alfredo, and Douglas Olson
2001 Accuracy and Coverage Evaluation: Effect of Targeted Extended Search. DSSD Census 2000 Procedures and Operations Memorandum Series B-18. U.S. Census Bureau, Washington, D.C. (February 28).

Owens, Karen L.
2000 Census 2000 Address List Review. Paper prepared for the Joint Statistical Meetings, Indianapolis. U.S. Census Bureau, Washington, D.C. (August).

Passel, Jeffrey S.
2001 Comparison of Demographic Analysis, A.C.E., and Census 2000 Results by Race. Memorandum prepared for the U.S. Census Monitoring Board, Presidential Members. Urban Institute, Washington, D.C. (February 27).

Prewitt, Kenneth
2000 *Accuracy and Coverage Evaluation: Statement on the Feasibility of Using Statistical Methods to Improve the Accuracy of Census 2000*. U.S. Census Bureau. Washington, D.C.: U.S. Department of Commerce. (June).

Raglin, David A.
2001 ESCAP II: Effect of Excluding Reinstated Census People from the A.C.E. Person Process. Executive Steering Committee for A.C.E. Policy II, Report 13. U.S. Census Bureau, Washington, D.C. (October 9).

Raglin, David A., and Elizabeth A. Krejsa
2001 ESCAP II: Evaluation for Results for Changes in Mover and Residence Status in the A.C.E. Executive Steering Committee for A.C.E. Policy II, Report 16. U.S. Census Bureau, Washington, D.C. (October 15).

Robinson, J. Gregory
    1991 Robustness of the Estimates of the Population Aged 65 and Over. Preliminary Research and Evaluation Memorandum No. 79. U.S. Census Bureau, Washington, D.C.
    2001a Accuracy and Coverage Evaluation: Demographic Analysis Results. DSSD Census 2000 Procedures and Operations Memorandum Series B-4. U.S. Census Bureau, Washington, D.C. (February 28).
    2001b ESCAP II: Demographic Analysis Results. Executive Steering Committee for A.C.E. Policy II, Report 1. U.S. Census Bureau, Washington, D.C. (October 13).

Salvo, Joseph J.
    2000 Data capture. Pp. 105-108 in *Encyclopedia of the U.S. Census*, Margo J. Anderson, editor-in-chief. Washington, D.C.: CQ Press.

Salvo, Joseph J., and A. Peter Lobo
    1998 The American Community Survey: Nonresponse follow-up in the Rockland County Test Site. Paper prepared for the American Community Survey Symposium. Population Division, Department of City Planning, New York, N.Y. (March).

Schindler, Eric
    2001 Accuracy and Coverage Evaluation (A.C.E.) Survey—Census Imputations by Poststratum. DSSD Census 2000 Procedures and Operations Memorandum Series Q-64. U.S. Bureau of the Census, Washington, D.C. (July 17).

Siegel, Paul M.
    1993 The Impact of Content on Census Coverage. Memorandum. Population Division, U.S. Census Bureau, Washington, D.C.

Starsinic, Michael D., Charles D. Stissel, and Mark E. Asiala
    2001 Accuracy and Coverage Evaluation: Variance Estimates by Size of Geographic Area. DSSD Census 2000 Procedures and Operations Memorandum Series B-11. U.S. Census Bureau, Washington, D.C. (February 28).

Steffey, Duane L.
    1997 A Review of the Census Undercount Issue. Faculty Fellows Program, Center for California Studies, California State University.

Thompson, John H.
    1992 CAPE Processing Results. Memorandum. U.S. Census Bureau, Washington, D.C.
    2000 Organization and administration of the census. Pp. 295-299 in *Encyclopedia of the U.S. Census*, Margo J. Anderson, editor-in-chief. Washington, D.C.: CQ Press.

Thompson, John H., Preston J. Waite, and Robert E. Fay
    2001 Basis of "Revised Early Approximation" of Undercounts Released Oct. 17, 2001. Executive Steering Committee for A.C.E. Policy II, Report 9a. U.S. Census Bureau, Washington, D.C. (October 26).

Treat, James B.
    1993 1993 National Census Test Appeals and Long-Form Experiment, Long-Form Component. Final Report. Census Data Quality Branch, U.S. Census Bureau, Washington, D.C.

U.S. Census Bureau
    1992a Assessment of Accuracy of Adjusted Versus Unadjusted 1990 Census Base for Use in Intercensal Estimates: Recommendation. Report of the Committee on Adjustment of Postcensal Estimates. U.S. Census Bureau, Washington, D.C.
    1992b *1990 Census of Population, General Population Characteristics*. 1990 CP-1-1. Washington, D.C.: U.S. Department of Commerce.
    1993 *1990 Census of Population and Housing—History, Part A*. Washington, D.C.: U.S. Department of Commerce.
    1994 Nonresponse Followup Reinterview. 1990 Census of Population and Housing Evaluation and Research Reports: Effectiveness of Quality Assurance. Washington, D.C. (February).

1996 *Statistical Abstract of the United States.* Washington, D.C.: U.S. Department of Commerce.

1999 *Census 2000 Operational Plan Using Traditional Census-Taking Methods.* Washington, D.C.: U.S. Department of Commerce.

2000 The Census 2000 Evaluation Program. Planning, Research, and Evaluation Division. Washington, D.C. (February 4).

U.S. Census Monitoring Board Congressional Members

2001 *A Guide to Statistical Adjustment: How It Really Works.* Report to Congress. Washington, D.C. (May 23, 2001).

U.S. Census Monitoring Board Presidential Members

2001a *Report to Congress.* Washington, D.C. (April).

2001b *Final Report to Congress.* Washington, D.C. (September).

U.S. General Accounting Office

1992 *Decennial Census: 1990 Results Show Need for Fundamental Reform.* GAO/GGD-92-94. Washington, D.C.: U.S. Government Printing Office.

2000a *2000 Census—New Data Capture System Progress and Risks.* GAO/AIMD-00-61. Washington, D.C.: U.S. Government Printing Office. (February).

2000b *2000 Census—Status of Nonresponse Follow-up and Key Operations.* GAO/T-GGD/AIMD-00-164. Washington, D.C.: U.S. Government Printing Office. (May 11).

Waite, Preston J., Sally M. Obenski, and Lisa E. Buckley

2001 2010 Census Planning: The Strategy. Paper prepared for the Joint Statistical Meetings, Atlanta. U.S. Census Bureau, Washington, D.C. (August).

Warren, Robert

2001 New Census Data and INS Estimates of the Unauthorized Immigrant Population. INS Release. Immigration and Naturalization Service, Washington, D.C.

West, Kirsten K., and J. Gregory Robinson

2001 The Use of Demographic Benchmarks to Ensure Census Data Quality. Paper prepared for the International Conference on Quality in Official Statistics, Stockholm. U.S. Bureau of the Census, Washington, D.C. (May).

Wetrogan, Signe I., and Arthur R. Cresce

2001 ESCAP II: Characteristics of Census Imputations. Executive Steering Committee for A.C.E. Policy II, Report 22. U.S. Census Bureau, Washington, D.C. (October 12).

Word, David L.

1997 Who Responds/Who Doesn't?: Analyzing Variation in Mail Response Rates During the 1990 Census. Population Division Working Paper No. 19. U.S. Bureau of the Census, Washington, D.C.

Wright, Tommy

2000 Sampling for follow-up of nonresponding households. Pp. 325-327 in *Encyclopedia of the U.S. Census,* Margo J. Anderson, editor-in-chief. Washington, D.C.: CQ Press.

Biographical Sketches of Panel Members and Staff

Janet L. Norwood (*Chair*) is author of *Organizing to Count: Change in the Federal Statistical System* (1995). Previously, she served as commissioner of the Bureau of Labor Statistics in the U.S. Department of Labor. She has written articles and monographs on statistical policy and on unemployment, price, and wage statistics, and has testified often on these issues before congressional committees. She has been a member of the Committee on National Statistics of the National Research Council and its Panel on Census Requirements in the Year 2000 and Beyond, is chair of the Advisory Committee for the Leading Indicators, and is a member of advisory committees at the National Science Foundation, at several statistical agencies, and at universities. She has received honorary LL.D. degrees from Florida International and Carnegie Mellon Universities. She has a B.A. degree from Rutgers University and M.A. and Ph.D. degrees from the Fletcher School of Law and Diplomacy of Tufts University.

Robert M. Bell is a researcher at the AT&T Laboratories. He became a member of the National Research Council's Committee on National Statistics in October 2001 and previously served on its Panel on Alternative Census Methodologies. Earlier, he worked at the RAND Corporation, where he examined and coauthored a number of studies on social policy issues. His work with RAND's Child Policy Project included research on such topics as prenatal substance abuse, adolescent drug use and the importance of social bonding among different ethnic groups, and the effects of the availability of condoms in a high school in Los Angeles. Dr. Bell earned a B.S. in mathematics from Harvey Mudd College and an M.S. from the University of Chicago and a Ph.D. from Stanford University, both in statistics.

Norman M. Bradburn is the assistant director of the National Science Foundation for Social, Behavioral and Economic Sciences. Formerly, he held positions as a senior vice president for research of the National Opinion Research Center (NORC) at the University of Chicago, director of NORC, and provost of the University. In his work as a social psychologist he has focused on the areas of survey and questionnaire design and related fields. He is also a past member of the Commission on Behavioral and Social Sciences and Education and the Committee on National Statistics and chaired the Panel to Evaluate Alternative Census Methodologies. He is a fellow of the American Statistical Association, the International Statistical Institute, and the American Association for the Advancement of Science, and a member of the American Association for Public Opinion Research and the World Association for Public Opinion Research. He received B.A. degrees from the University of Chicago and Oxford University and M.A. and Ph.D. degrees in clinical and social psychology from Harvard University.

Lawrence D. Brown is the Miers Bush professor of the Department of Statistics at the Wharton School at the University of Pennsylvania. He is a member of the National Academy of Sciences. He is also a member the National Research Council's Committee on National Statistics and a former member of the National Research Council's Commission on Physical Sciences, Mathematics, and Applications and its Board on Mathematical Sciences. He has been a critic of the Census Bureau's plans to incorporate sampling in the census. He received a B.S. from the California Institute of Technology and a Ph.D. from Cornell University.

Constance F. Citro is a senior program officer for the Committee on National Statistics. She is a former vice president and deputy director of Mathematica Policy Research, Inc., and was an American Statistical Association/National Science Foundation research fellow at the U.S. Census Bureau. For the committee, she has served as study director for numerous projects, including the Panel on Estimates of Poverty for Small Geographic Areas, the Panel on Poverty and Family Assistance, the Panel to Evaluate the Survey of Income and Program Participation, the Panel to Evaluate Microsimulation Models for Social Welfare Programs, and the Panel on Decennial Census Methodology. Her research has focused on the quality and accessibility of large, complex microdata files, as well as analysis related to income and poverty measurement. She is a fellow of the American Statistical Association. She received a B.A. degree from the University of Rochester and M.A. and Ph.D. degrees in political science from Yale University.

Michael L. Cohen is a senior program officer for the Committee on National Statistics, currently serving as the study director for the Panel on Research on Future Census Methods and staff to the Panel to Review the 2000 Census. He previously assisted the Panel on Estimates of Poverty for Small Geographic Areas. He also directed the Panel on Statistical Methods for Testing and Evaluating Defense Systems. Formerly, he was a mathematical statistician at the Energy Information Administration, an assistant professor in the School of Public Affairs at the University of Maryland, and a visiting lecturer at the Department of Statistics, Princeton University. His general area of research is the use of statistics in public policy, with particular interest in census undercount, model validation, and robust estimation. He received a B.S. degree in mathematics from the University of Michigan and M.S. and Ph.D. degrees in statistics from Stanford University.

Daniel L. Cork is a program officer for the Committee on National Statistics, currently assisting the Panel to Review the 2000 Census and serving as co-study director of the Panel on Research on Future Census Methods. His research interests include quantitative criminology (particularly space-time dynamics in homicide), Bayesian statistics, and statistics in sports. He holds a B.S. degree in statistics from George Washington University and an M.S. in statistics and a joint Ph.D. in statistics and public policy from Carnegie Mellon University.

William F. Eddy is professor of statistics at Carnegie Mellon University. His research concentrates on the computational and graphical aspects of statistics. He is particularly interested in dynamic graphics for the analysis and presentation of data, especially those dynamic graphical displays that cannot be rendered interactively. He is a former member of the Committee on National Statistics; a fellow of the American Association for the Advancement of Science, the American Statistical Association, the Institute of Mathematical Statistics, and the Royal Statistical Society; and an elected member of the International Statistical Institute. He was the founding coeditor of *CHANCE* magazine and is the founding editor of the *Journal of Computational and Graphical Statistics*. He has an A.B. degree from Princeton University, and M.A., M.Phil., and Ph.D. degrees from Yale University.

Robert M. Hauser is Vilas research professor of sociology at the University of Wisconsin-Madison, where he has directed the Center for Demography and Ecology and the Institute for Research on Poverty. He currently directs the Center for Demography of Health and Aging. He is a member of the National Academy of Sciences and a fellow of the National Academy of Education, the American Association for the Advancement of Science, the American Statistical Association, the Center for Advanced Study in the Behavioral Sciences, and the American Academy of Arts and Sciences. He has served on the National Research Council's Committee on National Statistics, Commission on Behavioral and Social Sciences and Education, and Board on Testing and Assessment. His current research interests include trends in educational progression and social mobility in the United States among racial and ethnic groups, the uses of educational assessment as a policy tool, the effects of families on social and economic inequality, and changes in socioeconomic standing, health, and well-being across the life course. He received a B.A. degree from the University of Chicago and a Ph.D. degree from the University of Michigan.

Ingram Olkin is professor of statistics and education at Stanford University. Before moving to Stanford, he was on the faculties of Michigan State University and the University of Minnesota, where he served as chair of the Department of Statistics. He has cowritten a number of books and been an editor of the *Annals of Statistics* and an associate editor of *Psychometrika*, the *Journal of Educational Statistics*, and the *Journal of the American Statistical Association*. He has also served as chair of the National Research Council's Committee on Applied and Theoretical Statistics and as president of the Institute of Mathematical Statistics. He has received an honorary D.Sci from DeMontfort University; a Lifetime Contribution Award from the American Psychological Association, Division 5; and a Wilks Medal from the American Statistical Association. His recent interest has been methodology for research synthesis, and he has published both theoretical and applied papers in medicine. He is currently a fellow in the Primary Care Outcomes Research Program. He received a Ph.D. in mathematical statistics from the University of North Carolina.

D. Bruce Petrie is vice-president and chief operating officer at the Canadian Institute for Health Information. From 1984 to 1999, he was the assistant chief statistician of the Social, Institutions and Labour Statistics Field at Statistics Canada, where he was responsible for conducting the census in Canada. Petrie has held several positions at Statistics Canada, including director general of the Household Surveys Branch from 1978 to 1984 and director of the Labour Force Survey (the Canadian equivalent of the Current Population Survey) from 1973 to 1978. He previously served as a member of the Committee on National Statistics' Panel to Evaluate Alternative Census Methodologies. He has a bachelor of commerce degree from Dalhousie University and an M.B.A. from the University of Western Ontario.

Michele Ver Ploeg is a member of the staff of the Committee on National Statistics, currently serving as the study director for the Panel on Data and Methods for Measuring the Effects of Changes in Social Welfare Programs and the Panel to Evaluate the USDA's Methodology for Estimating Eligibility and Participation for the WIC Program. Her research interests include the effects of social policies on families and children, the outcomes of children who experience poverty and changes in family composition, and individuals' education attainment choices. She received a B.A. in economics from Central College and M.S. and Ph.D. degrees in consumer economics and housing from Cornell University.

Meyer Zitter is an independent demographic consultant. Formerly, he was chief of the Census Bureau's Population Division and also served as assistant director for international programs. He is a fellow of the American Statistical Association and a member of the International Statistical Institute and the International Union for the Scientific Study of Population. He has a B.B.A. degree from City College of New York.